Masters of the

Masters of the GROTESQUE

*The Cinema of Tim Burton,
Terry Gilliam, the Coen Brothers
and David Lynch*

SCHUY R. WEISHAAR

McFarland & Company, Inc., Publishers
Jefferson, North Carolina, and London

LIBRARY OF CONGRESS CATALOGUING-IN-PUBLICATION DATA

Weishaar, Schuy R.
   Masters of the grotesque : the cinema of Tim Burton, Terry
Gilliam, the Coen brothers and David Lynch / by Schuy R.
Weishaar.
      p.   cm.
   Includes bibliographical references and index.

   ISBN 978-0-7864-7186-7
   softcover : acid free paper ∞

   1. Motion pictures — Aesthetics.   2. Grotesque in motion
pictures.   3. Motion pictures — Philosophy.   I. Title.
PN1995.W384 2012
791.4301— dc23
                                                                    2012036435

BRITISH LIBRARY CATALOGUING DATA ARE AVAILABLE

Front cover image: Michael Keaton in
Beetlejuice, 1988 (Warner Bros./Photofest)

Manufactured in the United States of America

*McFarland & Company, Inc., Publishers
   Box 611, Jefferson, North Carolina 28640
   www.mcfarlandpub.com*

For Felicia, Finn, Athan, and Kyle
"It is something to have been"

Acknowledgments

My interest in the grotesque began when, as an under-graduate, I had the good fortune to discover the works of Sherwood Anderson, William Faulkner, Flannery O'Connor, Tom Waits, Johnny Dowd, Nick Cave, Pieter Bruegel, Hieronymus Bosch, and surrealism at approximately the same time. (It was a good year.) This interest has been fostered by professors, friends, and colleagues in courses and conversations that haven taken place at and around Trevecca Nazarene University, Duke University, and Middle Tennessee State University: thanks to Rob Blann, Annie Stevens, Steve Hoskins, Holly and Boyd Taylor Coolman, Kevin Donovan, Carson Walden, Brannon Hancock, JJ Ward, Billy Daniel, Syndi and Mark Woods, Brandon Arbuckle, Jooly Philip, Graham Hillard, and Nate Kerr for their guidance, friendship, and support. I also owe a debt of gratitude to Linda Badley and Allen Hibbard for reading and providing helpful criticisms for an early draft of this work, as well as to David Lavery, under whose direction this work began.

Finally, special thanks to Mallory Carden for her attentiveness in finding my mistakes; to Kyle Weishaar for his mad genius and his music (Manzanita Bones); and, most of all, to my wife Felicia for her love, support, sanity, and brilliance.

Table of Contents

Preface

I would like my pictures to look as if a human being had passed between them, like a snail, leaving a trail of the human presence and memory of the past events as the snail leaves its slime.
— Francis Bacon, *Francis Bacon: Painter of a Dark Vision*

Here is lots of new blue goo now. New goo. Blue goo. Gooey. Gooey. Blue goo. New goo. Gluey. Gluey.
— Dr. Seuss, *Fox in Socks*

The grotesque is often conceived of as an aesthetic dimension divided in two, one side gravitating towards the dark, terrifying, and macabre, the other towards the bright, jovial, and ridiculous. These contrastive poles share certain elements of style, structure, pattern, form, etc.— all of the factors upon which the continuum of the grotesque itself is predicated — but, even while there may be minimal interplay between them (so continues this strain in the theory), most grotesquery in art gravitates towards the one side or the other. There is a kind of obviousness to this claim. When we look upon the paintings of Pieter Bruegel the Elder or Hieronymus Bosch, we probably perceive both as grotesque. But (as someone once explained to me during my college days) while Bruegel seems to dabble in the dark and horrifying, we may observe that the light and somewhat ridiculous seem more representative of his true vision, and while certain Bosch works retain an air of silliness, what we are arrested by are his obscenely grim triptychs.

But what happens when we pay slightly closer attention, or a different kind of attention, or when we multiply our critical perspective? What happens when we interpret the two painters from within the space of their contradiction? Do we not identify as much of the ludicrous in Bosch as in Bruegel and as much of the terrible in Bruegel as in Bosch? It is the contention of the present study that when we deal with the grotesque, we are faced with a multifaceted, polyvalent corpus of theories, traditions,

1

content (subject matter, etc.), images, themes, motifs, formal/structural apparatuses and patterns, and so forth, which problematize the notion of convenient conceptual bifurcations such as light and dark, good and evil, sacred and profane, beautiful and ugly, etc. Rather, it is my contention that, insofar as we approach the grotesque "in" something or insofar as we approach something "with" the grotesque, we must perceive these sides or poles of our evaluative or critical distinctions in new light, as, in a way, inverted twins of one another, as identical opposites. If this is the case, then to thoroughly explore the grotesque one must spiral towards the inward space of contradiction, of paradox, towards the midzones between identical opposites, before spiraling back out, as it were, into evaluations: this is grotesque *par excellence*.

We can perceive the aperture of such "spaces" in the world represented in the paintings of Francis Bacon, perhaps even more immediately and explicitly than in those of Bruegel and Bosch. The Baconian world is full of these tensions between any of a number of related binaries, perhaps most prominently dramatized in the repeated motif of his oozing, pearlescent, fleshily indistinct figures (Are they developing, becoming, or are they rotting, dying? Are they stuck in the middle? Are they coming apart, even as they are becoming?) trapped within "a demarcated area, an interior non-place" (Domino 70). These areas or "non-places" are angular constructions that resemble abstract cages, chairs, and pedestals, or, more frequently, they are simply furnished, lushly painted otherwise vacant rooms. The paintings image a vague, interior space, the abortive/developing flesh-figure, spilling or smearing out from itself, residing there in the room, perched aloft the toilet or chair, sprawled out across the bed or rug, or oozing from a square on the wall down onto a table. These are troubling spaces to be sure, spaces rife with the potential for the grotesque. One critic has written that the "darker, more disturbing use of the grotesque" is critical in Bacon's work, "functioning as a means of pushing us beneath the surface of reality to a deeper dimension," one concerned essentially with "the reality of despair" (Yates, "Francis Bacon" 163, 161).

But, if we can perceive this despairing grotesque opening out from within the space of the Baconian world — if we can "feel" it here — must we not also admit that we can feel its inverted twin yawning within the preposterous world of Dr. Seuss?[1] The Seussian world is populated with grotesque evolutionary degenerates and malformed, human-like (in one way or another) fusions of beast and bird and reptile, etc., who are set adrift in a meaningless, menacing world, which seems itself to be alive, one which seems to be pieced together in a flimsy architecture of knobby, furred joints and cavities, walkways, train tracks, and habitations perched rather precariously on its elbow-like bumps and knee-like bends or baroquely structured in, around, or upon its orifices and protuberances. The Seussian world surely dwarfs the medieval bestiaries and devilries in the sheer variety of its creatures; it surely outstrips the worlds of Bruegel or Bosch in its portrayal and enumeration of human vice. In some ways, we may even perceive the Seussian world as more subversively grotesque than Bacon's, for while both image the humanlike figure as some mimetic maceration of the original upon which it is based in some "other," alienated, contradictory "space," Seuss more thoroughly distorts and alienates this world itself as well. In general, there are none of the banal comforts offered to Bacon's smeared subjects in lieu of their missing meaning — no bourgeois domestic accoutrements or possessions: no plush couches, no toilets, no (proportionally adequate) beds — no place to sit or shit or screw (all behaviors that Bacon's figures engage in). Seuss's protagonists have no time for bourgeois trivialities or pleasures. They are constantly on the run, careening through a world which looks like it could fall apart at any moment or swallow them whole or brush them away, a world of absurdity and despair, one in which they have been given a role in some ludicrous game that they do not understand — and that game is their life. And more radical still: the protagonists in the Seussian world still (sometimes grouchily) hope, without whining; they hope, not for meaning per se, but for justice, peace, and community.

The grotesque as such necessitates a persistent mode of resistance to the contraction of conceptual spaces of contradiction; it thrives on the logic of paradox. It requires a certain degree of irreverence in order to drag the sacred into the profane, the beautiful into the ugly, the elite into the popular, the high into the low, and so on. From the perspective of the grotesque, the critic is obligated to compress, compare, contrast contemporaries like Bacon and Seuss, both of whom provide rather distressing "pictures from life's other side" (to borrow a line from Hank Williams), but "other" pictures which must be "othered" themselves in the layering of one dimension of contradiction across another. And just as the worlds evoked through appeals to the grotesque by these artists effectively drag human being through the muck, they can also be perceived dynamically to tug correctively at one another, not as poles on opposite ends of a continuum ("dark" and "light," etc.), but as inverted manifestations of twinned approaches: we can perceive Baconian dread in the Seussian cosmos, and, by then redirecting or inverting our critical gaze back at the Baconian world via our revised view of the Seussian, we must perceive a bourgeois solipsistic form of navel-gazing in Bacon's existential dread. The grotesque is the prism at the center of this process, constantly fragmenting and obfuscating, but in such a way that it adds variety, intensity, and color to the visions we perceive.

Just as the prism refracts all light that tries to penetrate it, the grotesque effects a kind of leveling of those worlds that writers/artists "shine" through it, the worlds of art, philosophy, ideology, etc. This initiates the critic/theorist of the grotesque on a spiraling journey both into and out from the seats of contradiction and/or paradox. This book attempts to trek just such a circuitous journey with and in and towards the grotesque with respect to its intersections in contemporary American film, specifically, the films of Tim Burton, Terry Gilliam, the Coen brothers, David Lynch, and a few early films of the slasher genre. So, even more than being a book "about" film, this is a book about the grotesque, one aimed at exploring what it does in film art — in slapstick farce, drama, fantasy, realism, horror, comedy, in the blockbuster and the art film, in the independent project and the multimillion-dollar production, and in the Academy award winners and the universally despised.

Introduction

Imagine human beings living in an underground, cavelike dwelling ..., able to see only in front of them. Light is provided by a fire burning far above and behind them. Between the prisoners and the fire, there is an elevated road stretching. Imagine that along this road a low wall has been built.... Also imagine, then, that there are people alongside the wall carrying multifarious artifacts that project above it.

— Plato, *The Republic*, Book VII

Cinematic Grotesquery, Genre and History

In an accompanying sketch that demonstrates Athanasius Kircher's "magic lantern" in the 1671 edition of his *Ars Magna Lucis et Umbrae*, he has drawn a dark room divided in half: on one side is the box containing his invention; emerging from the other side of a partition is a shaft of light projecting an image on the brick wall some distance away (Parkinson 10–11). And what is the content of that image, now a foundational one in the prehistory of the cinema? It is the macabre figure of grinning death: a human skeleton standing erect, a sickle tucked under its right arm and a portentous hourglass in its left hand (10). The grotesque, defined succinctly and judiciously by Phillip Thomson as "the unresolved clash of incompatibles in work and response" or "the ambivalently abnormal," has been a part of the movies since their conception in or out of other art forms and manners of visual representation (27). While it can be glimpsed across the history of popular film in America from the silents through the 1960s, allowed to explore variations amenable to various generic requirements (in the incorporation of grotesquery in the depiction of the monsters of horror or of ridiculousness in comedy, etc.), it is also chained in a way, tethered to the concept of genre.[1] Even so, the collision of opposites on which the grotesque thrives is present in early American film, especially in comedy and gothic/horror (and, later, in science fiction/fantasy as well), though

Introduction

only to a certain degree. The demands of genre allow glimpses, elements or aspects, of the grotesque, but rarely on the scale of what is possible after the studio system falls apart and the production code with it.

Silent slapstick comedies of the Sennett Keystone variety appeal to the grotesque in their reliance on clownish comic violence and play with the threat of death. The mild, Dickensian grotesquery of Chaplin's Tramp in *The Gold Rush* or *Modern Times* makes satiric comedy out of dehumanizing situations (Cook 202). Chaplin extends this trajectory even further in *Monsieur Verdoux*, his brooding, grimly comic masterpiece in which a middle aged clerk takes to romancing and murdering rich women in order to acquire money to support his family. The most disturbing scene in this film may be the final one in which Verdoux walks away from the camera to his death at the guillotine, but suddenly he is limping slightly, his toes turned outward — Chaplin as lady-killer and Chaplin as lovable Tramp merge uneasily. Buster Keaton, too, plays with the comic grotesque, particularly in scenes like those in *The Navigator* or *Steamboat Bill Jr.* when the world seems, quite literally, to be crashing down around him, and he escapes death, often by what seems like sheer chance, but remains apparently unaffected, as he maintains his characteristic stoic, deadpan gaze. And others (W. C. Fields, Laurel and Hardy, the anarchic Marx Brothers, et al.) extend this trajectory in their various ways.

Whereas early comedy arrives at a light sense of grotesquery by engaging in humor through the incorporation of threats of violence, the deleterious effects of social problems, and menace of catastrophe into comic situations, narratives, and structures, early film horror and gothic invert this strategy. The grotesquery in these films seems to rely on the mismatch of humor, ridiculousness, and the like within a gothic/horror aesthetic visual context reliant on the ominous style of German Expressionist cinema (Bordwell and Thompson 103). The films by directors such as James Whale (*Frankenstein, The Invisible Man*, and *Bride of Frankenstein*), Tod Browning (*Dracula* and *Freaks*), and Karl Freund (*The Mummy*), among others, rely on exotic, threatening presences, represented in these films by actors like Boris Karloff and Bela Legosi, whose performances can at times cross the border from the terrifying into the laughably ridiculous. At other times, films such as these seem to cast an ironic eye on their own subject matter, as the example of Browning's *Freaks* demonstrates.

Freaks is a film that takes experimentation with the grotesque in this era of American filmmaking about as far as it could have gone within the limitations of the Hollywood studio production system. With a cast composed mostly of actual circus performers (circus "freaks," to use the parlance of the variety of "show" they are associated with), Browning inverts the usual thematic structure of the horror film in a way that is similar to what Whale does with *Frankenstein*. He makes monsters out of the cruel, "normal" people in the film. While his camera lingers, perhaps fetishistically, over the variously "freakish" bodies of his performers (a "human torso," a set of Siamese twins, a legless boy, a "human skeleton," a few "pinheads," a "he-she," some dwarves, and others), he does allow them to be perceived as a kind, caring, life-loving carnival family. That is, until they are wronged. Then they become a murderous, vengeful throng of xenophobic monsters and are, therefore, pulled back within the normative function of the monster in the genre. In both cases (in comedy and in gothic/horror), then, one of the functions of generic conventions seems to be to provide a "coherent baseline," as David Bordwell puts it in "The Classical Hollywood Style, 1917–60," which allows for "bursts of stylization," but only insofar as such bursts fit within the "range of permissible stylization" and thus remain oriented around classical normativity (71).

As with any broad, sweeping theory of the history of anything, this narrative is only suggestive of what seems to be a prominent trend in American filmmaking within the system from the rise of the studio until its fall. There are surely examples (probably especially among the B-movie catalog) that would provide challenges to this notion. One very famous and prolific exception is Alfred Hitchcock, who, after directing twenty or so films in England and rising to considerable popularity there, came to Hollywood in 1938, where the film industry was booming and able to sustain his big budget popular art films (Cook 326). Over the next twenty years, Hitchcock redefined the sufficiently vague genre of suspense/thrillers, establishing his ownership over it, all the while engaging in unparalleled experimentation with nearly every facet of the filmmaking process.

His films portray the integration of traditionally comic aspects, such as clever verbal banter, chase sequences, and visual gags, into filmic narratives centered on murder, espionage, and identity crisis. In *Shadow of a Doubt,* he plays with subtle contrasts between the threat of a murderous psychotic and his perceived normality in a provincial town full of overly agreeable people who fail to realize how dangerous he is. *Spellbound* integrates a surreally warped dreamscape constructed by Salvador Dali to illustrate a trip through a very Freudian unconscious. The narrative of *Rope* is constructed around two young men who attempt to prove themselves worthy Nietzschean supermen by killing a friend and then serving their dinner guests from the makeshift coffin that holds his corpse. *Strangers on a Train* examines an initially rather silly doubling of Guy with the awkwardly humorous Bruno, but Hitchcock allows Bruno to retain his ridiculously pathetic quality even as he becomes a serious threat, that is, after he kills Guy's wife (satisfying Guy's fleeting unstated wish?) and then attempts to frame Guy for it after Guy refuses to "repay" him the favor by murdering his father. *Vertigo* and *Psycho* feature Hitchcock's interest in madness and doubles, as well as his experimentation with tone, cinematography, editing, and characterization in films in which he also seems to relish depicting the unraveling of a mind and its mutually crushing effects on the self and others. By the 1960s, when Hitchcock is experimenting with the grotesquery of cross-dressing killers, animated corpses, an avian apocalypse, and neurotic obsessions with thunderstorms and the color red in *Psycho*, *The Birds*, and *Marnie*, the production code is being scrapped, foreign art films are pouring into American cinemas, and 80 percent of films are either being made by Hollywood's finest in foreign countries ("runaway" productions) or are being financed independently (Cook 512–14).

As David Cook observes, when the financial troubles in Hollywood worsened in the sixties, a multiplicity of industry forces coalesced to generate sweeping changes to the American film scene: an increased tolerance for independent (European style) art films; independent producers, like Roger Corman (whose own Poe cycle explored the grotesque in the fifties), began promoting young filmmakers (Kubrick, Penn, Lucas, etc.) with their own creative visions; foreign art films (Fellini, Antonioni, Bergman, Bunuel, et al.) began to run in major theaters throughout the United States; and film studies courses began to emerge in the college classroom (920–22). Cook also observes a major shift in the movie-watching demographic:

> This audience was composed of the first generation in history that had grown up with the visually, if not intellectually, sophisticated medium of television. Through hours of watching television as children and teenagers, its members knew the language of cinema implicitly, and when filmmakers like Frankenheimer, Lumet, Penn, and Peckinpah began to move out of the studios in the

mid- to late-sixties and to employ the New Wave techniques of French and Italian cinemas for the first time on the American screen, this young audience liked what it saw [922].

Cook describes the crumbling of the old structures — the studio, the production code, the changes in the viewing public — as affording an open and wider space (literally and figuratively) within which new filmmakers could experiment. Generic changes through the sixties and seventies in the war film (Kubrick's *Dr. Strangelove*, Coppola's *Apocalypse Now*), the western (the films of Sergio Leone and Sam Peckinpah), the road movie (Penn's *Bonny and Clyde*, Hopper's *Easy Rider*), romantic comedy (Woody Allen films), horror (the films of Toby Hooper, George Romero, Wes Craven), and drama (Altman, Scorsese), etc. reveal heretofore unparalleled experimentation with symbolism, imagery, scoring/use of music and sound, pacing, cinematography, degree and depiction of violence/gore and sexual content, atmosphere and tone in which filmmakers situate extreme images, degree of adherence to generic trends, etc. This was an era when up-and-coming filmmakers already viewed themselves as auteurs. They were film artists who were familiar with film history, foreign film, and movie making and who were ready to make their mark in the art form by strategically breaking conventions, by shocking, by carefully depicting life in the extreme — the weird, wild, and terrible — in order to find something good in it or just because it had never before been done that way or just to piss people off.[2] This was an era of filmmaking ripe for the grotesque, and it saw David Lynch and Terry Gilliam begin their careers in the movies, Burton and the Coens to follow them a little over a decade later. And it is the presence and character of the grotesque, as the work of these four (five including both Coens) filmmakers elucidates it, that the present study will focus on.[3]

Establishing Shot

Thomson's definition of the grotesque (quoted above) conveys his attempts to establish some common ground in a subject of critical inquiry and theorization in which common ground is difficult to find. The ambivalent, oppositional, and contradictory nature that he identifies in his definition of the grotesque carries over as one of the key features in the wider literature on the subject. Part 1 (Chapters I and II) provides a thorough examination of the theories of the grotesque that have been prominent in recent scholarship on the subject. Most contemporary theorization on the grotesque returns to the work of Wolfgang Kayser and Mikhail Bakhtin, who aim their critical gazes in opposite directions at nearly every turn, Kayser toward the grim, malevolent incubus of the modern, and Bakhtin toward the raucous, life-affirming reveries of the medieval and Renaissance eras. Part 1 follows this precedent and extends the discussion from Kayser and Bakhtin to the various attempts to close the gap between them or to banish them to opposite sides of a critical continuum for which there is no bridge.

The subsequent chapters in Part 2 on Tim Burton and Terry Gilliam and Part 3 on Joel and Ethan Coen and David Lynch build on facets of theory extrapolated from the philosophy of the grotesque. Each chapter begins by delineating a critical direction from within the more eclectic theory section and specifying and then extending the theoretical approach taken in interpreting the material. Part 2 initiates the application of the grotesque to film by invoking an (inter)polar approach to the grotesque in an attempt to invoke but problematize the banishment of "light" and "dark" grotesque (and related binary distinctions inherent in the "philosophy" of the grotesque) to opposite ends of a theoretical continuum. Chapter III focuses on locating a Bakhtinian relationship between the "official" and the "carnival" in Tim Burton's films. Chapter IV explores the connection and overlap of the mythic (in Harpham and Danow), madness (in Foucault's *Madness and Civilization*), and the grotesque as a prominent feature of Terry Gilliam's films.

Part 3 explores the ways in which the grotesque must be conceived beyond categories placed in binary distinctions on a continuum. Consequently, Part 3 is concerned with examining the invasiveness of the philosophy of the grotesque — moving from the outer polarities of contradiction to within the "moments," intervals, and metaphysical and psychic spaces (subjectivities, identities, fantasies) at their heart. Chapter V interprets physically manifested responses to catastrophe and violence via the acting style through which they are presented in the films of Joel and Ethan Coen as they are related to Geoffrey Galt Harpham's notion of "the grotesque as interval," a site of alienation and confusion, one to which excessive physicality in the Coens' films point (14–15). Chapter VI investigates the modernist grotesque in the cinematic world evoked in David Lynch's films through figures and functions (associated with the concepts of the double and the abhuman) that threaten human and/or subjective identity and that also suggest overlaps between the uncanny, the gothic, and the grotesque.

Part 4 concludes this study of the grotesque with contradiction (of course): Chapter VII turns a sharp gaze upon the "world," while Chapter VIII follows the route, one rife with paradox, of the Melvillian contemplative. Chapter VII is intended as a kind of intervention against any manner of stricture that even a "soft" adherence to an auteurist approach may entail. Here, relying on reflections from the writings of Theodor Adorno, Frederic Jameson, Robin Wood, and Bertolt Brecht, I am interested in unfolding the grotesque via an unholy trinity of "hippie horror" films. The point of this exercise is to provide a glimpse of the grotesque from the (largely anti-auteurist) perspectives of genre and (broadly Marxist) cultural theory, which will provide a brief exhibition of what the grotesque is capable of when utilized for deducing the aims of genre or politics rather than for probing a director's artistic output in an attempt to recognize some aspect his or her aesthetic philosophy. Finally, this study closes in Chapter VIII by turning to a philosophical thread from Herman Melville's *Moby-Dick* to sustain a meditation which situates the grotesque, its vagaries and contradictions, with humanity itself. Throughout this study, my thesis is that the work of these filmmakers (variously "established" representatives from two generations of American filmmaking) demonstrates a multifaceted but consistent engagement and experimentation with the grotesque. Beyond and within this is an elaboration of the grotesque in theory and in these filmmakers' work that progresses incrementally towards demonstrating that the notion of polar oppositions in the grotesque is ultimately untenable and that we must find a way to theorize the grotesque in a way that gives full attention to the contrastive and contradictory nature of grotesque art, which can be glimpsed at the borders, at the center, outside, and within.

Matte Shot: Auteur/Grotesque

Filmmaking is, almost necessarily, a collaborative art form. Even so, the four filmmakers whom I have selected for this study (one of them, in fact, being a pair of collaborating brothers with a seemingly consistent and unitary artistic vision) have achieved auteur status to such a degree that their films often bear their names in commercials and advertisements as a "brand name," inviting potential viewers to come see the next install-ment "from the mind of" Tim Burton, the Coen Brothers, Terry Gilliam, or David Lynch. Each filmmaker (or in the Coens' case, pair of filmmakers) has repeatedly collaborated with some of the same writers or co-writers, producers, cinematographers, etc., but this is evidence that has fueled arguments for or against auteurist approaches to their work.

This study of the grotesque in the films of these directors *is* an auteurist approach: I am "looking for stylistic and thematic connections from film to film," and, at least to some degree, I am interested in "dis-covering a worldview, a philosophy" that seems to extend across the breadth of their films (Grant 57). But I am aware of the debates in the back- and foreground of such an approach, debates which Barry Keith Grant sets out nicely and succinctly in *Film Genre: From Iconography to Ideology* (56–79). If my approach is from the perspective of auteur criticism, however, it is a "soft" auteurism, one balanced by an acknowledgement of and appreci-ation for the wider economic, political, and ideological challenges to it, as well as the contributions of the various collaborators who aid in bringing a film to life. Further, if an auteurist approach is interested in "discovering a worldview, a philosophy" in the works of a filmmaker (57), and if the worldview I find is one that demonstrates a particularly consistent engage-ment with the grotesque — a philosophy that extends, not only across the works of one director or directorial team (in the case of the Coens), but also across the works of at least three others (six, including Romero, Craven, and Hooper)[4] — then the auteurism of this study is one that is also balanced by wider philosophical and aesthetic concerns that place any artist within an aesthetic/cultural heritage — the philosophy of the grotesque in art — a hydra-headed coil of ideas and formal qualities which must be acknowledged and interpreted along with any individual artist's navigation of it. Consequently, the present study is more immediately con-cerned with exploring the grotesque and pursuing its theoretical corollaries via critical engagement with these cinematic visionaries than it is with a more traditional, more narrowly defined "film studies" approach to think-ing about film.

PART 1

The Philosophy of the Grotesque

I believe that there is no test of greatness in periods, nations, or men, more sure than the development, among them or in them, of a noble grotesque.

— John Ruskin, *The Stones of Venice*

The grotesque has often been invoked or implied in various philosophical discussions, frequently, as might be expected, of those to do with aesthetics, as in the writings of Kant, Hegel, and Schopenhauer, among others, but rarely do such philosophical accounts elevate the grotesque to the foreground, meditating upon it, its formal properties and its effects intact, as an object of philosophical speculation in its own right. Rather a conceptualization of the grotesque is fit into systems: it is made to occupy this or that position in a hierarchy or process or theory of something else.[1] As will be shown below, the grotesque has received most of its attention from cultural theorists and literary and art critics, but writers from any number of domains have proffered their reflections on the grotesque. Further, as with any "cultural theory" worth its name, theories of the grotesque have been developed with inspiration from philosophy, psychoanalysis, theology, etc.— from "culture." While what follows attempts to give a somewhat orderly account of contemporary writing on the cultural phenomena of the grotesque and argues for a particular kind of engagement with the various domains from which and towards which the grotesque comes and goes, I do not pretend that it is any manner of systematic philosophy. And while I am interested in the philosophical "weight" of the grotesque and in what an understanding of philosophy can contribute in order to make that weight more bearable, I do not pretend to be a philosopher.

13

Part 1. The Philosophy of the Grotesque

Rather, I name this section "The Philosophy of the Grotesque" for a few reasons. First, as I have already alluded to, there is some degree of dynamism between the grotesque and philosophical speculation. The grotesque often accosts us with art that demands response or interpretation or that we cannot help but respond to or that we must reflect upon before judging; thus, philosophy, as a discipline interested in the ways in which we think about, interpret, respond to, and engage the world, is a useful tool in thinking through what and how the grotesque means to us, which, of course, thereby implicates it in a number of philosophical categories and discussions. Second, there is a dearth of other appropriate critical rubrics under which to title what the grotesque is, does, does to its viewers/readers, to and with its subjects and components, etc. The grotesque is too bound up with the physical to be completely abstracted as a "theory" and too much concerned with bodies to be dematerialized into a "mentality." So, three, I choose to use the phrase "The Philosophy of the Grotesque" because it entails more than sheer theory; it goes deeper than speculation alone. Perhaps the least worst understanding of what I am trying to articulate by the use of the term "philosophy" here is less immediately associated with the specialized, often academic, meaning of the word: I am after something closer to "philosophy" understood as a set of values or beliefs and practices through which one engages the world, a viewpoint or lens through which one perceives the world, a peculiar sensibility, which, as will be shown, may be born out of or in response to related qualities in one's experience of the world. After all, it was initially such a way of perceiving or being in the world from which grotesque art first emerged when ancient humans reached out to the rocky walls around them. It seems appropriate, then, that a loving attempt to learn the wisdom of this terrible beauty might call itself a philosophy.

I. Art, Being and Contrast

Glaucon: It is a strange image you are describing...
— Plato, *Republic*, Book 7, 515a.4

In a tin box the grit of her —
ash and bone. The biscuits
are fluffy today...
— Allison Pelegrin, "Funeral Dawn"

The Grotesque and Theory: Beginning When There Is No Beginning

There is no single comprehensive theory of the grotesque that accommodates the presence of the swirl and undulation of the often divergent or contradictory theories and definitions associated with the term. There has been, among such attempts in criticism and theory, associated with a number of disciplines (literature, painting/visual/plastic arts, cultural studies, anthropology, psychology, philosophy, theology, to name a few), as much agreement as disagreement about what the grotesque is or what its basic principles or effects are, among other questions that arise around it. Further, a starting place for a concentrated effort at discussing the grotesque with any seriousness also proves difficult, as Geoffrey Galt Harpham notes in *On the Grotesque: Strategies of Contradiction in Art and Literature* (xvi). Harpham observes that, regardless of the phenomenological approach taken toward defining the grotesque, its lack of clarity persists. Direct apprehension of the grotesque is often quite tricky, while recognition of its effects "in" art is typically rather immediate. This conceptual aporia, Harpham insists, inverts the pattern by which most critical notions function. He identifies that, even at first approaching it, the grotesque is rife with paradox: it is immutable but elusive; it emerges from within a multiplicity of forms but is somehow as distinguishable from such semblances

15

as a wave is as it curls along the water — the grotesque is always identifiable as itself. And the final paradox Harpham cites among these preliminaries is the originary one: the grotesque has no historical departure point, so, consequently, one cannot adequately narrate its history (xvi).

In light of these abortive fundamental complications, many theorists/ critics (including Harpham) include, as an initial component of their studies, an excavation of the word itself, stalking the word "grotesque" and its roots, mutations, and derivatives through the history of its uses in texts. This also proves to be a kind of false foundation, for, as Harpham observes, the first objects to earn the attribution of the term, wall frescoes in Nero's Golden Palace, were not to be described as such until the palace itself was exhumed from its fifteen-hundred-year repose around 1480, which would mean that the first application of the word "grotesque" nearly coincides with the (perhaps arbitrary) borderline between the late medieval and the early modern periods (23). Thus at its inception, the word is born out of an aesthetic and/or ideological conflict between ideas associated with a burgeoning modernity and those reflected in ancient artifacts from a culture in the remote past. Wolfgang Kayser cites the word "*grotta* (cave)" as the root of various applications of "grotesque," designating these weird, decorative fusions of plant, animal, and human forms by association with the "cave," the underground excavation site, where they were discovered, rather than with the form or content of the images themselves (19–24). The word, then, only begins to accumulate more specific meaning as a descriptive or aesthetic term as its original denotative meaning shifts in use from "from the cave" to a designation applied to various artworks that were taken to be related in some way to the qualities of those works from the cave. Moreover, as both Kayser and Harpham write, the style of these ancient frescoes from Nero's palace predates Rome (Kayser 19–20; Harpham 23). Although they retain a prominent position as inaugural objects for the grotesque and its study, these works of art indicate relationships with ideologies that predate Roman culture considerably. Thus, they were not novel expressions of artistic style concomitant with Nero's era; in fact, Harpham states that these frescoes contain formal features that can even be traced back to the most ancient cave paintings, that is, to the very birthplace of art (Harpham 23, xvi). "Grotesque," then, as a word is a "modern" one, and at its inception it is one whose origins seem almost completely functional or linguistically denotative. The word seems only to become the basis of a theory

16

when it merges with cultural conflicts aesthetic, metaphysical, ideological, etc.—a road which leads grotesque detectives back to the very origins of art, which itself surely has any number of trap-doors and secret passageways to places farther away from the light, taking them deeper and deeper into the dark caves of history.

A notable exception to the notion that some form of the grotesque is as old as history itself, or even as old as human consciousness, is included in a theory propounded by Ewa Kuryluk in *Salome and Judas in the Cave of Sex*. She delimits the grotesque to art produced within the particular historical period, beginning with the unearthing of the ancient frescoes mentioned above during the Renaissance and ending in the nineteenth century. Her theory of the grotesque turns on the notion of "anti-worlds," any number of underground oppositional "worlds" that exist in contradistinction to official culture's accepted ideological "worlds." Such bifurcations include the anti-worlds of femininity, childhood, the heretical and apocryphal, and hell and Satan as they are opposed to "official" worlds controlled by men, adults, the canonical and orthodox, and heaven and Jesus (and there are others that fit the form of opposition between dominant culture and subculture, etc.) (3). I tend to agree with Wilson Yates's critique of Kuryluk in "An Introduction to the Grotesque: Theoretical and Theological Considerations," which states that Kuryluk's rather arbitrary rationale for the relegation of the grotesque to this particular period is contingent on a similarly arbitrary determination of when Western culture dominates and when it does not. This allows her to stack the deck for how to perceive the grotesque simply by aligning its expression as contingent on her delineation of "anti-worlds" and their corresponding dominant worlds in Western culture (38–39).

Rather than to risk founding a theory of the grotesque upon any number of possible historical "false bottoms," I will begin by considering the two works of modern grotesque theory that catapulted the concept into its current position, as Phillip Thomson observes, as an "object of considerable aesthetic analysis and critical evaluation": Wolfgang Kayser's *The Grotesque in Art and Literature* and Mikhail Bakhtin's *Rabelais and His World* (Harpham xvi–xvii; Thomson 11). While this methodological strategy of beginning with relatively recent theories seems most fitting for a study of the grotesque in contemporary culture, it only deceptively makes for a firmer foundation for my attempt to elucidate the concept, for as is well known to those familiar with these texts (and as Harpham reminds), Kayser's and Bakhtin's theories are utterly contradictory down to their most elemental assumptions (xvii–xviii). Moreover, though these works are the two most influential and most referred-to texts in subsequent meditations on the grotesque, the very possibility of an authority in the "field" of such studies is put into question, since the grotesque is so pervasive that one can support just about any theory by judiciously choosing examples to support it (xvii–xviii).

I shall begin, then, by building first from Kayser's and Bakhtin's theories before moving to more recent studies on the concept (by Dieter Meindl, David K. Danow, and Geoffrey Galt Harpham), in an attempt to ascertain a theory that is broad enough to encompass the various filmic employments of the grotesque from the group of filmmakers I have selected for the latter part of the book. I hope, too, that my rendition of grotesque theory will also allow enough conceptual "space" to bring together at least some of the contradictory, divergent, or opposing aspects of the various theories that I put into conversation with one another. My goal is neither to "stack the deck" merely by proposing a theory that seems convincing only according to my judiciously chosen examples, nor is my intention necessarily to present a synthesis of all previous theoretical attempts at defining, delineating, and delimiting the grotesque. Rather, I want to present the philosophy of the grotesque as a kind of conversation, as a many-sided discussion, one that, like all good conversations, thrives because of the agreements (synthesis) and disagreements (contradictions) among its interlocutors. It is this tension between the parity and disparity, between unity and contradiction, between agreement and disagreement, which makes this and every good conversation interesting and fruitful.

The Exorcist and the Clown: Wolfgang Kayser and Mikhail Bakhtin

Kayser's and Bakhtin's theories of the grotesque, as I mentioned above, do not hang together well. Kayser's reflects an aesthetic theory influenced by a modernist existentialism, while Bakhtin's theory emerges from an existential premise about the meaning of life that he sees as the animating principle in a multitude of aesthetic works, kinds of performance, cultural events, and phenomena in culture (Meindl 18). Kayser maintains that "grotesque," as a word, can be applied in three domains connected with art: the process by which art is created, that art work itself, and the reception of the work of art. Accordingly, because of its universal applicability to each domain in the life of the work of art, the grotesque can be appropriated into aesthetics proper as a conceptual designation in its own right (180). The three-part aspect of art itself sets the work of art apart from various other forms of production because it marks the art work as "created." This structure uniquely preserves the identity of the work of art, even as its "cause" may be absorbed in the final product; art thereby transcends its own "occasion." Finally, then, the work of art must be "received," which, Kayser says, sets it apart from various other sorts of use. Moreover, it is only in this act of being received that the work of art can truly be experienced, regardless of how or whether it is modified upon reception (180).

For Kayser, the grotesque, as an aesthetic category is a kind of metaphor for the "work of art" itself. If one takes into consideration Kayser's attempts to contrast the art-work from other modes of production and interprets his employment of the phrase "work of art" literally — the work that goes into producing the art, which is embodied in the piece of art, as well as the work that the art does in impinging itself upon the receivers of the art, who must do their own work in its terms in order to "experience" it as fully as possible — then one begins to apprehend the nature of the grotesque as art in its most radical form (180). The grotesque reveals art as a seething, tension-ridden cultural cauldron in which each of these three "realms" is in conflict with the others. Though the grotesque, because it is an aesthetic designation, can only be experienced in being received, Kayser remarks, contemporary aesthetic and poetic theories necessitate that the concept be theorized as a "comprehensive structural principle of works of art," which entails some kind of discussion or consideration of the creative processes of artists as well. But with the grotesque, these realms often cut against one another, for the art in which practitioners of a particular culture may normally express themselves may strike those of another culture as grotesque upon reception even though such a response may seem incongruous, given the structural make-up of a given piece of art (181). Kayser notes that the resultant experience of the grotesque from such misunderstandings of the artistic principles of foreign cultures still merits the moniker, even in cases in which the application of the word "grotesque" is justified only by sheer ignorance on the part of the receivers (181). He relates that such experiences warn us away from defining the grotesque only according to its effects upon reception, but Kayser reminds that there persists an unavoidable "vicious circle" in defining the term for aesthetic theory. His more general points on aesthetics as such dictate that the three aspects of interpreting what art is are mutually inclusive, so, any attempt to define the grotesque's structural properties must imply some manner of reference to its reception (181). It seems that this sense of fundamental uncertainty regarding the relationship between the artist, the art work, and the receivers of art undermines and opens up theoretical considerations in Kayser's (and perhaps all) aesthetics.

Composer Arnold Schoenberg provides a helpful summation of this problem in a reflection entitled "An Artistic Impression" in *Style and Idea*:

> An artistic impression is substantially the resultant of two components. One, what the work of art gives to the onlooker — the other, what he is capable of giving to the work of art. Since both are variable magnitudes, the resultant, too, is variable, so that with the same work of art it can vary from one individual to the next. Thus the effect exerted by a work of art depends only in part on the work itself [189].

Schoenberg goes on to suggest that the "forces" in the art awaken "forces" within the receiver, which mingle in tension with the forces from the art to be "sensed by us" as an artistic impression (189). The "forces" residing in each component, that is, in the art-work and the onlooker/receiver, are, for Schoenberg, equal in latency and intensity, and the commingling of these forces in tension "explodes"; this explosion *is* the artistic impression (189). Further, the intensity of this incendiary impression is contingent on the onlooker's capacity to both give and receive simultaneously (189).

The point that Kayser makes here in his preliminaries, before coming to his definition of the grotesque, and the point that I am attempting to elucidate using Schoenberg, is that the grotesque as an aesthetic theory bears the same marks as any aesthetic theory: it must consider what the work art is and does at every point, from its inception to its reception, and it must acknowledge the multivalent, and often contradictory, results of the unruly dynamism present in the relationship that inheres among the three "realms" of the work of art. Further, the grotesque, as an aesthetic category and "structural principle" that embodies the work of art itself (taken in both literal and figurative senses) in its most radical form does so self-consciously and self-referentially. It embodies the work of art self-consciously because it highlights and polarizes the problematic relations among the "realms" of art, forcing Kayser's own aesthetics into the "vicious circle" of interpretation in which analysis of "structural properties" associated with the grotesque requires an account of the reception of those very properties, the effect they have on the receiver, though this cannot account exclusively for the application of the term "grotesque" (180–81). Thus, the paradox or contradiction of this circular hermeneutical logic sits at the very heart of aesthetics, and, for Kayser, the grotesque realizes this and makes it present in a peculiar way.

The grotesque embodies the work of art self-referentially in its radical depiction of the "createdness" of the art, its fictive quality as artifice, which is inscribed within grotesque art in the "repetitions of subject matter," including monsters, fantastic creatures, the synthesis of mechanical and organic components, human forms reduced to automata, the petrification of faces into masks, and many other motifs that turn on a certain degree of ambiguity regarding the actual and the artifice (180–83). Such self-referentiality also functions in what Kayser calls the "*Schaffenspoetik*," a "poetics concerned with the creative process," which Kayser sees as a substantial expression concerning the grotesque's formal structure that operates in many of the frequent literary encounters with madness from Romantic and Modernist writers (184). Kayser's theory of the grotesque is, then, a theory of aesthetics, insofar as this latter term relates to discussions pertaining to the Greek word *aesthesis*— sensual and intellectual perception — though it is perhaps a theory that "stands for" art in the sense I described above by "standing against" art. That is, by offering an alternative logic, structure, and beauty to those that dominate "our world," the grotesque applies a corrosive but corrective funhouse mirror to the dominant aesthetics (185).

Kayser claims that "the grotesque is a structure... [It] instills fear of life rather than fear of death. Structurally, it presupposes that the categories which apply to our world view become inapplicable" (184–85). The grotesque, for Kayser, alienates people from the world in which they live by making that world absurd for them, turning its order upside down, crippling any sense of certainty or stability, and finally leaving them in the throes of a disorienting, dejecting madness (185). Kayser's grotesque, as critic Dieter Meindl writes, refashions reality as "the sphere of the unfathomable, a familiar world in the process of dissolution or estrangement, diffusing an aura that instills insecurity, revulsion and terror" (15). "THE GROTESQUE IS THE ESTRANGED WORLD," Kayser states dramatically (185 emph. orig.). He continues this line of thought by observing a key difference between the world of the grotesque and the world of the fairy tale. Fairy tale worlds may indeed be considered alien and strange from an external viewpoint, but these worlds are not "estranged" in the way that the world of the grotesque is (185). In approaching the world of fairy tales, it is our world that must undergo transformation; we must adjust what is natural and familiar there according to the logic of fairyland. The world of the grotesque essentially relies on the sudden surprise and shock of inscribing the natural and familiar from our world into a context in which these comforting, reliable elements become ominous and strange (185). The grotesque world affects us so dramatically, terrifies us even, because of its strategy of shattering our confidence in our own world, which in light of our recognition of its substance in the grotesque parallel, makes us wary about our ability to live in either, for our view of both changes in the process (185).

So, for Kayser, while fairy tales relate to us an innocuous parallel reality that calls for us to amend our worldview in order to make meaning in this different reality, the grotesque relies on the often terrifying disjuncture between our world, what we know of it, and our ability to interpret it, and the grotesque world's inimical or indifferent relation to our world (185–86): "The grotesque world is — and is not — our own world" (37). The ambiguity by which the grotesque functions is left also in its wake in the way it affects us. We are thus left with the cold awareness that our world — one which we previously perceived as harmonious and familiar — is alienated from us, or we from it, as we are made to acknowledge the disintegration of its now fragmented coherence under the sway of the dreadful forces made plain in its juxtaposition with the grotesque world (37). The ways in which we would normally orient ourselves become useless because the grotesque thrives on the fusion of those domains that we assume are separate, the eradication of statistical probability, the obliteration of identity, distortions of "natural" proportions, the interruption of the process of categorizing objects, the annihilation of personality, and the breakdown of chronological order (185).

Kayser argues that the grotesque is that aspect of artistic expressions that engages contradictions, sometimes playful and usually dreadful, toward a depiction of the dissolution of the familiar world that is ruined by the "abysmal forces" active in the grotesque (35–36). This form of expression in art inspires a sense of terror and alienation, thus increasing the intensity of various related oppositions in works of art (35–36). He claims that the grotesque thrives in holding contradictory impulses, ideas, and responses together in an uneasy fusion of characteristics in an artistic structure that allows the clashes of these qualities to bear heavily upon receivers, preventing them from orienting themselves in the world of the "text," which, paradoxically, is and is not their world (37, 184–86). Kayser observes that the grotesque is especially likely to function in depictions of distorted or dismembered human bodies, madness, violence, and death, for which the world of the fiction offers little rationale — or an absurdly unsatisfactory one — both of which serve to heighten tensions for readers by alienating them further from explanation (in general) and from a reliability on the explanations offered up for the contradictions in their own world (185–86). For Kayser, the grotesque shocks us with its absurdity, but its resonance effects aftershocks that point both to the depths of the absurdity in the world of the grotesque and to the existential absurdity of our own world as it is grimly mirrored in grotesque art. Kayser marks this ambiguous sense of uneasiness and disorientation as the central effect of the grotesque.

"But who effects the estrangement of the world, who announces his presence in this overwhelming ominousness?" Kayser asks (185). His answer is interesting and perplexing because he answers the questions by observing that there should be no answers (185). Moreover, Kayser claims that this conundrum transports his discussion to the deepest levels of the horror that these altered worlds inspire (185). The agent of estrangement in the world of the grotesque must remain "incomprehensible, inexplicable, and impersonal" in order for the grotesque's essential mystery and horror to remain intact (185). Kayser calls this force in the grotesque the objectified "It," or the "ghostly 'It,'" which he posits as the impersonal pronoun's third meaning, in contrast to the "psychological 'It'" ("it pleases me") and the "cosmic 'It'" ("it rains"), and which, as Kayser explains in a footnote, is the "It" by means of which we form expressions that attempt to capture those objects or phenomena that outstrip the signifying capacities inherent in language (185, 208). Kayser does seem to apply some metaphysical valuation to this "ghostly 'It,'" in whatever guise it appears in works of the grotesque, in his definitive pronouncement on the grotesque, which states the grotesque's association with "the demonic aspects of the world":

> In spite of all the helplessness and horror inspired by the dark forces which lurk in and behind our world and have power to estrange it, the truly artistic portrayal effects a secret liberation. The darkness has been sighted, the ominous forces challenged. And thus we arrive at a final interpretation of the grotesque: AN ATTEMPT TO INVOKE AND SUBDUE THE DEMONIC ASPECTS OF THE WORLD [188, emph. orig.].

Thus, Kayser does sense in the grotesque that, despite its terrifying grimness, it ultimately contributes to an aesthetics of hopefulness. In this light, the "secret liberation" that the grotesque can enact is a kind of aesthetic exorcism of the "ghostly" or "demonic" It, which defies our explanations and throws us into existential disorientation. But, as Wilson Yates observes, Kayser fails to elaborate on his use of the term "demonic," which is little more descriptive than any other of his synonyms in this passage: "dark forces," "darkness," "ominous forces." All beg for further explanation as to the nature of such evil, as well as to the historical or ontological character of these "demonic aspects" (Yates 19). Yates also provides a concise recapitulation of Kayser's grotesque aesthetic, stating that Kayser's definition of the grotesque has almost entirely to do with experiencing the various guises of the alien, the ominous, and the negative (in general). The grotesque's only redeeming quality, Yates remarks, is that in experiencing it, we are afforded an opportunity to invoke the "it" and its sinister mysteries; we may internalize it and, in doing so, vanquish it, respond to it in some way. But, Yates concludes that, for Kayser, the grotesque collects those aspects of life which have no real positive function, but, instead, remain those facets of life which we should attempt to overcome (19–20).

While Kayser appeals mostly to Romantic and Modern art and literature for his conception of the grotesque, the other foundational theorist for the contemporary study of the grotesque, Russian philosopher Mikhail Bakhtin, grounds his theory in the popular carnival culture of the Middle Ages and Renaissance. Bakhtin argues in *Rabelais and His World* that grotesque images refer to phenomena in various states of transformation, to arrested metamorphoses of becoming, between birth and death, growth and maturity (24). He highlights two particular indispensable traits, or

24

determining elements: the way in which grotesque images are related to time and their characteristic ambivalence. These aspects are always already implicated in those images given to picturing processes of becoming, for such images represent opposite extremes of transformation, the new and the old, reproduction and death, beginnings and endings, forever locked in moments of transition (24). For Bakhtin, grotesque images from folk carnival culture function by their contrariety to "classic aesthetics," that is, the theories of beauty formed by the "official" cultural power, which conceive of human beings as completed and perfected, purified of the remaining residue of birth and maturation (25). The ideal of "classic aesthetics" is the isolated, individual body, one that is alone, confined to itself, and separated from all other bodies (29). In contrast to this body, the grotesque body transgresses the confines of its own proportions as it persists in growing beyond itself (26). Consequently, the most important parts of this body are those through which the body opens to the world around it, those parts from which the world emerges or enters, and those through which the body itself extends from itself to meet the world (26).

Bakhtin's theory of the grotesque takes the concept, from the very start, into an existential realm of social reality. From this foundation Bakhtin develops a theory of culture that necessarily encompasses aesthetics, which itself entails concepts used for interpreting artistic phenomena that reflect the nature of human existence purported in his theory of the grotesque. For Kayser, the grotesque in art and literature may lead people to considerations of existential questions about the ultimate issues that concern human life, but Bakhtin's conception of the grotesque turns the problem exactly the other way. As Dieter Meindl notes in *American Fiction and the Metaphysics of the Grotesque*, the conceptual underpinnings of Bakhtin's philosophy of the grotesque have to do with "life as a whole," absolute existence, in which the world and bodies and bodies and other bodies are ever involving one another in constant interchange (17–18). This is the existential premise for which Bakhtin's reflection on the human corporeal form emerges as a semiotics of that body, by which grotesque images in literature, the visual and plastic arts, and other cultural phenomena may signify certain aspects of the interconnectedness of people with each other and with the world itself (17–18).

Wilson Yates identifies Bakhtin's theoretical work in *Rabelais and His World* as an extension of the philosopher's theory of dialogue and the dialogic imagination. Yates observes that for Bakhtin ideology and language are approximations of one another that demonstrate the ways in which people carry a dynamic social world in their language and dialogue, which, through their voice and discourse, fashions and refashions the self (21). This means that someone can never be an isolated, independent individual who generates her own speech apart from her social context, for the whole social world is within who she is; therefore, when she speaks, she always speaks out of that world, which, even as she is speaking, is embedded in her identity (21). Dialogue, in Bakhtin's sense, illustrates the dynamism of social identity through language that is "regenerative, corrective, and relative," and it is in this perpetual discourse that we devise ever-changing ways to imagine and think through our experience of the world, even as we receive, construe, and revise ideas in the dialogic realm of discourse (Yates 20). The "dialogic imagination" is how Bakhtin describes the presence of such dialogue in literature. When he finds the dialogic imagination at work in literature, Bakhtin is able to interpret more certainly what dialogue is and how it functions (Yates 20). Dialogue's enemy is monologue, which, as Gary Saul Morson claims, is "constructed so as to restrict or ignore the dialogic possibility" (qtd. in Yates 20). Monologue attempts to fashion a closed reality that "constricts, abstracts, objectifies, casts the other into social roles, and presumes power over the other" (Yates 20). It stands as the antithesis to dialogue.

The grotesque, or, as Bakhtin sometimes calls it, "grotesque realism," the name which he ascribes to literary uses of the aesthetics of carnival, in its purest form, operates according to the dialogic imagination. It images the existential totality of life that Bakhtin's conception of dialogue describes in terms of discourse, as Terry Eagleton observes in a discussion of Marxist theory and comedy in *Walter Benjamin or Towards a Revolutionary Criticism*. In employing a "socialist collectivism," says Eagleton, Bakhtin is after a realization of the comic truth of social dialogue, that what I say to the other always already entails what that other says to me, and this, too, implies what I may say and have said to him or her (*Walter Benjamin* 149). Eagleton observes that Bakhtin's theory of dialogism is constructed on the foundation of this irony, which in Bakhtin's carnival grotesque becomes the dialogic "decentering of the discrete subject that explodes the authoritarian solemnities of monologue." Carnival's discourse always entails receiving speech back from those others it was first addressed to: The subject is thus constantly implicated "in a pleasurable play of shifting solidarity with others" (149–50).

Bakhtin observes that, while grotesque realism first flowered as the medieval carnival culture's catalog of popular imagery and then reached its zenith as a Renaissance literary genre when more learned art and literature began to incorporate bastardized images from the folk carnival culture found in motifs from the décor of Nero's rubble, modernity trudged on, and bourgeois culture took over as a dominating force. This left an atomized, individual conception of selfhood to replace the dialogic notion of the "self as social self" (Bakhtin, *Rabelais* 31–34; Yates 21). This modern, monologic view of the self assumes that existential authenticity of human identity is possible only insofar as the individual can free itself from the constraints of the social and cultural tethers that "classic" aesthetics perceives as outside of and alien to the individual (Yates 21). Bakhtin's thought seems to rely on a kind of dialectical relationship between related binaries: social self and individual self, popular carnival culture and "official" culture, body as "unfinished metamorphosis" and body as completed and isolated, dialogue and monologue, the "classic" (or neoclassical) aesthetics of modernity and grotesque aesthetics of the carnival spirit. The second term of each set, along with related values and social structures ("hierarchy, dogmatism, formalism, and absolutism"), reflect modernity's increasingly bourgeois and totalitarian impulse toward creating a world that seeks to divide the self from the other, from social reality, from its own body: from itself, in a systemic ideological shift that undercuts dialogue (Yates 21). The first term of each set of binaries, along with their related values and social structures, reflect Bakhtin's Marxist attempts to theorize ways to disinter or devise strategies to imagine a world built around a more life-affirming ontology (Yates 21). Yates interprets in Bakhtin's project a philosophical reorientation, which provides a course of life aimed more directly at participating in social structures amenable to the creation of this new world than merely at representing it in art. And once this new world becomes a possibility, the grotesque can instill radical visions of its core values of dialogue and participation, a constant prophecy of a realizable revolutionary dream of a utopia freed from totalitarian and bourgeois cultures (Yates 21–22). In a discussion of "popular-festive forms" associated with the grotesque and its roots in carnival, Bakhtin puts the matter this way: The forms and images of carnival are capable of envisioning and performing the victory of the future over the past; they cast this victorious future as one in which "the people" live lives of equality, freedom, and brotherhood in a world of abundant material resources (*Rabelais* 256). Bakhtin then situates carnival's vision of what is to come within his broader philosophy of "the whole." He writes (rather poetically) that the new being born is as necessary and unavoidable as the old dying; one is transmitted to the other; that which is better ridicules and kills the worse, for the only entry-place for fear is through some segment that has been cut off from the whole. Bakhtin goes on to say that this "whole" is always speaking in images of carnival, making participation in awareness of itself available to all (*Rabelais* 256).

The grotesque world Bakhtin describes in *Rabelais and His World* is the utopian "second life" of the carnival counter-culture in which the popular body conquers the world by achieving union with it (9, 370). Thus, carnival functions historically and politically as a circular, festal dimension in which linear time and official culture and its aesthetics are conquered as well (at least temporarily) by a radical freedom that flourishes with aberrancy, intemperance, and contradiction. Bakhtin theorizes the grotesque, which he alternatively calls the "carnivalesque," through an exhaustive analysis of the medieval and Renaissance culture of popular folk humor that he finds at work in the writings of Rabelais, as well as in the works of Shakespeare, Cervantes, and numerous others in less concentrated forms. He identifies the central purpose of the grotesque with an aesthetics of "degradation," which functions to materialize the abstract; embody the "spiritual"; and displace the high gestures of ritual and ceremony, forcing them back in to materiality (25). The grotesque achieves these aims through its reliance on the body; on tropes and characters associated with popular carnival forms, the clown and fool especially; and a metaphysics of contradiction and ambivalence that works to make "classic" aesthetics untenable (25). The theory, then, has what Eagleton calls a "somatic root": carnival grotesque, more than anything else, involves "pluralizing and cathecting" the body (which is always in transgression of its material confines), making fresh and movable parts of its dismantled unity (*Walter Benjamin* 150). The body itself, Eagleton continues, is opened up to the social world surrounding it, transforming its cavities and protuberances into organs of erotic exchange with that world "outside," which is in some way "inside" too. A bodily materialism — one based on vulgar but shameless depictions of genitals, buttocks, bellies, anuses, etc.—waylays the civilities of the dominant class (150).

From the perspective of the "classic aesthetics" of the ruling classes, the grotesque images are not only contradictory and ambivalent, but they are also ugly, revolting, and monstrous (Bakhtin, *Rabelais* 25). According to Bakhtin's conception, the grotesque attempts to show in its deployment of such shocking images that death and restoration cannot be separated in "life as a whole," and life, so conceived, is nearly incapable of inspiring fear (50). For Bakhtin, it is in the spirit of carnival and in folk humor and culture where true grotesque raucously thrives as a utopian vision of social and cosmic human unity and equality (47). It is a festive realm in which human existence is rooted in the complexities of bodily experience in and of the world. It defies and surprises the uninitiated by its comprehensive enjoyment of life. It does not morbidly wallow in Kayser's alienating world of horror.

Bakhtin accuses Kayser of ignoring the thousand years of development that the grotesque underwent before the Romanic era and instead devising a warped interpretation that relies exclusively on Kayser's own modernist aesthetic and philosophic sensibilities (Bakhtin, *Rabelais* 46). Bakhtin observes that Kayser never explains his silence regarding the veritable essence of the grotesque, which is inseparable from carnival spirit and folk culture (47). Kayser, according to Bakhtin, reads the history of the grotesque backwardly, beginning with the modernist grotesque, which inspires Kayser's notion of the concept. This error ignores or forgets the grotesque's past by anachronistically allowing a formalization of its carnival heritage to eclipse its foundation and using this exceptional form of the grotesque instead to judge its previous manifestations (47). This interpretive methodology leads Kayser to draw lines between the darkness, fear, terror, and alienation in modernist works and what he sees as similar invocations in earlier works (47). Bakhtin critiques Kayser's theory by arguing for rather unsurprising alternative interpretations of Romantic forms of the grotesque, which emphasize the importance of the body in grotesque art and literature, of madness, of laughter, and of Kayser's "it" (49). Bakhtin reaches the crux of his disagreement with Kayser in his examination of the latter's general tendency toward existentialism (49). His discussion of Kayser's view of the grotesque's relation to death is characteristic of the nature of the debate and is more detailed than some of the other points in the argument.

Part 1. The Philosophy of the Grotesque

Bakhtin takes issue with Kayser's existentialist assertion that the grotesque begets a general sense of dread concerning life more than it does a fear of death (*Rabelais* 50). Bakhtin argues that Kayser's claim contradicts completely the system according to which grotesque imagery functions because it relies on an opposition of death to life (50). For if life is interpreted in terms of "the whole," then death cannot be seen as its negation; rather, because "the whole" incorporates the vast social body, the body of all people, death fulfills the role of the condition that facilitates the constant rejuvenation and renewal of that body: it is, therefore, a component of life, and an indispensable one at that (50). To rightly theorize death's place in the grotesque, Bakhtin infers, one must remember that grotesque images always relate death to birth and the grave to the fructifying womb of the earth (50). Further, if fear for Bakhtin reflects a stupid and narrow-minded seriousness, which if met with laughter is utterly defeated, and if complete freedom is only possible in a world without fear, then another disjuncture emerges in addition to the disagreement about the metaphysical nature of death and the grotesque: one's orientation to that nature, and, further still, to the thorough-going political dimension of Bakhtin's grotesque, which in Kayser's theory never receives much elaboration.

II. Metaphysics, Myth and Purgatory

Opposition is true Friendship.
— William Blake, *The Marriage of Heaven and Hell*

Whence come you, from what spheres, or inky deeps,
What careless hand joy and distress to strew?
— Charles Baudelaire, "Hymn to Beauty"

Of Gaps and Bridges

All of the terrifying storm and stress of Kayser's grotesque starkly contradicts Bakhtin's playfully irreverent grotesque carnival aesthetic. And Kayser's "secret liberation" of shining a flashlight on the devil does little to bridge the gap between the theories. An undeniable disconnection remains. But Dieter Meindl casts doubt on the possibility for the grotesque to exist in the absence of this fundamental contradiction or paradox, this collusion or collision of the serious and playful, of dread and fun (14). He appeals to John Ruskin's similar point in *The Stones of Venice*:

> [I]t seems to me that the grotesque is, in almost all cases, composed of two elements, one ludicrous, the other fearful; that, as one or the other of these elements prevails, the grotesque falls into two branches, sportive grotesque and terrible grotesque; but that we cannot legitimately consider it under these two aspects, because there are hardly any examples which do not in some degree combine both elements [qtd. in Meindl 14–15].

Further, Meindl proposes that the historical regression of the "carnivalesque grotesque" (Bakhtin's grotesque), which in romanticism begins to be replaced or displaced by something more akin to the grotesque as Kayser theorizes it, leaves much of the grotesque's "life-affirming message" to fall away (19). The location of the "bright pole" becomes less discernible.

Primeval human involvement with "the whole" of life and the world does not necessarily disappear in the more modern grotesque, but Bakhtin's life-affirming existential implication — that death does not negate life but that it, rather, participates in it when we see life appropriately, as the total body of all — no longer seems consistent with the grotesque's literary manifestations (19). Modern literature becomes preoccupied with the definition of the individual, and the individual is obliterated by "total existence" because consciousness is cancelled out by Being as such (19). Thus the individual is rightly terrorized when confronted with "the existential dimension" because it is the "sphere of his or her annihilation" (19). The modernist grotesque becomes oriented towards its darker pole of horror and anxiety in order to reflect this change in consciousness (19). Meindl goes on to observe that, as I noted above, these two theories emerge from different foundations: Kayser's develops from aesthetics, whereas Bakhtin's emerges from an "existential premise" based on participation in the grotesque carnival that reveals the "totality of life" (18). Meindl attempts to integrate these two foundations, the aesthetic and the existential, while not dissolving the inherent contradictions in each of the theories. What emerges is a metaphysics of the grotesque that leans heavily on the philosophy of Martin Heidegger.

For Meindl, the "horror-oriented" modernist grotesque, too, recognizes an existential "totality of life," but one which precedes the self and hedges itself against this conscious subject. This dimension — "life as a whole" — in existing as the context and foundation for patterns of human consciousness and cognition decenters (or, as Kayser would have it, "alienates") the self, requiring a reorientation of our relation to knowledge, which culminates in a "new metaphysics, existential and this-worldly" (28). Heidegger's philosophical work, Meindl claims, represents the culmination of this new metaphysics. Meindl suggests that Heidegger's philosophy essentially displaces humans as subjects, and within subject/object relationships altogether; instead, Heidegger strives to consider elemental human primordial essence (31). Heidegger's philosophy represents the summit of this line of thought, which Meindl attempts to show in a brief genealogy of philosophical meditation on "the primordial element" from Cartesian metaphysics to Schopenhauer, and finally to Nietzsche and Bergson (29–31). For Heidegger, this "primordial" thought is thought that "descends":

When thinking of this kind speaks the truth of Being it has entrusted itself to what is more essential than all values and all types of beings. Thinking does not overcome metaphysics [in other words, subjectivist, Cartesian metaphysics] by climbing still higher, surmounting it, transcending it somehow or other; thinking overcomes metaphysics by climbing back down into the nearness of the nearest. The descent, particularly where man has strayed into subjectivity, is more arduous and more dangerous than the ascent [qtd. in Meindl 31].

Meindl connects this tendency to plunge beyond the "subject/object matrix" in metaphysics to the inclination in literature to mine human "existential depths" by exploring a subterranean web of myths, dreams, terror, and madness, and one cannot overestimate the part of the grotesque in the exhumation of such material from these depths (31). This "descending thinking" and desire for the primal in modern works of art results in a new conception of evil, death, and aberrancy that explores these regions intending to put their flames and exotic fancy to imaginative use (32).

It is interesting to observe, as a side note, that Meindl, in connecting the modern grotesque to such "downward thinking," effectively makes the original, denotative application of the word "grotesque," "from the cave (*grotta*)," function metaphorically as well: but, in this sense, the "cave" toward which such "descending thinking" is oriented is the cave of human consciousness, the all-but-lost primal impressions of a reality that somehow defines us but from which we are also alienated. In this subterranean pursuit, Meindl, then, brings together the horror and madness of Kayser's theory and the anarchic joy and sacrilege of Bakhtin's carnival theory without reconciling them per se. He unites these two concepts of the grotesque, each with its own vision of the "totality of life" (Being), in a shared "downward" philosophical trajectory. This "downward" thinking functions to plumb the depths of prerational human thought in myths, dreams, fears, and whatever is dreadful in the world in order to depict Being itself in its "eternal, incomplete unfinished" act of becoming (Bakhtin, *Rabelais* 52). What is essential about Meindl's marriage of these theories is his suggestion that, to best participate in the grotesque, they must hold their clash, their dissonance, with one another.

The other side to Meindl's theory concerns the artist's production. He writes that the "new metaphysics" imagines a totality and unity of life that is posited in opposition to the human capacity for language and the faculty of the mind. This leaves writers in an epistemological quandary and challenges them with an arduous task (210). How does the artist portray Being itself? Many modern artists turn to the grotesque, which relies largely on the metaphor (a sense of language that often abandons assertion as such) and circumvents the reliability and exactitude traditionally associated with narrative perspective (210). These developments, Meindl posits, along with Heidegger's suggestion that works of art should display their own createdness — a facet of meaning which should be expressly experienced and discovered in the work of art itself, one not unlike Kayser's *Schaffenspoetik* (Meindl 135, Kayser 184) — leads modernists to exploit the *mort vivant* (Meindl 210). This kind of grotesque presents the arrested lives of human figures. Appealing to the *mort vivant* allows artists to capture the, heretofore, ungraspable flux of "life itself" in narrative but also to fashion it in such a way that it bears the marks of its medium in its sense of grotesque absurdity and metaphor, as well as in its narrative self-consciousness (210).

David K. Danow connects the exploration of the nether realm of pre-rational, or preconscious, human thought to Jung's theory of the archetypes. In his book, *The Spirit of Carnival: Magical Realism and the Grotesque*, Danow devises a theory of the carnivalesque-grotesque, which effectively polarizes Bakhtin's theory (which he calls "the carnivalesque") and Kayser's theory (which he seems only to get second-hand from Bakhtin and calls "the grotesque") to opposite ends of a continuum that is demonstrative of what Danow calls an "anthropological constant" with roots in a particular "reiterative human tendency or impulse" that surfaces in various manifestations in nearly all known cultures (137). A couple of things here are worth drawing out more clearly within the discussion so far: namely, Danow's notions of a continuum on which the grotesque functions and his definition, or description, of what the grotesque is and of where it emerges from.

First, Danow's appeal to the metaphor of a continuum to conceive of the contrastive aspects of the grotesque, "one ludicrous, the other fearful" to borrow from Ruskin, seems helpful for differentiating between these two intonations of the grotesque in a work of art (literary, visual, plastic, etc.), and Meindl seems to invoke something similar in his discussion of the historical regression of the "bright pole" and its replacement with the "dark pole" during the age of romanticism (Meindl 19). Thus both Danow and Meindl take critical steps towards the inclusion of both "poles" within the same continuum of the grotesque. Second, Danow offers yet another definition of what the grotesque is. For Kayser, Bakhtin, and Meindl, the grotesque is, respectively, an aesthetic — a particular way of seeing the world — which can be apprehended in art and literature in various ways; a guiding cultural principle that reflects a worldview of the existential totality of being, which boils over into art, literature, and various other cultural phenomena; and an artistic phenomenon that reflects a particular metaphysics concerned with mining the depths of human knowledge and consciousness. Danow, extending Bakhtin through Jung, treats the grotesque as an "anthropological constant," which is rooted in some kind of (largely undefined) basic "human impulse" (137). This is similar to Meindl's Heideggerian metaphysics of the grotesque, but whereas with Meindl, the grotesque reflects some level of adoption of the "new metaphysics," as he demonstrates by pointing to a number of works of American fiction that bear it out, Danow's claim digs deeper into the cave of consciousness by positing, not only that the arduous concentration on the depths of the primal mind may deliver us in some way from subjectivist metaphysics, but that the grotesque is one way to reconnect to that primordial "collective consciousness" (Bakhtin), or "collective unconscious" (Jung) (Meindl 31, Danow 137, 150).

Danow extends his theory by establishing a link between Bakhtin's notions of "great time" and "collective consciousness" and Jung's theories concerning archetypes and the "collective unconscious" (Danow 149). "Great time" names the spiritual notion that every utterance from the remotest past to the most distant future is linked with every other utterance. Bakhtin relates this idea to literature by identifying that it is primarily revealed in the "differentiated unity" of the culture and era in which it was produced, though the work cannot be partitioned off within its own culture and era alone: its true richness and meaning is only revealed in "great time" (Danow 149). Danow claims that the same relationship between time and significance can also be applied to interpreting those archetypal notions, like carnival, which have stood the test of time, that is, those "texts" that, in Jungian thinking, have outlived all others in their productivity and resiliency as constitutive components of the "human psyche — both in its efforts at survival and in that other great, related project of making art" (149). Danow identifies a reference to "collective consciousness" in *Rabelais and His World* in Bakhtin's discussion of carnival's protagonists. (Bakhtin identifies them as "the people.") Here Bakhtin explains that the central concern of carnival for its protagonists does not lie in their "subjective awareness but in the collective consciousness" of their immortality, in their earthly and historic significance as a people, and in their perpetual rejuvenation and growth (Danow 150; Bakhtin 250). The difference here between Bakhtin's term, "collective consciousness," and Jung's "collective unconscious" is "essentially negligible," Danow claims, since, for Jung the nature of archetypes is to remain unconscious, while the "archetypal representations" that the unconscious mediates to us frequently surface into consciousness (Danow 150; Jung 653). Danow quotes Jung to conclude his argument: "The concept of the archetype, which is an indispensable correlate of the idea of the collective unconscious, indicates the existence of definite forms in the psyche which seem to be present everywhere" (Jung qtd. in Danow 152). Danow's fundamental claim, then, is that the "carnivalesque, with *its* 'indispensable correlate,' the grotesque," is one of these thought-forms that Jung alternatively calls "categories of the imagination" or "primordial thoughts" (Danow 152; Jung qtd. in Danow 152).

In a similar way to Danow, Geoffrey Galt Harpham, in *On the Grotesque: Strategies of Contradiction in Art and Literature*, appeals to the grotesque as "a given," or "an element," of the cultural mind, one that remains the same in essence and function, but one whose constituent features are shaped by its necessary contrariety to the cultural circumstances regarding coherence and order against which it surfaces (xx). Further, by connecting motifs from Renaissance and modern grotesques to similar motifs in the frescoes from Nero's palace, and by drawing an interpretive line between these and comparable patterns in prehistoric cave drawings (particularly the fusion of plants or animals with human bodies), Harpham demonstrates the primordial and mythic character of the grotesque as a basic "element" in the human mind (65). Wilson Yates observes that Harpham's major contribution here is in theorizing the scope of the grotesque in a way that perceives its almost total transcendence of culture and history, exceeding its Renaissance and Roman roots, and perhaps even Western culture as such, seeing even non–Western structures as sources that may contribute to comprehending the grotesque's character and function (34–35).

Harpham identifies the core of the grotesque to be its position on the "disorderly margins" of Western aesthetic conventions and the culture that they constitute (xxi). Harpham recognizes the grotesque as "a species of confusion" that in popular usage is recognized and defined by a peculiar range of obstructions to logical and organized thinking (xxi). The word itself, in a turn perhaps analogous to Kayser's theory of the objectification of the "It," serves as a signifier for those entities and objects that no noun seems to appropriately capture, and this corresponds to sense of formal irregularity observable in grotesqueries, artful distortions in which generic, logical, or ontological categories are egregiously jumbled together (xxi). Harpham carries further this notion of the grotesque as the illegitimate fusion of opposites to include not only generic, logical, and ontological categories, but also more totalizing values of "high" and "low," the normative and the abnormal, the fully formed and the unformed, the ideal and the degenerate, and often such fusions are *con*fusions, marked by affinity or antagonism of the fused objects, or indeed sometimes grotesque fusions subsist with seeming indifference to the incongruity of the copresence of high and low (9). Time and size, too, are often markedly irregular, compressed or elongated to accentuate a dysmorphic quality in narrative structure, characterization, depiction, or description in relation to the rest of a text, story, painting, etc., upsetting the formal balance of a work (9, 14).

Harpham presses the concept further, noting the tendency of the grotesque to occupy gaps and intervals, to subsist within the conceptual center of "a narrative of emergent comprehension" (15). Or, borrowing from George Santayana's *The Sense of Beauty*, he suggests that the grotesque occupies a purgatorial phase of understanding throughout which the perceived object appears as a distorted mishmash of various forms. Something like this frequently occurs in normal thinking processes, but usually the interval between perception and comprehension is relatively insignificant and easily spanned by anticipation and memory that it is virtually unrecognizable (15–16). The grotesque object thrives in that interval, elongates it, explodes it, resists its closure, and "impales us" on that moment of confusion, voiding the past and precluding the future (16). Again, Harpham conceives of the grotesque as something so natural to human consciousness — the gap between the appearance and the apprehension of something — but so foreign to consciousness in its tendency to make that gap its focus, its center; but it does so for a purpose and at a price.

Artistic representation that relies on fragmentation, confusion, rupture, and corruption steers us into the grotesque, Harpham argues, but it also generates the interpretive practices and energy by which we may navigate our return from it through the kind of theoretical speculation that pursues closure in attempting to find an explanation through appeals to metaphor or allegory or in discovering new forms with which to identify this kind of art (18). But the personal toll paid for the experience, Harpham reminds, is considerable. Baudelaire characterized his reaction to the "absolute comic" as a swoon, an agony, and a paroxysm (qtd. in Harpham 18). G. Wilson Knight states that the "demonic grin of the incongruous and absurd" that one feels in the "grotesque comedy" of Shakespeare's *King Lear* "wrenches, splits, gashes the mind till it utters the whirling vapourings of lunacy" (qtd. in Harpham 18). Harpham observes that these are accounts of the mind suspended between death and renewal, madness and discovery, ruin and revelation (18).

This passage in Harpham's study is reminiscent of an analogous episode in Kayser's approach — the grotesque as an "attempt to invoke and subdue the demonic aspects of the world"— but Harpham's emphasis on interpretation, rather than on exorcism, is somewhat more precise and leaves a more positive role for the grotesque than does Kayser's aesthetic *via negativa* (Kayser 188, Harpham 18). Moreover, while Kayser's approach, in the end, suggests that we, through our artful rendering of it, attempt to subdue the threatening powers and unfathomable forces that loom large in the grotesque, Harpham turns the matter on its head (Kayser 188). Harpham suggests that it is we who are subdued by the grotesque, and our artistic invocations of it do little to change or chain the demonic that we encounter through or in it; what they do instead is to pull us deeper within them, within the troubled liminal space of our own experience of the grotesque (Harpham 18). And it is we who change as a result of the descent into the grottoes of contradiction: "interpretative activity"— imaginative intellectual energy— emerges as the hard-won wisdom we earn through this dark night of the soul (18). We are only led out of the grotesque when we embrace a hermeneutical wisdom that refuses to give in to the wrenching agony of our experience of it and instead use that psychic energy towards interpreting the wrecked reality it impinges on us.

Harpham unpacks these claims, or indeed packs them quite full, in a conclusion about what he calls the "mythic or primitive" character of the grotesque: the grotesque entails "the manifest, visible, or unmediated presence of mythic or primitive elements *in* a nonmythic or modern context. It is a formula capable of nearly infinite variation" (51). He elaborates this thesis by spelling out the contradiction more precisely. In the domain of myth, metaphors may be literalized, for example nothing prevents Acteon from turning into a stag, Philomela from becoming a bird, or Hyacinthus from transforming into a flower. Myth traverses categories and is also capable of plowing the human and the natural together: animals may marry, stars may organize themselves into families, and water may speak. But it is on the fringe or margin where the figurative touches the literal that the grotesque lies: it is neither, and it is both; it reflects their mingling and their unity (53).

Harpham argues further, relying on Levi-Strauss and Edmund Leach, that, while myth thrives on contradiction and uses narrative to mediate it, everyday modern logic relies on an evasion of contradiction (53). In a claim not far from Danow's Jungianism, Harpham theorizes that the mythic depends on the notion that everything that exists is somehow relatable to everything else: Primitive thinking is ceaselessly ordering and reordering the world as it attempts to discover a comprehensive system of connections that webs all things together (52). Fusions of opposites are necessary because the "mythic mind" seeks the ultimate unity of everything (52). Invoking Freud's *Beyond the Pleasure Principle*, Harpham draws connections between the qualities associated with mythic thinking and those associated with the unconscious, and, merging the two, he asserts that this mythic unconscious is what emerges as the imaginative energy that drives the interpretive element in encounters with the grotesque (67, 18).

Harpham also suggests an interesting political aspect of the grotesque. Following Erich Auerbach's examination of the persistent cultural tension between "the high" and "the low" in Western cultural history in *Mimesis: The Representation of Reality in Western Literature*, Harpham asserts that cultures design "systems of decorum" (political, cultural, artistic, etc.) to maintain order of the status quo and to keep the low and the marginal in their places (74). But these systems necessarily short-circuit because they rely on the assumption that meaning and value are not distributed in the world at random but rather through systems that devise methods to discriminate the meaning of everything that contributes to the greatness and stability of the state through "high style" (73). This regulated form of mediation is characteristically "grandiloquent, stylized, and highly rhetorical," and, consequently, it is cordoned off from the officially meaningless and disdainful real world "life of the everyday," which is associated with vulgarity, carnality, and indulgence (73). The "high" customs and traditions associated with such methods always eventually decay, and they too become meaningless clichés (74). Harpham concludes that meaning in culture is always migrating toward the low and marginal. Revolutions are based on the goal of resetting the standard opposition of the meaningful and meaningless, transferring what is at the bottom to the top under the banner of a renewed faithfulness to "reality." The grotesque, Harpham continues, names that "dynamic state of low-ascending and high-descending" (74). Those who situate themselves with the "low," like Bakhtin, formulate theories of the grotesque in terms of "realism," while those who speak from the perspective of the status quo, like Kayser, discuss the grotesque in terms of its horror, its nightmares. But the real problem at the base of these distinctions concerning definition of what is real has to do with the "systems of decorum" that we create for the specific purpose of avoiding the kinds of experiences the grotesque is made for (74).

One manner of escaping this problem, Harpham suggests, is to form a system of decorum that is centered on ambivalence and indeterminacy (74). Auerbach claims that Christianity was once such a system, based around a monstrous Christ figure that essentially fuses the sacred and the profane, pure and impure, the incandescent light of the transfiguration and the grim and bloody darkness of the passion — contradictions which can only cohere in or by the logic of myths — and Auerbach analyzes this tendency in the content and style that Dante, Rabelais, and others bring into play to fashion their works. Harpham's theory of the grotesque, too, is an attempt at a similar system of decorum, one that sees that on the margins of experience expressions of the real take the form of the grotesque. Such expressions are out of joint with the world that has rejected them, but they can become metamorphoses of that world through their grotesqueness (Yates 41). Further, Harpham's "final paradox" for the grotesque entails its self-annihilation, for if the grotesque leads to a peculiar kind of wisdom, then, truly comprehending what the grotesque is precludes us from regarding its form of expression as grotesque any longer. He invokes Coleridge's final line of "This Lime-Tree Bower My Prison" to drive home the point: "No sound is dissonant which tells of life" (76).

It is interesting to observe that this paradox seems to be a different conclusion than the one Harpham discusses in the preface to his book. There, he suggests that a burgeoning "soupy tolerance" in Western culture is having an effect on the grotesque by allowing it everywhere and in increasingly diluted forms, thus making it ubiquitous, invisible, and innocuous all at the same time (xx-xxi). Interestingly, the statement from the preface is also rather paradoxical and further demonstrates, for Harpham, the importance of the grotesque as revelatory of a kind of hidden knowledge, the possibility for the realization of which may be slipping away as we lose our aesthetic capacity for perceiving it. Umberto Eco, in his *On Ugliness*, remarks on one such instantiation of this "soupy tolerance": "We hear repeatedly from all sides that today we coexist with contrasting models [of beauty and ugliness] because the opposition beautiful/ugly *no longer has any aesthetic value*: ugly and beautiful would be two possible options to be experienced neutrally" (426 ital. orig.). Eco goes on to suggest that such clichés are indeed trite fictions that ultimately result from a misunderstanding of the real relationship between the existential and the aesthetic, or which see no need for the reconciliation of the two. Eco argues that our world is often ugly beyond the cliché notions of "aesthetic relativity," even if that ugliness is somehow marginalized, ignored, suppressed, or repressed (436).

Many of the images and texts compiled in Eco's book could be or have been integrated into discussions of the grotesque. Eco's point here seems to be that the stark and personal reality of these kinds of ugliness in the world are recent manifestations of an existential form of ugliness that has plagued human history, and to which art has responded, and to which art will continue to respond, by invoking such ugliness in images and words (436–37). By pushing the examples of ugliness to extremes, Eco makes absurd the notion that such ugliness (or its correlate) could be experienced neutrally, or, perhaps, that it could be experienced neutrally somehow only through some kind of aesthetic detachment and only in works of art, a conclusion that, for Eco, would seem to miss the significance of art as a signifier of culture, thereby ultimately rendering aesthetics itself meaningless.

Grotesque, Paradox and Dialectic

In an interesting discussion between Anglican theologian John Milbank and Slovenian philosopher Slavoj Žižek, collected and published

Part 1. The Philosophy of the Grotesque

under the title *The Monstrosity of Christ*, the "monstrous" fusion of "high" and "low" in the Christian savior (in essentially the same terms as suggested in Harpham's discussion of Auerbach), a fusion that exceeds explanation in rational terms alone, becomes the center around which the debate between the Christian and the atheist revolves within a contemporary discourse, which both agree is defined, at least in part, by the decay of secular reason (17). Midway through, John Milbank resets the debate as one that begs the question of what kind of logic best suits the subject:

> [I]s the claimed truth of Christian revelation better presented in terms of a paradoxical or dialectical logic? Does it announce the coincidence of the ordinary with the extraordinary, or rather a necessary journey through the extraordinary illusion, which finally leaves us in an ordinary forever alienated from the extraordinary — even if we console ourselves, as Žižek does, with the thought that this is the most extraordinary thing of all? [177].

Is this question of the kind of logic with which to perceive Christian revelation not like the question that must arise at some point in a discussion of the grotesque? Discourse surrounding Christian revelation must reach this point between these two interlocutors both because of the very different uses to which a Milbank or a Žižek would put it, but also because, if Auerbach is to be taken seriously, Christianity functions according to a conceptual system of decorum based on ambivalence and contradiction with a "monster" at its center (Harpham 74, Žižek and Milbank 82). Such monsters also populate the ambivalent and contradictory world of the grotesque, regardless of whose theory one discusses, or what sort of inflection those monsters receive, or how the presence of monstrosity as such affects those who find themselves on the receiving end of such art. To discuss the function or use of the grotesque in a more general sense, before suggesting how it can be seen as functioning for contemporary American film (to be addressed in the parts 2 and 3), I should first like to reiterate a few points regarding grotesque theory so far. In order to finally come to some conclusions, I will attempt to close this chapter with an admittedly oversimplified inquiry into the grotesque's definition and phenomenology that will provide a brief summary of the theories by attempting to issue responses to the questions "What is the grotesque?" and "Where does it come from?" I will then return to the question or consideration with which I began this section: "Where does the grotesque go?" (conceptually) and "By what logic (paradoxical? dialectical?) does it get there?"

Philip Thomson, in his very brief introduction to the concept, *The Grotesque*, defines the term this way: It is *"[t]he unresolved clash of incompatibles in work and response"* (27 ital. orig.). He notes that this clash is significantly paralleled by an essential ambivalence and abnormality in grotesque art, and this connection leads him to a correlated definition of the grotesque as the "ambivalently abnormal" (27). His "definition," perhaps, over-generalizes, but it does so in a way that reflects the ambivalent vagueness at the core of the problem of defining this slippery concept, which makes it a relatively judicious definition, inviting as much agreement as is possible among the various divergent statements in the field. Thomson's definition identifies the sense of the contradictory as the center of the grotesque, which can also be glimpsed with more or less emphasis and to different ends in each of the theories I have discussed here. Thomson identifies this sense of the contradictory as the animating principle of the grotesque in the work itself as art, which Kayser calls its "structural principle" (Kayser 180); in our emotional response to it, as it elicits from us conflicting and contradictory emotions (Thomson 5–7); and in the ways in which it clashes with our sense of normalcy and with the stability and certainty of meaning, which could lead into the already traversed byways of cultural aesthetics, ideology, epistemology, mythology, etc. I have also attempted to point out, in addition to "what it is," some of the theoretical assertions that attempt to describe "where the grotesque comes from," though, again, I should like to reiterate the artificiality of these categories, as there is a significant degree of overlap and transposition in setting things out in this manner.

For Kayser, the grotesque arises as an aesthetic principle, which is a figure of sorts for the processes of art itself. As such, it informs the work of art from its inception in/with the artist, through its production as a "structural principle" in the work of art, and on into its reception by viewers/readers that may interpret the work according to an aesthetics of the grotesque (180–85). For Bakhtin, the grotesque (or carnivalesque) goes a step deeper: it emerges from a cultural awareness, especially visible in the Medieval and early Renaissance eras, of the existential relatedness of humans with each other and with the world that surfaces in cultural phenomena (festivals, kinds of humor, kinds of and uses of language, performance, literary and visual arts, etc.) as well as in theories of aesthetics, which might inform artistic production and reception. Meindl's theory attempts to situate the grotesque, as it can be recognized in modern American fiction, within a particular (Heideggerian) metaphysical outlook, which philosophically engages in a kind of "downward thinking" that attempts to give precedence to a more organic, prerational, primal, and impulsive kind of thought process, which appeals to myth and raw imagination (31–32). Danow discusses the genesis of the grotesque by applying Bakhtin's concepts of "great time" and "collective consciousness" to the Jungian notion of the "collective unconscious" in order to position the grotesque among the archetypes as an "anthropological constant," which may be activated into consciousness from the collective unconscious through art (137–52). Finally, for Harpham, the grotesque is an elemental aspect of the human mind that reaches back as far as is demonstrable through analyses of culture — back to scratches and drawings on cave walls (65). Harpham's notion of the grotesque is like an archetype, though he avoids restricting it within a Jungian vocabulary and instead seems more comfortable with the haziest possible phenomenological explanation of it. Harpham merges the grotesque's phenomenology with epistemology, reaching back to a primordial past and locating the grotesque with the most ancient forms of mythic thinking, which seek to unify reality by relating everything to everything else (52–53). He extends these discussions into a consideration of the grotesque in the modern era by theorizing the subsistence of these mythic forms of thought in the modern mind where they clash with a context for which they are not suited and seem shockingly inappropriate (51). He thus effectively keeps intact both Kayser's and Bakhtin's versions of the grotesque in a theory that is not unlike Meindl's but with this catch: while Meindl asserts the grotesque in terms of a subject's metaphysical understanding of the ancient and primal thoughts of humankind, Harpham's theory treats the grotesque as the object of such consideration, an element within the mind that persists from the dawn of human consciousness to the present.

But if the grotesque "goes" anywhere, where does it go, and how does it get there? How do theories of the grotesque delineate the ends for which the concept functions and logic according to which it operates? Thomson's last chapter presents the "Functions and Purposes of the Grotesque" in terms of its impact, "the sudden shock which it causes," that is, as it may be used to jolt the reader/perceiver of the grotesque out of his customary ways of interpreting the world and "confront him with a radically different, disturbing perspective," or as it may be used to issue an irresolvable tension between comedy and tragedy or for the sake of experimental "playfulness" with language, characterization, or narrative (58–65). He also discusses the "psychological effect" of the grotesque, which provides a psychoanalytic approach to the interruption, the shock, that grotesquery imposes upon its perceivers. To elucidate this appellation, Thomson relies on Michael Steig's Freudian formulation of the power of the grotesque to arouse anxiety at the same time that it provides some sense of liberation from fear in its attempts to manage the uncanny by or through the comic, in effect, returning us to childhood modes of thought in which threatening material is eased by the comic and vice versa. As an example of such "tension and unresolvability," Thomson refers to G. Wilson Knight's reading of *King Lear* in the essay "*King Lear* and the Comedy of the Grotesque," but he also cites the works of Samuel Beckett and Franz Kafka (Thomson 62). Thomson observes that these works underscore difference between tragicomedy and the grotesque: "Tragicomedy points only to the fact that life is alternately comic and tragic, the world is now a vale of tears, now a circus. The grotesque ... has a harder message. It is that the vale of tears and the circus are one, that tragedy is in some ways comic and all comedy is in some way tragic and pathetic" (Thomson 63).

To extend the discussion beyond these more formal traits or literary or psychological effects, I would like to suggest that another tension that seems to be at work in theories of the grotesque is between an orientation towards the social and/or political and one that seems more inwardly inclined towards a meditative, almost mystical, telos, though I do not think these are totalizing tendencies, as any theory that I have mentioned so far or that I intend to mention in the remainder of this study, with the appropriate contextualization, can reflect both poles of such a continuum, as I intend to demonstrate. Further, these different emphases of the political or the meditative seem to work according to a certain emphasis of predominantly dialectical or paradoxical logic (respectively). Kayser, Meindl, and Danow, at first glance, seem to reflect attempts to engage in and advocate the grotesque as a largely meditative strategy for sustained consideration or exploration of contradiction according to a paradoxical kind of logic. They treat the grotesque's play with absurdity and contradiction as gateways to metaphysical or anthropological speculation about the nature of human consciousness in a way that leads to further meditation on the character of that consciousness and speculation about what it means to be human, but which never really emerge from the caves of the grotesque.

Bakhtin, on the other hand, by emphasizing the contrariety of the grotesque carnival to the dominant "classic" aesthetics of Medieval and Renaissance Europe, as well as to the "official" culture of that era, offers a dialectically oppositional politics of the body and of the body politic to the ones that dominate in the history of Western culture (*Rabelais* 25–29). He demonstrates how the cultural practices of medieval popular folk humor and the carnival spirit function as historical and cultural antitheses to the "official" practices and ideologies, and how these factors form a kind of synthesis in grotesque literature as a "literary genre" (Bakhtin 34). This synthesis had become accepted as a formal strategy in writing to the extent that its patterns emerged in the literary culture as generic formal strategies but also remained connected to "carnival-grotesque" in its tendency to sanctify the freedom of invention; to encourage the admixture and recon- ciliation of various oppositional elements; and to enact and occasion lib- eration from the dominating forces in the world, from truths associated with conventions and traditions related to those forces, and from the broadly "understood" or "accepted" truths of the banal and cliché (34). Bakhtin extends this dialectical reading of history to a broader treatment of the laughter of the people as antithetical to the dominant seriousness that pervades official power, and he uses his study of Rabelais to shed light on the popular (folk) culture and humor of other ages as a particularly incandescent recapitulation of what is possible in the literary grotesque, a genre which continues to offer the chances to look at the world anew, to perceive the relativity of all things, and to receive the grotesque's invitation to a completely novel ordering of the world (474, 34). Thus the political and dialectical receives much emphasis in Bakhtin, as it does in those who have applied and extended his theories into the domains of post-colonial and feminist studies, as Alison Milbank observes in an essay on "Divine Beauty and the Grotesque in Dante's *Paradiso*," noting the work of Mar- garet Miles, Christine Ross, and Mary Russo on feminism and Elizabeth C. Childs and Leonard Cassuto on race and post-colonial studies (155, 166).

Harpham complicates things by offering what may be the most med- itative analysis of the grotesque in the group. His theory relies on irresolv- able contradictions of subject matter, imagery, formal properties, modes of thinking, and social/ideological context, and functions according to a self-defined, paradoxical logic that seeks an almost gnostic truth at the "bottom" of the grotesque. This "bottom," however, drops out when Harpham asserts that the hidden truth of the grotesque reaches a point of synthesis that necessarily moves beyond the conflicts of its defining contradictions, birthing a new outlook on the world in even more precise terms than does Bakhtin's theory, though with much of Bakhtin's politics attached (76). Further, Harpham resets Kayser's and Bakhtin's debate about the essential nature of the grotesque as one that emerges from the class positionality of each writer and the constituent points of interest that accompany the bourgeois and the working class intellectual, thus politicizing Kayser's theory by setting it within a dialectical social framework (74). Danow or Meindl, too, could be interpreted according to a more political end that operates according to dialectical logic simply by emphasizing their uses of Bakhtin's or Kayser's theory as significant influences on their own theories. And other works, such as John C. Clark's *The Modern Satiric Grotesque and Its Traditions* and Robert Doty's *Human Concern / Personal Torment*, rely on political tensions of the literary and artistic avant-garde in modern and postmodern literature and visual/plastic arts with the culture at large and its bourgeois sensibilities and its myths of rationalism and individualism, but often towards a shocking stasis (as Thomson describes it) that affords readers / viewers a conceptual space from which to meditate on their own culture and the artificiality of its myths as a result of the "satiric grotesque" or politically informed utilization of the grotesque in art (Clark 2–4, Doty 5–8).[1]

Perhaps an alternative to the thinly worn notion of the various continuums on which the grotesque appears to function (dark pole / light pole, "high" / "low," form / formless, "official" / popular, paradoxical / dialectical, etc.) would be to think about these sets of ultimately irresolvable contradictions in a way that gives more credence to their incompatibility but that keeps them in relation, still realizing the close connection between them. Such a theoretical move is possible by appropriating Slavoj Žižek's rendition of the notion of parallax (which he uses in a different context) as a hermeneutic to think through the concept of the grotesque. In *The Parallax View*, Žižek introduces the logic of a parallax perspective and the parallax gap at its center as the method of situating two phenomena that are strictly incompatible each to the other on the same level, in a move analogous to Kant's notion of "transcendental illusion" (4). Žižek argues that the illusion at the heart of this transcendental logic entails "being able to use the same language for phenomena which are mutually untranslatable and can be grasped only in a kind of parallax view," a perspective that operates according to a constant and methodical shifting between points "between which no synthesis is possible" (4).

> Thus there is no rapport between the two levels, no shared space — although they are closely connected, even identical in a way, they are, as it were, on the opposed sides of a Moebius strip.... [The] parallax gap [represents] the confrontation of two closely linked perspectives between which no neutral ground is possible [4].

In many ways, to suggest such a logic for interpreting the grotesque is not unlike the claims in Harpham's theory that grotesque imagines "liminal" images in which opposing developments and assumptions exist simultaneously in a solitary representation, which figure, occupy, and explode an interval or gap in the Santayanan "narrative of emergent comprehension" discussed earlier (14–15). Accordingly, the grotesque would function as both a kind of illusion, a language — or to borrow from Kayser, a "structural principle" — that allows for "incompatible phenomena which are mutually untranslatable" to be grasped according to a parallax logic, which constantly shifts from one perspective to another in order to make interpretable phenomena represented in the grotesque, for which there is no other mediation, for which there is no synthesis (Žižek 4). Theorizing the grotesque in such a way would liberate grotesque art to thrive specifically on the union of things, ideas, images, values, etc. in contradiction, but would also necessitate an interpretive logic that attempts to analyze this parallax clash-gap as an impossible coincidence of phenomena that makes possible new interpretations of the world through a kind of play. A parallax view of the grotesque would accordingly allow the possibility of marrying the opposite poles of this or that continuum, essentially, by reconceiving the continuum as something like the Moebius strip — by adding two more dimensions to the concept and theorizing the twist that allows both nearly identical relation to concepts that would otherwise be banished to opposite ends of a line, as well as the dimensional boundary that maintains their essential incompatibility. Under the rubric of parallax, paradoxical and dialectical logic may drive theories of the grotesque in contradictory directions, for ends that are incompatible, or to no end at all: what such a

48

method would allow is a refocusing of the grotesque — in art, in life, as aesthetics, as philosophy, towards meditation, towards the political, etc. — as an object of interpretation that always already entails interpretations within itself in its uneasy fusion of contradictions within the very gap that seems to make such fusions impossible, ludicrous. A parallax perspective, then, would not necessarily seek to solve the riddles of the grotesque, or to get lost in its tormenting effects, but, rather, it would seek to experience them and pull back from them in a way: to feel the grotesque's effects and refuse them, to suffer its terror or enjoy its sacrilege or to bear the crushing weight of its hardest lessons, but also to negate them in order to create a new interpretive space that relies on position and negation but which lies outside of these by exploding them through interpretation — through imagination — attempting to see from as many angles as possible (Žižek 381–82).

PART 2

Interpolarity: Binaries of the Grotesque

The Grave shrieks with delight & shakes
Her hollow womb...

— William Blake, *The Song of Los*

The epigraphs that introduce the two chapters of which Part 2 is composed are instructive, not only for setting the tone and theme for each, but also for illuminating how these chapters contribute to the overarching, more theoretical, argument that is slowly unwinding throughout the pages of this book. The meaning hiding in Bakhtin's and Carroll's words (below) only emerges when we interpret each of the binary distinctions implied in their sentences in the hermeneutical light that the others give, that is, of each in dynamic relation to its other. To the official acts that make the history of the world Bakhtin appends a scoffing carnival chorus. Carroll's Alice identifies the queerness of the present moment as she impulsively compares it with the context of the past, the wild world of Wonderland with the banality of the "real" world. And in each case, poles of agency, experience, and/or reflection are invoked that introduce certain oppositions, but these oppositions retain an air of simultaneity or equivalency: each pole is clearly oppositional to its other, but each also, within the logic of this opposition, refers to its other; implies its other; interferes with it; corrects, undermines, or qualifies it. We see each emerge as the other's identical opposite, the other's other. The polarity implied in the establishment of such binaries is necessarily a form of interpolarity: meaning here cannot be driven into isolation at poles that will never intersect, for they nearly touch, even as they remain irreducible to one another.

Likewise, Harpham's words, which initiate Chapter IV, complete the thought. He speaks to the energy generated when there is friction between such identical opposites, in the context of his discussion: between the mythic and the modern and the art born of a rupture in the progress of the narrative of history. I am after something similar in the two chapters that follow. In Chapter III, I appeal to the films of Tim Burton as visions of the fraught relations between a number of related binaries associated with a largely Bakhtinian distinction between the carnivalesque grotesque and the official. And in Chapter IV, I examine the themes evoked through the preoccupations with the binaries of the mythic and the modern and of madness and rationality in Terry Gilliam's films. In both cases, that is, with respect to Burton's and Gilliam's work, the grotesque seems to subsist in these interpolar frictions, in the dredging up of polar oppositions which seem never to be completely synthesized nor completely displaced, but, rather, tend to send meaning into a perpetual reverberation between them.

III. Tim Burton's Two Worlds

Every act of world history was accompanied by a laughing chorus.
— Mikhail Bakhtin, *Rabelais and His World*

How queer everything is today! And yesterday things went on just as usual.
— Lewis Carroll, *Alice's Adventures in Wonderland*

Burton, Bakhtin and the Carnivalesque-Grotesque

"The carnivalesque — a liberating mix of comedy and the grotesque in defiance of the status quo — is a significant component of Burton's work," Ron Magliozzi writes in one of the introductory essays to the companion book published for the Museum of Modern Art's 2009 exhibition of works by Burton (14). Magliozzi highlights Burton's apparent fondness for the grotesque and documents his visual references to festive images associated with the Day of the Dead, Halloween, and Christmas; to the circus; to extravagant bodily manipulation and mutation; and to his tendency to utilize a dazzling palette of primary colors to signify attractions that are sinister and/or unsettling (13–14). One needs only to recall Burton's take on death in *Beetlejuice* and *Tim Burton's Corpse Bride*, his weirdly threatening and amusing incarnations of the Joker or Penguin from *Batman* and *Batman Returns* and their armies of mimes and clowns, or the absurdly cartoonish blood-spatter in *Sleepy Hollow* and *Sweeny Todd: The Demon Barber of Fleet Street* in order to see the appropriateness of Magliozzi's invocation of Bakhtin's key terms as a fruitful approach to understanding Burton's film aesthetics (He 21).

When he is asked in interviews to provide explanations of these tendencies in his films, Burton frequently responds in a manner best summed up in his response to the particular manifestation of the question in an interview with David Breskin: "It's about duality" (qtd. in Breskin 79).

The poles of such "duality" in Burton's film corpus sometimes shift from one film to the next, but often the director's interest in oppositional polarity approaches something akin to what Bakhtin describes in his analysis of the relationship between "official" culture and "carnival" culture. In his discussion of festivity in *Rabelais and His World*, Bakhtin demonstrates the duality of the festal dimension in the Middle Ages and its extension into the culture of the Renaissance by contrasting the ideologies associated with official and carnival feasts. He argues that, while the official feasts functioned to maintain the existing social and cultural hierarchies and the proscriptions, standards, and values associated with the dominant moral, political, and religious structures in order to ensure that the ideological cycle of life retained its invariable stability, carnival feasts were temporary celebrations and performances of liberation from these established truths of the dominant order; they denoted that hierarchical rankings, class privileges, and the prohibitions and norms associated with the prevailing powers had been suspended (9–10). The feasts of official culture were marked by a rigidly serious tone to which laughter was completely alien, an attitude in which official culture fundamentally distorted and betrayed the real essence of the festive realm.

But laughter, the true center of festivity as Bakhtin understands it, thrives as the organizing principle of carnival (10–11). This laughter, though, is not the guffaw at a particular comic event; it is complex: the laughter of carnival is the laughter of all, which is universally aimed in all directions, at everyone, at the world itself, even at those who participate in carnival (11). Further, this laughter is systematically ambivalent — it is gleefully triumphant, even as it mocks and derides, denies and asserts, revives and buries (11–12). Such laughter enacts the liberation that its performance in carnival denotes. Bakhtin claims that the aesthetics of the grotesque is predicated upon this kind of festive laughter, which organizes around itself particular phenomena associated with the grotesque. These phenomena include swearing and other carnivalesque patterns of speech associated with the market place. The principle of the materiality of the body, in which bodies are rendered, in grotesque imagery, as exaggerated, grandiose, and immeasurable, also numbers among such phenomena. Bakhtin also discusses the degradation of all of the lofty forms of abstraction, spirituality, and idealism as well as a cyclical, reproductive conception of time, all within the context of the grotesque's ambivalent and contradictory nature (11–24). But, from the perspective of the official culture — and its monolithic seriousness, hierarchical regalia, elegantly polished language, spiritual and intellectual strivings, individuated bodies, historical/linear notion of time, and its "classic" aesthetics — the grotesque reflects a hideously repulsive threat to its ideological rule over culture (21–29). In essence, then, the multivalent tension between official rule and the power of carnival hinges on the ideological, social, cultural, etc. threat represented in carnival to the standards of the official.

Jenny He, in "An Auteur for All Ages," specifically applies this notion of conflict of oppositional realities in her discussion of how the drama of Burton's films frequently relies on the simultaneous existence of dual worlds, regardless of whether these worlds exist only in the characters' minds or in some kind of parallel reality or netherworld (18). She goes on to state that "the 'normal' world is exposed as claustrophobic and suffocating while the 'topsy-turvy' world is colorful, imaginative, and revelatory," and often turns out to make more sense than its counterpart (21). Of Burton's work to date, the films that can most benefit from this particular kind of Bakhtinian approach are *Beetlejuice, Batman* and *Batman Returns* (along with his short-lived internet animation experiment in *The World of Stainboy*), his two feature length stop-motion animation films *The Nightmare Before Christmas* and *Corpse Bride*, and *Sleepy Hollow, Ed Wood, Mars Attacks*, and *Planet of the Apes*.[1] The social aspect of the poles of Burton's rendition of "duality" in these films is more pronounced than his similarly conceived use of such devices in *Vincent, Edward Scissorhands, Charlie and the Chocolate Factory, Pee-wee's Big Adventure*, and *Big Fish*. The films that compose this second group all retain some version of the Bakhtinian clash of worlds, but in these works the "other world" seems to be positioned with, or as He suggests, "in the mind of," a particular character, an individual, rather than an entire cultural or social group (18). I will discuss them in the latter part of the chapter.

Worlds Divided: Beetlejuice, Batman *and* Batman Returns

In Burton's incorporation of the theme and structure of duality in the world of *Beetlejuice*, as Edwin Page observes in *Gothic Fantasy: The*

Films of Tim Burton, "life and death are far from distinct as the opposing sides" (42). Rather, they mimic and reference one another; each subsists as the other's identical opposite. Further, Burton fuses the comic with the tragic, the ghastly with the amusing, by situating the film "somewhere between fantasy, horror and comedy," as Helmut Merschmann notes in *Tim Burton: The Life and Films of a Visionary Director* (90). Merschmann continues by arguing that Burton's generic defiance in *Beetlejuice* allows him to draw freely on the usually divergent conventions of these genres to suit his purpose in making a film that invites a response "on an intellectual level," as Burton puts it in an interview with Marc Shapiro, to things "that are basically so stupid" (Merschmann 90, Shapiro 8). But without the freedom to traverse from the horrifying to the ludicrous or his freedom to throw both into the same sequence, the film's presentation of the conflicting worlds would suffer. The film would be "stupid" without the ironic "intellectual level" that makes it an interesting movie.

The realm of the dead in *Beetlejuice* reflects a tension between the real freedoms that being dead affords characters in the film — most notably represented in the Betelgeuse character, but also in the ability the dead have for spontaneous metaphysical travel and corporeal malleability — and the fact that the realm of the dead is populated by dead humans, whom the film paints as almost universally boring, even to the point that they have formed a bureaucracy to manage the afterlife as poorly as they had managed things in the realm of the living, complete with typists, complaint departments, waiting rooms, case workers, and instruction manuals for the newly deceased. But these forms of ruling the afterlife are mere fictions. Being dead seems to come with nearly unchecked freedoms, which the character of Betelgeuse embodies, while the governing bureaucracy that presides over day to day existence in the world of the dead are more concerned with keeping those freedoms as much of a secret as possible, as evidenced when the Maitland's case-worker, Juno, warns them that they should by no means hire Betelgeuse (the bioexorcist) to help them get rid of the new (living) family that has moved into their house.

Betelgeuse's powers seem almost without limit, and his alienation from the status quo — the bureaucracy of the world of the dead, which may effectively serve as a holdover and comfort from the world of the living — grants him such a freedom that even those who, it would seem, share in his powers (the dead as such) are wary of him. The makeup, dress, and characterization of Betelgeuse, as David Denby puts it, makes him more of "an unsettling, ambiguous cross between a benevolent clown and decadent Weimar era nightclub entertainer" than a ghoul, though, together with some of the visual references in the set design of the world of the dead to Robert Wiene's Expressionist masterpiece, *The Cabinet of Dr. Caligari*, Betelgeuse's countenance may also reflect some of the threat (though perhaps parodically) of the murderous, somnambulant, Cesare from Wiene's film (38). Betelgeuse demonstrates his "supernatural strength," as Merschmann observes, in becoming an enormous snake, as well as when he makes himself into a kind of one-man circus (93). His head sprouts a macabre merry-go-round, and his arms unroll like fire hoses to reveal two enormous mallets in the place of his hands, which the bioexorcist uses in a "prove your strength" carnival game of his own making to catapult two offensive Manhattanites through the ceiling of the Maitland's home. The dead Maitlands, too, demonstrate this carnivalesque supernatural ability to modify their bodies, though to less effect, in their attempts to scare the living out of their house when Barbara Maitland decapitates her husband or when they physically pull at their heads, contorting their faces into grotesquely misshapen visages, not unlike those of the demonic beasts in Hieronymus Bosch's *The Last Judgment* or *The Altar of the Hermits*. But all of this, which in horror films would be exploited to appeal to the fears of audiences, in *Beetlejuice* is placed in the context of an inverted spoof on the haunted house movie, one in which the ghosts are attempting to rid their house of the living.

As outsider, Betelgeuse explores those freedoms deemed prurient or repulsive by the "normal" representatives of the status quo. Page points to Betelgeuse's "overtly sexual nature," which is highlighted in his "repeated and lustful molestation of Barbara Maitland" and of the disembodied legs of an unfortunate magician's assistant, as well as in his attempt to wed himself to the Deetzes' teenage daughter (50). Another critic points out that Betelgeuse's tendency to belch, fart, and grab at his crotch align him with what "every twelve-year-old boy wants to be" (qtd. in Page 50). Michael Keaton, who plays Betelgeuse, even comments in an interview with David Edelstein on the sense of liberation he experienced in acting for the role: "There are no bars, I can do anything I want under any rationality I want .... You show up on set and just go fuckin' nuts. It was rave acting. You rage for twelve or fourteen hours ... It was pretty damn cathartic. It was rave and purge acting" (12–13).

Beetlejuice presents "official" culture, such as bureaucratic business culture of the world of the dead, the Wall Street and avant-garde cultures of the Deetzes and their circle of acquaintances, and the provincial middle-class culture of the Maitlands as ultimately absurd, pretentious, or just boring. Betelgeuse is the only character that completely embraces the freedoms afforded to him, and his only goal in the film seems to be enjoyment of those freedoms. Ultimately, Betelgeuse functions as a living-dead critique of official culture in accordance with Bakhtin's theory of festive reality: he represents the carnival spirit in his manifestation of the material bodily principle, derisive language patterns, and degradation of the realm of spirits in defiance of the various guises of the official. The Maitland's employment of the freedoms available to the dead in service to their attempts to get rid of the Deetzes, and their fear of what lies outside the familiar confines of their own home, undercuts their uninhibited enjoyment of those freedoms, effectively locking the couple within a purgatory of their own making in the official confines of the social and cultural forms of the living to which they are accustomed. It is they and the Deetzes who must change in order to get along with one another by agreeing to a kind of social contract at the film's end, while Betelgeuse, even after having been eaten by a desert snake (in an overt reference to David Lynch's *Dune*) in the film's finale, remains the same wild character in the waiting room scene that ends the movie, as he tries to entertain himself with bad jokes and a prurient sense of eroticism. The conclusion of the film also situates Betelgeuse within carnival time: his "death" scene in the film is ultimately regenerative; it is a rebirth that brings new opportunity, while the Maitlands seem to impose a kind of historicity or linearity on time (even though they apparently share Betelgeuse's metaphysical state), agreeing with the Deetzes to put the past behind them and forge a relationship that is stable and predictable, an orderly relationship that they can sustain for the future.

Betelgeuse is one of many references that Burton makes in his films to clowns, which also factor, in a rather menacing way, in the protagonist's neurotic hallucinations in *Pee-wee's Big Adventure* and in the construction of the villains in *Batman* and *Batman Returns*. In an interview with David Breskin, Burton provides some explanation for his appeals to clowns and clown-like figures to establish weirdly threatening characters, often without clear motivations for their behaviors: "I grew up with a fascination for people that were dangerous. Why a fascination with clowns?" And he answers: "Why are they so powerful to children? Probably because they are dangerous" (66). Later in the same interview, Burton picks up a similar thread discussing the duality between Batman and Joker:

> BURTON: ... [The Batman character has] got good impulses, but he's not integrated. And it's about depression. It's about going through life, thinking you're doing something, trying very hard. And the Joker represents somebody who gets to act however he wants.
> BRESKIN: He's playing the Beetlejuice character.
> BURTON: Yeah. There are two kinds of people, even with double personalities. The ones that are fucked and they're still trying to muddle through life, and then the ones that are fucked and get to be completely free, and scary. And they're basically two fantasies. There are two sides [79–80].

In Mark Salisbury's *Burton on Burton*, the filmmaker describes *Batman* as a "duel of freaks. It's a fight between two disfigured people." He continues,

> The Joker is such a great character because there's a complete freedom to him. Any character who operates on the outside of society and is deemed a freak and an outcast then has the freedom to do what they want. The Joker and Betelgeuse can do that in a much more liberating way than, say, Edward Scissorhands, or even Pee-wee, because they're deemed disgusting. They are darker sides of freedom. Insanity is in some scary way the most freedom you can have, because you're not bound by the laws of society [80].

Burton's clowns, mimes, and crime-world circus performers from *Batman* and *Batman Returns* represent what Bakhtin describes as the carnival spirit's perpetual and certified representatives, those whose everyday lives perform the carnival spirit (*Rabelais* 8). He posits that fools and clowns signified a certain kind of life that was at once ideal and real: they lived on the boundary between art and life in a peculiar liminal space (8). But whereas Bakhtin's medieval clowns were neither eccentrics nor idiots, to describe Burton's Joker or Penguin as "eccentric" would nearly amount to a compliment. Even as they represent the grotesque "otherness" of carnival life, as well as the freedoms and images with which it is associated, they, at the same time, give credence to a malicious, often sadistic, violent threat that goes beyond the one Bakhtin identifies in the subversive relationship that carnival has with official culture (8, 11–12). Burton's incarnation of the carnivalesque in the Batman films, then, requires a slight adjustment in the application of the theory so far, for while Bakhtin's theory of the carnivalesque grotesque from *Rabelais and His World* still seems as appropriate as it did for *Beetlejuice*'s lighter, more playful tone — for that weirdly humorous, giddily adolescent spark is still present in characterization and in the aspects of art direction, set design, color scheme, etc. that accompany the grotesque characters in all three films (*Beetlejuice, Batman*, and *Batman Returns*) — the darker tone and texture of the Batman films requires a theory closer to Dieter Meindl's, which is inclusive of both Bakhtin's "bright pole" as well as Wolfgang Kayser's "darker pole," one more attuned to a modernist grotesque and its preoccupations with violence, alienation, and anxiety (Meindl 19). So, while I will continue to draw out the carnival culture as the freeing social "other" of official culture, as Bakhtin argues, I will attempt to do justice to Burton's shift in tone in the Batman films as well.

Danny Elfman's scores for *Beetlejuice* and *Batman* are signposts of Burton's overall shift in tone towards what Meindl calls the darker pole (19). Edwin Page and Smith and Matthews comment on a "slightly sinister air" in the score for *Beetlejuice* and point to Elfman's reliance on a minor key and an "angular melody" to achieve dissonance; however, they also observe that the frantic, dance-like pacing contrasts the sinister tone with a "bright quality," more along the lines of Elfman's work in *Pee-wee's Big Adventure* (Page 32, Smith and Matthews 66). This juxtaposition of contrasting elements within the same score, often at the same time, effectively mimics the film's visual and narrative appeals to a brighter pole of the grotesque, for death and Betelgeuse are threats but not serious ones. In *Batman*, Elfman's score is markedly more operatic; it is darker and unrelentingly ominous or tragic, attributes which garnered for Elfman some comparisons with Wagner (Smith and Matthews 88). *Batman*'s inclusion of several pop songs, many composed by Prince, and "department store muzak," as Dirk Schaefer remarks in "Danny Elfman's Film Music," are jarring departures from Elfman's orchestral score and usually serve to musically connect "the wit, irony and fun" in the film with Joker, in keeping with his role as a representative of carnival life in an otherwise dismal and oppressive Gotham City (Schaefer 156; Bakhtin, *Rabelais* 8). The score of *Batman Returns* (also Elfman's), described by Richard Corliss as "discordantly lush," achieves an uneasy synthesis of the two styles, which perhaps contributes to the film's overt appeals to grotesquery (79). Elfman relies more on orchestral themes for the major characters; thus, much of the Wagnerian menace extends from the *Batman* score into sequences in *Batman Returns*, but so do aspects of the *Beetlejuice* score. Elfman utilizes variations on circus waltzes as themes for Penguin, but these musical circus references come across in disjointed melodies that are heavily accented with deep brass and woodwinds and off-beat percussion, relaying musically the sinister spectacle that Penguin and his low life circus represent in plot and character.

The Joker and Penguin characters subvert attempts, such as Meindl's, however, to situate Bakhtin's and Kayser's theories as representative of bright and dark poles on a continuum of the grotesque, for they are both completely Bakhtin's clown and Kayser's madman. If Joker's and Penguin's function as Bakhtinian clowns accounts for their subversive appeal as living, breathing symbols of the carnival spirit, and the vibrancy, flamboyancy, vulgarity, freedom from official convention, derisive humor, and bodily principle that accompany it, then it is their function as Kayserian madmen that elucidates their freakish menacing quality. Kayser writes, in *The Grotesque in Art and Literature*, that in madmen it is human nature itself that becomes menacing. The sheer existence of the insane inspires ominously spiritual interpretations (such as demon possession, for example): some force or spirit — impersonal, inhuman, or alien — Kayser says, appears to have penetrated and subjugated the human soul (184). Kayser concludes that encounters with the insane are confrontations with the grotesque that life itself imposes on us (184).

Joker's slapstick terrorism in poisoning Gotham's vanity products (shampoos, lotions, hairsprays, makeup), his declaration that "the pen is truly mightier than the sword" after he murders a man with a gaudy feathered pen, or his gassing of patrons and staff in the Flugelheim to enable his unfettered defacement of Gotham's prized art collection reflect the satirical wit and degradation principle of the carnival spirit, but it does so in a context closer to the impersonal, inhuman threat of the grotesquely insane, as do Penguin's biblical-scale revenge plots in *Batman Returns*. Arthur Clayborough seems to suggest some vague correlation between this uncanny, nameless energy and the id of psychoanalysis, a notion that may seem suitable for an interpretive analogy for the ominous overtones in these villains' versions of clowning: they represent, to apply the psychoanalytic analogy along with Plato's "analogy between the city and the soul," as Simon Blackburn puts it in his *Plato's Republic: A Biography*, the dark side of Gotham City's id (Kayser 185, Clayborough 65, Blackburn 130).

In his *New Introductory Lectures on Psycho-analysis*, Sigmund Freud describes the id as "a chaos, a cauldron of seething excitations" in which "contrary impulses exist side by side," while the super-ego's task is to "strengthen the ego, to make it more independent..., to widen its field of perception and enlarge its organization" so that it can keep the id in check, appropriating from the id only what serves its own purposes: "Where id was, there ego shall be" (91–92). Perhaps even closer to the point are Freud's reflections on the human psychological economy in *Civilization and Its Discontents*. There, he characterizes the struggle that civilization as such represents and dramatizes: it entails the perpetual battle between the Eros and Thanatos. Civilization "must present the struggle between Eros and Death, between the instinct of life and the instinct of destruction, as it works itself out in the human species" (111). If, following this slightly convoluted analogy, the villains may represent Gotham's unruly id, then it is Batman himself that figures as Gotham's shadowy, corrective super-ego, attempting to work with the city's officials when possible, but overstepping whatever legal or social strictures stand in his way when necessary, in order to achieve the balance between decadent cravings in the city and the rule of law. In both films, Batman's regulatory function does little more than to reset the status quo of the city when a threat surfaces from within its (criminal or, in the case of Penguin, literal) depths.

Bakhtin's critique of Kayser's id-language refers to its sense of the existential, for which the id is associated with an inhuman otherness that is within us, secretly controlling us, our lives and behaviors—the world itself—and it is this id that Bakhtin sees Kayser pointing to in the madman (*Rabelais* 49). He counters by arguing that the motif of madness for the grotesque is used quite differently: it is employed in order to provide a fresh view of the world through eyes that are free of this world's counterfeit truth (49). According to this logic, the madness in Joker or Penguin could be interpreted as merely an absurd exaggeration or extension of the day-to-day life in Gotham: the city's aristocracy masks their power grabs, violent instincts, acts of vengeance, and greed with a façade of respectability, of which Max Shreck of *Batman Returns* is the most obvious example. The difference for the villains—what makes them villains—is their adherence to the carnival spirit—their particular incarnations of impulses that would otherwise be perfectly at home in Gotham City are deemed offensive because of their scale, their lack of seriousness or normalcy, and the fact that they are particularly public (often interrupting official Gotham festivals and holidays in both films).

Batman/ Bruce Wayne has a lot invested in Gotham City (personally, financially), and he, as aristocrat playboy and as the city's "Dark Knight," is also given official sanction to exercise his baser desires. Such a conception of Batman's role adheres almost precisely to Freud's explanation of civilization's invention and employment of the superego within the psyche to inhibit the antisocial aggressiveness of Thanatos (*Civilization and Its Discontents* 114). Freud writes, in *Civilization and Its Discontents*, that the function of the superego is to introject and internalize thanatic aggressiveness and redirect it back towards the ego itself (114). Thus, it is by employing this "harsh superego," which is given license to utilize "the same harsh aggressiveness that the ego would have liked to satisfy upon other, extraneous individuals," that civilization "obtains mastery over the individual's dangerous desire for aggression by weakening and disarming it and by setting up an agency within him to watch over it" (114).

So if he stands over the city as Gotham's superegoic force, then Batman is not so much the "primary benevolent figure" in the film, as Cory Reed claims in "*Batman Returns*: From the Comic(s) to the Grotesque," as he is an impersonal and ultimately static henchman of the official status quo, to which his alter ego is subject (48). Reed's analysis of the city is insightful, though perhaps overly dramatic: "Burton's Gotham City is an overwhelmingly ugly, oppressive, and depraved metropolis where apocalyptic disorder reigns over a city about to collapse under its own weight" (39). And his observations of the architectural shifts from neo-gothic in *Batman* to largely fascistic styles mixed with pop kitsch in *Batman Returns*, as Merschmann also notes, are helpful for pointing at visual/spatial representations of the misdirected aspirations and decadence at work in Gotham City (Reed 39, Merschmann 70–71). But to state that this is "the director's satirical conception of a dysfunctional society in which the only true justice is vigilantism" simply ignores the role of the superhero in Burton's films (39). Burton's baldest representation of the superhero role is in *The World of Stainboy*, in which the pathetic protagonist, whose only "superpower" is the dark stain he leaves in his wake, serves the city of Burbank by acting as catalyst for the self-destruction of a number of his freak peers, many of whom, like Stainboy himself, originated as characters in Burton's *The Melancholy Death of Oyster Boy & Other Stories*, have disrupted daily life in the suburbs. Burton's perspective on the superhero's relation to his city is obvious at the end of "Chapter Three" when, after Stainboy has out-witted a giant bowling ball and his army of pins at the Burbank Bowl, Sergeant Glendale thanks Stainboy for making the "streets safe again for overweight bowling losers who consider themselves athletes because they can roll a ball in a straight line."

The Living and the Dead: The Nightmare Before Christmas *and* Corpse Bride

The two simplest renditions of Burton's various "duality-centered" films that relate to tensions between official culture and the carnival spirit are his stop-motion animation features, *The Nightmare Before Christmas* and *Corpse Bride.* The drama of both films relies on tensions caused by the grotesque world of the carnival transgressing its boundary with its official opposite. These films make for relatively simple analyses because each world is so clearly distinguishable from the other, and the grotesque world in each film — Halloween Town in *The Nightmare Before Christmas* and The Land of the Dead in *Corpse Bride* — is so raucously instilled with images and motifs associated with carnival spirit, and the contrast between the grotesque and the official is so obvious that these aspects of the films are nearly impossible to miss.

Nightmare relies on tensions that arise between Halloween Town and Christmas Town when Jack Skellington, the Pumpkin King of Halloween Town, gets bored with his life's work, and, after discovering Christmas Town, decides to give "Sandy Claws" an involuntary vacation, Jack taking on Santa's duties for the year in an attempt to stave off his doldrums. The film's grotesquery comes in the form of the variously distorted bodies of the inhabitants of Halloween Town (skeletons, a mad scientist/ Frankenstein figure with an external brain, a living doll with detachable parts, zombies, vampires, a hunchback — the usual Halloween fare) and in the superimposition of Halloween imagery and prank pulling on the contexts of Christmas. Of the latter category, a notable sequence is the one in which Jack flies his coffin-sleigh, which is pulled by the reanimated skeletons of reindeer and led by a ghostly dog with a glowing red nose, and delivers bats, vampire dolls, shrunken heads, and a living snake that eats an entire

Christmas tree as Christmas presents for the good boys and girls, effectively "subverting the customary iconography of Christmas," as Merschmann puts it (167). The only real threats in the world of *Nightmare* arise from overzealous attempts taken in the "real" world to bring Jack's Christmas haunt to an end by shooting down his sleigh and by Oogie Boogie's equally overzealous attempts to scare a captive Santa Claus to death by cooking him.

Corpse Bride functions according to a similar sense of duality, and its drama, likewise, relies on transgressions of the boundary that would normally keep the inhabitants of two worlds — in this case the Land of the Living and the Land of the Dead — within their rightful jurisdictions. But *Corpse Bride*'s invocation of the grotesque is more complicated visually and thematically than *Nightmare*'s. As Page remarks, "The land of the living is loosely based on the Victorian era, its houses tightly crammed along the streets and the society tightly crammed into norms of behavior straight-jacketed by a firm class system" (230). The classes are visually represented in the puppets used in the film. The stuffy, old world rich have grotesquely oversized heads, markedly grim expressions, and they are costumed in simple gray and black clothes that nearly completely hide their bodies, while the nouveau riche are slightly smaller and thinner and seem to adorn themselves in more "fashionable" attire, baroquely accessorizing their ensembles with fans and jewelry. The lower classes are exaggeratedly hunch-backed with distorted bodily proportions. The color scheme of the Land of the Living is limited to grays with hints of sepia tones and very pale blues here and there, giving the "living" world the visual texture of daguerreotype photography. The Land of the Dead, by contrast, bursts into the film with lush blues, lavenders, greens, and reds. This world is peopled with skeletons and partially rotted corpses, many of which wear brightly colored costumes from which their bones protrude here and there, while others wear little or nothing at all. The corpse bride herself, in a tattered wedding dress with a plunging neck line, relates, as Stephanie Zacharek observes, a "disconcertingly erotic" image, as is prominent when the long slit or tear in the dress reveals her legs, one of which has rotted away, exposing her bones (188). Zacharek also observes that "her lips have a pout that suggests not even death can fully destroy the human sex drive" (188).

Zacharek's comment hints at a major motif in the film: *Corpse Bride* elucidates the linkage between life and death by a kind of bodily semiotics.

While the land of the dead seems mostly to be about enjoying the afterlife and the company there, the raucous abandon of which is obvious in the musical numbers (again, parts of a score supplied by Danny Elfman) by General Bonesapart and Mr. Bonejangles, who at one point even manipulates marimba music from the boney bodies of a number of his friends, the bodily (de)composition of the inhabitants of this place provide visual signs of any number of terrible things in the Land of the Living. The logic of this aspect of the film is not unlike the function of Mexican Day of the Dead iconography; as Burton acknowledges in an interview with Edward Douglass, "it's all about humour, music and dancing and sort of a celebration of life, in a way, and that always felt more like a positive approach to things" (184). The Land of the Dead in *Corpse Bride* is a celebration of life *in death*— death as a kind of Bakhtinian rebirth, but one that still bears the marks of life's troubles and grim realities — as Burton's puppets signify, one with a knife in its head, another with a yawning hole in its torso, not to mention the number of children running around with their pigtails and sailor suits. The Land of the Dead seems to celebrate the new freedom death offers — freedom from the harsh consequences of those realities: it is ruled by the carnival spirit through the logic of grotesque imagery that connects this film with the theme of death as rebirth, the combination of birth and death, and the images of joyous death and their liberating and rejuvenating sense of laughter, all of which, Bakhtin reminds, play a role in the aesthetics of the grotesque tradition (*Rabelais* 51).

A Gang of Freaks: Sleepy Hollow *and* Ed Wood

Sleepy Hollow and *Ed Wood* reveal Burton's tendency to work in the vein of the grotesque in markedly different but related ways. *Sleepy Hollow*, like *Beetlejuice* and *Corpse Bride*, appeals to the worlds of the living and the dead and the transgressions of the boundary that separates them, but it does so with imagery and content more closely aligned with the gothic and horror traditions, situating the film closer to Kayser's description of the grotesque than Bakhtin's, though one can still glimpse a liberating "second life" that subverts official rule. In *Sleepy Hollow*, Burton incorporates witchcraft, a topic he toys with as a narrative mechanism in the séance scene in *Beetlejuice* and in the fairytale magic with the wedding ring in

Part 2. Interpolarity: Binaries of the Grotesque

Corpse Bride, as a life-affirming means by which women may wield power, realize a kind of union with nature, and subvert the official patriarchies in the religious and political spheres. The opposition between witchcraft and religion in the film finds its narrative center in the construction of the Ichabod Crane character.

Burton provides an evocative set of dream sequences to invent a biography for Crane in which religion and witchcraft clash in the personages of his father (a pastor) and mother (a witch), leaving him without a mother and without faith in his father's religion. Crane, then, brings into the film the more prominent thematic polarity between superstition (of any stripe: including both religion and witchcraft) and reason, to which Crane has dedicated his life in lieu of the superstitions that ruined his childhood. Burton's intention in *Sleepy Hollow* is to elucidate this conflict by situating its poles with two absurd character representations of the terms (reason and superstition): "What I liked about the Ichabod character was it was very much a character inside his own head," and this character is "juxtaposed against a character with no head" (Burton qtd. in Salisbury, "Graveyard" 153). Interestingly, these two characters emerge as the film's most notable players in visual and situational grotesquery, mostly to do with the sheer absurdity of the headless horseman figure and the sometimes cartoonish ways in which the heads he lops off spin and roll around before he is able to collect them, as well as with Ichabod Crane's tendency to become the butt of the bloody equivalent to pie-in-the-face gags during analytical procedures with his "Cronenbergian surgical implements and complex optical devices that never enable him to see anything" (Newman 157).[2]

The Bakhtinian turn on witchcraft goes largely undeveloped, apart from the scene in which the inhabitants of Sleepy Hollow take refuge from the prowling horseman in the church near the end of the film. At first, it seems that the horseman is unable to tread on consecrated ground, in line with the underlying conservatism in certain traditions of the horror film, but with a couple of quick shots of Katrina Van Tassel sketching protection spells on the floor of the church, Burton ascribes the real metaphysical power in the film to the witches rather than to the church. The drama is brought to an end through the cooperation of reason and superstition, represented by Ichabod Crane and Katrina Van Tassel. The cooperation or synthesis or agreement between seeming opposites in Burton's films is a strategy that recurs frequently; just to name a few: in *Frankenweenie* between suburbanites and Victor and Sparky, in *Beetlejuice* between Maitlands and Deetzes (the dead and the living), in *The Nightmare Before Christmas* between Santa Claus and the inhabitants of Halloween Town (signified in his well-wishing and gift of snow in the finale), in *Planet of the Apes* between humans and their evolutionary ancestors, and in *Corpse Bride* between the living and the dead (in the marriage scene near the end). These endings retain specific meanings according to the contexts in which they emerge in each particular film; but what does seem consistently held over across the films as a group is that such endings tend to bring Burton's films to a comfortable close, not so much a "happy ending" all of the time, but one which most audiences probably find satisfying enough. In *Sleepy Hollow*, just such a theme is confirmed when Ichabod and Katrina are revealed to have become lovers in the film's final seconds, which show their return to Ichabod's New York City, young Masbath in tow: they, for different reasons, have been alienated from Sleepy Hollow, but together they form a little family of orphans, a community of outsiders.

It is this notion — the family of "orphans" — which becomes the predominant theme in *Ed Wood*, Burton's biopic of "the alcoholic, heterosexual transvestite and sometime pornographer known affectionately as 'the world's worst director'" (Hoberman 118). Burton's film traces Wood's career from his attempts to write, produce, and direct his early plays and films through his premiere for *Plan 9 from Outer Space*, but *Ed Wood* centers on the throng of odd-balls that gather around Wood to help him achieve his creative "vision." Wood's girlfriend, Dolores Fuller, after discovering Wood's transvesticism and meeting his circle (composed of a hack TV psychic, a colorblind cameraman, an oversized Swedish wrestler, a drag queen, and an aged morphine addict and washed up horror film star), says in an attempt to give Wood a reality check, "Ed, this isn't the real world. You've surrounded yourself with a bunch of weirdoes." Another telling bit of dialogue in the film comes later when Wood's new girlfriend, Kathy O'Hara, comes to his defense: "Eddie's the only guy in town who doesn't pass judgment on people." Wood adds, "That's right. If I did I wouldn't have any friends." In this way, *Ed Wood* demonstrates Burton's attraction to outsiders and the liberation and acceptance available in communities of "weirdoes," a theme he also addresses in *Batman Returns, Nightmare, Corpse Bride*, and *Sleepy Hollow*.

Mars Attacks! *and* Planet of the Apes *as Satirical Grotesque*

As with many of his films, Burton's *Mars Attacks!* and *Planet of the Apes* incorporate visual and narrative motifs associated with both Bakhtin's and Kayser's oppositional renditions on what the grotesque entails. Philip Thomson comments on this paradoxical quality of the grotesque, identifying its "unresolvability" as one of its identifying traits: it both liberates and produces tension at once; the grotesque jolts the reader or viewer out of habitual ways of interpreting the world and confronts him or her with an alternative that is disturbingly and radically different (59–61). In the world of *Ed Wood*, for instance, Wood and his weirdoes are *mere* weirdoes from the perspective of those who identify with the ideology of what is "normal" (even for Hollywood), which Burton demonstrates in depicting the reactions that studio executives, Dolores, potential investors, and most moviegoers have to Wood and his works. But, while viewers of *Ed Wood* may identify or sympathize with the "normal" perspective's tendency to be repulsed, confused, or frustrated by Wood, his gang, and his films, Burton's film requires a shift in perspective for interpreting the weird because the film confronts the viewer with the weird — but from the perspective *of* the weird, a perspective which requires viewers to "read" Wood and his gang in a way that probably cuts against the ways in which "normal" viewers tend to interpret those things that are offensive to status quo normality. It is a film about the "other" from a perspective sympathetic to the "other," a perspective that sees nothing alien in them.

Mars Attacks! and *Planet of the Apes* rely on a similar function of the grotesque, though one that ultimately alienates viewers by playing on their tendency to identify with the least weird point of view offered in the film. Thomson writes that in addition to being used as an "aggressive weapon" in parody and satire, the grotesque's shock effect may also be utilized to disorient, bewilder — in essence, to alienate — readers in order to exaggerate and shine light upon the disgusting and horrifying qualities of life, which in being illumined, may also, by the simultaneous employment of some comic aspect, be made less harmful (58–59). Kim Newman refers to one such instance of Burton's penchant for alienation in closing his review of *Mars Attacks!*

> Like *Batman Returns* it's the sort of thing that alienates far more people than it converts, but it has so much verve packed into its admittedly incoherent

frame that it's hard not to take something cherishable away from it, whether it be the severed heads of Pierce Brosnan and Sarah Jessica Parker shyly kissing as their flying saucer crashes, or the chortling Martians erecting a mammoth and complicated ray-canon to point at one little old lady's head [145].

Mars Attacks! and *Planet of the Apes* engage these textures of the grotesque in ways that also fit the Bakhtinian notion of the "otherness" of a social body to the official status quo, and otherness signified in images that, according to the official, dominant culture, seem disgusting and horrifying (Bakhtin, *Rabelais* 6; Thomson 59). Both films hinge on humans finding themselves in situations where the "other" culture is a kind of parallel but ultimately blank other, a culture upon which humans project their own cultural values in their attempts to orient themselves when confronted with sheer otherness. Kayser's discussion of the grotesque as "the estranged world" brings this notion into focus, as he delineates between strangeness in fairy tales and in the grotesque: "Viewed from the outside, the world of the fairy tale could also be regarded as strange and alien. Yet its world is not estranged, that is to say, the elements in it which are familiar and natural to us do not suddenly turn out to be strange and ominous" (184). This is precisely what Kayser says the grotesque does: "it presupposes that the categories which apply to our world view become inapplicable" when faced with parallels that estrange them (185). This happens in *Mars Attacks!* and *Planet of the Apes* because of the unwillingness or inability of humans to suspend their worldview and leave blank the conceptual space their encounter with sheer otherness opens up.

In *Mars Attacks!*, this becomes the engine of the comic destruction of American civilization. In the run-up to the first official meeting with the Martians, professor Donald Kessler, an advisor to the president, assures President Dale, "Logic dictates that, given their extremely high level of technical development, they're an advanced culture, therefore peaceful and enlightened." The government sets up a welcoming ceremony for the Martians where the dignitaries of each culture are to meet for a photo opportunity in the midst of a congregation of onlookers. When a hippie releases a dove to celebrate the occasion, the Martian Ambassador shoots it with his ray gun, and then Martians level the entire gathering. Kessler and the Americans are confused, so they conclude that the hostility must have been the result of a "cultural misunderstanding." The Martians agree and wish to apologize to congress. But when the Martian ambassador begins incinerating the congress with what obviously seems like joy, Kessler is still per-plexed: "Mr. Ambassador, please! What are you doing! This does not make sense! This is not logical!" This sort of satirical slapstick sets the tone of the entire film. Not only do the aliens not act according to Kessler's flawed correlation of "advancement" and "enlightenment," they also seem to bring together a decadently adolescent sense of enjoyment and a highly sophis-ticated technological superiority, as evidenced in their experiments with Kessler's and Natalie Lake's living but decapitated heads and their attempts at barbecuing a live herd of cattle — or just adolescent, as in the scenes of Martians peeping on lovers in a trailer, flipping through pornographic magazines, and in expressing a true gamer's elation as they ray people in the streets while their translation devices advise gently, "Do not run. We are your friends."

Planet of the Apes employs a similar use of the grotesque in a science fiction/action-adventure context. Here, Captain Leo Davidson finds him-self the alien on a planet in which the official culture is both markedly pri-mate but betrays a striking similarity to a version of the human culture with which he is familiar. The difference is that humans are disallowed from participating in any of the luxuries of cultured ape civilization, and the humans are relegated to slavery or life in the desert, outside of the offi-cial rule of the civilization. Davidson's worldview cannot account for the shift in perspective, and the film does not force the issue, since Burton provides a *deus ex machina* to allow for his escape, only to suffer the same sense of alienation upon his return to earth with which the film ends. The function of the grotesque is essentially the same for the two films: both rely on Kayser's notion of alienation and estrangement. In both films, aspects of human culture are exaggerated and intensified, but they are also displaced from a recognizable, human context — they are realigned with a culture of monsters whose motivations evade human understanding. They are, as Kayser would have it, unable to orient themselves in the alienated world because that world has become absurd (Kayser 185). But Bakhtinian grotesque reminds that perspective makes a difference: perhaps Bakhtin's notion that grotesque "degradation," which at once debases the "high" and elevates the "low," incarnating grotesque images that bring high and low to a "crossroads," both conceptually and materially, allows for a reading of these films that extends beyond Kayser's rendition of the grotesque as sheer estrangement and disorientation that evades meaning (Bakhtin,

Rabelais 21 and 24; Kayser 186). Can we not interpret a critique of the false pretenses involved in rationality or the inhibitive nature of the concept of maturity in the Martian excesses of enjoyment, most of which are paralleled in the representation of American political culture in *Mars Attacks!*? Does painting excessive militarism, oppressive cultural codification, and "race" protectionism as monstrous in *Planet of the Apes* not make the desert-dwelling humans freer, in some sense, than those in the sanitized, technological military culture from which Captain Davidson comes?

Burton's Alienated Subject

Ron Magliozzi, in "Tim Burton: Exercising the Imagination," writes, "creativity is the saving grace of Tim Burton's heroes.... Their example of imaginative activity, as a response to conditions of disconnection and isolation, is the overarching message of Burton's work" (14). But to leave the statement here is to leave it incomplete, for some of Burton's characters thrive in their alienated states, as these states become occasions in which they become capable of manifesting their imaginations as the reality within which they are isolated, while others, no less eccentric, perhaps, are almost pathologically social. Society seems unable to resist them, and by the time these films end, it may be unclear whether society, as represented in the film, has been radically transformed by such characters' charisma and imagination or the other way around. These themes still fit within the overall motif of a conflict of two worlds, a duality, but in *Vincent, Edward Scissorhands, Charlie and the Chocolate Factory, Pee-wee's Big Adventure*, and *Big Fish*, one of those worlds is or is within an individual subject; the other is the world, and imagination is the mysterious force that drives these two worlds towards some kind of union or separation.

Vincent, Edward Scissorhands, and *Charlie and the Chocolate Factory* feature Burton's alienated subject, and in each film, part of the drama relies on this individual's strained relationship to a version of the world that cannot understand him. Two other films that I should mention in this discussion (but that I will mostly ignore) are Burton's *Frankenweenie* and *Sweeney Todd: The Demon Barber of Fleet Street*. For while the dog in *Frankenweenie* is certainly misunderstood and vilified as monstrous, it is Victor that effectively figures out the science to resurrect him, mostly out of a sentimental attachment to the dog. In *Sweeney Todd*, it is not Barker/Todd's creativity or imaginative eccentricity that sets the official world against him in the person of Judge Turpin. But when Barker returns as Todd to London, he certainly represents an alienated figure and gains a freedom from the official demands of the civilized world, but only out of blind dedication to vengeance. And while his modified barber chair and plan to sell the excess bodies he has around as meat filler in Mrs. Lovett's pies show ingenuity and thoughtfulness, imagination is not really the center of the narrative. So while these two films do indeed appeal to much that qualifies them as grotesque in one way or another — notably, sewing and resurrecting a monstrous dog corpse, only to have it be the same sweet dog it was when it was alive in *Frankenweenie*, as well as the stylized blood-letting and grisly human-pie plotline in *Sweeney Todd*, especially against the backdrop of Mrs. Lovett's middle class beach house aspirations — they only fit loosely within this particular scheme of the grotesque that I see as the overarching motif in Burton's films. These films may serve as a very early and a mid-to-late "exception to prove the rule."

The dramatic tension that arises between the alienated subjects and their oppressive, stultifying worlds in *Vincent, Edward Scissorhands,* and *Charlie and the Chocolate Factory* seems to function similarly to Thomson's notion of "unresolvability," discussed above with reference to *Ed Wood, Mars Attacks!,* and *Planet of the Apes,* in which some "other" becomes the "norm" within the world of the film, in one way or another, in order to effect a jarring shift of perspective from which whatever was judged to be normal before is now shown with a degree of derision or judgment because of its alienation of the "weirdoes" for whom Burton quite obviously has affection. The difference is that Vincent, Edward, and Wonka are individual subjects — particular characters — each with his own eccentricities and history, his own emotional hang-ups, family, dreams, etc. They are not part of a socially outcast group; they do not band together with others like themselves. And to emblematize them for this or that purpose would be to miss something essential about them. Each of them is the alienated "other": each is a particular instantiation of Albert Camus's "stranger to myself and to the world" (*The Myth of Sisyphus* 15). The theme of alienation in these films is heightened by Burton's tendency to demonstrate these characters' isolation from the societies in which they find themselves by constructing the films in such a way that viewers experience these "others" from a perspective in which camera position is frequently utilized in order to evoke sympathies with representatives from the official culture, which clash with similar strategies used to build identification with these protagonists. Further, Burton's films center on crises in which these characters get caught between who they are and who they want to be, the second of which throws real knowledge of the first into question, leaving these characters with a feverish impulse to express themselves (often "artistically") as immediately and as boldly as possible.

In this impulse to express — to externalize imagination — these characters communicate both diegetically and extradiegetically. But these expressions, most frequently, serve to alienate the characters further. The boy, Vincent Malloy, in *Vincent*, an early Burton short, wishes to be Vincent Price, and for a brief few minutes he is — kind of. The narration (read by none other than Vincent Price) keeps the conditional language of what the boy could or would do — what macabre possibilities he wishes for — but his imagination is expressed as already fulfilled desire in stop-frame animation. Viewers see Vincent Molloy become his hero, do his grisly deeds, wear his mustache — his imagined reality intermittently cuts into the day-to-day life he lives with his family and pets so distinctly that his cat seems to recognize it at one point, leaping from the boy's arms as he makes his imaginary transformation. His mother is exactly right when she states that Vincent's melancholia and impending insanity are "all in your head," and this seems to be a major point in the film: it is only in and through his imagined life, which for him is his "real" reality, one so powerfully conceived that his imagined world breaks into his day-to-day life, that he can be as he wishes. And it is telling that even after the motherly reminder that he is just a young boy and that he should go outside to play, Vincent seems to treat the mother and her reality check as a mere intrusion in his imagined world of horror and madness.

In *Edward Scissorhands*, the alienation of the title character is deepened by his ontological separation from humanity, as Slavoj Žižek points out in *Enjoy Your Symptom: Jacques Lacan in Hollywood and Out*: Edward is "a failed, aborted, Frankensteinian monster with scissor-like hands" (149). Edward's constitution as "Frankensteinian monster," as a fusion of man and machine, also appeals to what Kayser sees as a more horrifying modern equivalent to the fusion of plant and animal/human life in earlier grotesquery. He argues that the human and the mechanical are "alienated" from

73

their respective natures in their collision in such grotesquery: "The mechanical object is alienated by being brought to life, the human being by being deprived of it" (183). Accordingly, Edward is another in a long line of grotesque man-machines.

In unfolding how this troubling ontology affects Edward, Žižek describes him as "a melancholic subject condemned to pure gaze since he knows that touching the beloved equals causing him/her unbearable pain" (149). This aspect of Edward's alienation factors into the narrative when he, in a flashback to his "father's" death, attempts to rouse the old man, and even with the gentlest touch, he cuts the dead man's face. Again, near the climax of the film, after Edward saves Kevin from being hit by Jim's van, he manically fusses over the boy to see if he is hurt, frightening and cutting him a number of times. He is largely relegated to the role of voyeur, and this is the role to which he returns after his failure to integrate into suburban society as a novelty of the grooming world. At this highpoint of his integration into society, he, like Vincent, is engaged in the process of manifesting his imagination, but in a world that is ultimately unable to bear its weight. He finds no acceptable outlet in suburbia for the angst and despair that his relation to that culture brings him, emotions that he needs to externalize in art, which is his only real means of communication with the other. Burton touches on this idea when he extrapolates Edward's thematic meaning as having to do with "the inability to communicate, the inability to touch, being at odds with yourself" (qtd. in Smith and Matthews 101). If this is true, and if the aesthetic impulse to sculpt with his scissorhands is an attempt to express himself to the culture around him, then Edward's most intensely expressive scene in the film comes near the end when Edward kills Jim, a moment punctuated by Burton's anxious reverse tracking shot, when the wobbling camera shifts to Jim's perspective as Edward runs him through, ending forever his brief foray into a world beyond his own. But this alienated context seems to be exactly what Edward needs in order to thrive, for when he is alone in his dilapidated mansion on the hill, he has the freedom to unleash himself artistically, which viewers experience for the first time through Pegg Boggs near the beginning of the film. The conclusion returns Edward to his previous state, but by this point, he has achieved a kind of mythic separation from a world in which he does not belong. We see him through an aged Kim: he is unchanged by time, sculpting ice, the chips of which create the magical snowfall in the world below. His isolation is necessary because his imagination requires the complete freedom that only isolation affords him. His imagination cannot be fully expressed without certain pain to others, which would require it to be suppressed or repressed in some form, but in the absence of an immediate relationship with others, he is able to bypass expression as such. In isolation he merely manifests his imagined reality by cutting away those parts of his world that do not line up with his vision, and what he cuts away brings magic and delight to the world below.

The duality in *Charlie and the Chocolate Factory* works in a strikingly similar way. Wonka's history with people is a troubled one, leading him to isolate himself as the benevolent ruler of his own candy kingdom, peopled by tiny chocolate addicts who work tirelessly in exchange for an endless supply of their drug of choice. The pain caused in Wonka's relationship with the normal world of candy commerce is unidirectional: unlike Edward, Wonka, in the film's back-story (provided by Grandpa Joe), represents no real threat to others. He is merely an eccentric chocolatier who becomes disillusioned after the theft of his trade secrets by insiders cheapens his art. He isolates himself and cuts off all relationships. Burton calls him "the Citizen Kane or Howard Hughes of candy — somebody who was brilliant but then was traumatized and then retreats into their own world" (qtd. in Salisbury, *Burton* 228). But as with Vincent and Edward, it is only within the context of such thoroughgoing alienation that he is able to become "the amazing chocolatier" he wants to be, constructing an alternative world in which his fantastic candy dreams are realized, a world built on candy logic, where a chocolate river or televisual candy transporter is an end in itself, as Charlie, the only child pure enough to figure it out, realizes: "Candy doesn't have to have a point. That's why it's candy." Wonka's success seems directly related to his isolation — when his imagination is left unfettered, able to make manifest whatever wild candy-laced idea comes into mind.

It would be a mistake to ascribe this theme of the fruitfulness of social alienation to some kind of masturbatory imaginativeness — for in these films, Burton issues rather biting visions of what is "normal," of how the official culture in each case thwarts, impedes, and ruins imagination in its attempts to normalize it, use it, or defuse it. Consider the grotesque representatives of the "normal" world in these films: the patronizing maternal figure in *Vincent* is so tall compared to her son that she literally does not fit inside his perceived world, speaking to her son from a head that does not fit within the frame onscreen; the parodies of the "high school jock" or the almost archetypal variations on the "suburban housewife" in *Edward Scissorhands* (not to mention the sickly pastel houses with their tiny windows and obsessively trimmed, overly green yards); or the moralistic variations on the vices of children (and parenting) in *Charlie and the Chocolate Factory*, each flawed to monstrous proportions, Charlie being the notable exception. The normal, or the status quo, of official culture in these films is judged as inadequate for fostering the flamboyantly imaginative individual subjects in these films — and it is this aspect of the ruling culture that drives these characters towards near total isolation within worlds of their own making. Burton's creative subjects are represented as dangerous because they do not fit within the bounds of the status quo; they represent an imaginativeness that extends beyond the base line assumptions about what is appropriate, reasonable, or useful — about what is normal. As such, they subvert the status quo just by being themselves, but in so doing, they are also alienated by normal, official culture in their attempts to express themselves to a world that is not equipped with a way to make sense of them because it is too small to allow anomalies to thrive in its midst.

Pee-wee's Big Adventure and *Big Fish* reflect similarly constructed characters in more receptive contexts. These films seem to reverse the paradigm between the eccentrically imaginative individual and society. Here, "normal" culture gets sifted through the subject's imaginative reality, often to the extent that the protagonists' larger-than-life personalities tend to obfuscate delineations between subjective perception and objective "truth." Ann Lloyd, in her review of *Pee-wee's Big Adventure*, observes that the "preternatural quality to the imagery" invites viewers to "rediscover our capacity for wonder through our identification with Pee-wee's point of view" (qtd. in Smith and Matthews 47). The film is nearly unrelenting in remaining locked within Pee-wee's point of view, and, with few exceptions, by the close of the film, Pee-wee is able to recapitulate the world he finds in his travels, first through actual America and then through the virtual world of "the movies" (in the elaborate chase scene through various soundstages and movie sets on a production lot), in the wide-ranging circle of new friends who come to see the 007-style film adaptation of his recent exploits.

And just as the world is for Pee-wee a big room full of toys to play with and enjoy, a notion hinted at in the initial sequence of the film, for Edward Bloom of *Big Fish*, the world is a sequence of tall tales, each featuring Edward Bloom as the hero that finds a way to tie them all together. And the content of these tall tales is particularly grotesque. They feature giants, werewolves, witches, mermaids — all figures at home in the grotesque tradition's frequent appeals to images that marry the human form to an animal counterpart, as well as play with the "material bodily principle" in order to image the carnival aesthetic. *Big Fish*'s grotesquery is also particularly Bakhtinian. Even those figures that frequently function as fearful characters in horror here retain a sense of benevolence amid some kind of misunderstanding. Edward is able to befriend them because of his gregarious nature and because the ebullient character of his imagination precludes the possibility of making hasty judgments about even the oddest people.

Even though Edward's serious-minded son, Will, attempts to track down, ground, or disprove the subjects and characters of his father's wild autobiography, he is unable to do so with any completeness, leaving the two worlds — the fantastic story-formed world of Edward Bloom's perception and the stark, colorless world of his son's "objectivity" — to clash in juxtaposition. Burton vivifies Edward's stories by slightly and playfully distorting logic and visual proportion and by relying on a rich and brilliant palette of bright colors, while for those scenes in which Will's point of view dominates, the world appears in less contrast; colors are muted; the visual quality reflects a "personality-free style," as Manohla Dargis puts it in her review (174). Burton, in *Big Fish*, highlights the appeal of the almost mythic world of Edward Bloom's imagination, one that Will eventually comes around to appreciating. Taken together, then, Burton's, perhaps nearly bi-polar (in the clinical sense), rendition of the duality of the world of imagination over against attempts to explain or account for events in rational, objective terms — his attempts to contextualize the imagination and how it does and does not function in relation to the status quo of "normal" or dominant society/culture, aligns his work with Bakhtin's description of the purpose of the carnival's grotesque form: to sanctify the freedom of invention, to allow for the combination of various elements, to liberate from the dominant perspective of the world, from the conventional, the traditional, the banal, the cliché, from all that is understood or assumed in the normative thinking that sustains the status quo (34).

The Grotesque: The Aesthetics of Burton's Underlands

Burton's 2010 film adaptation, *Alice in Wonderland*, provides a synthesis of most of the aspects of the Bakhtinian "clash of worlds" motif that I have drawn out in the argument so far. This film reflects Burton's aesthetics, but it also represents, perhaps, his most consistently grotesque film to date. So, I will conclude this chapter in offering an analysis of this film according to the arguments I have already put forth.

Roger Ebert observes that Burton gives Carroll's characters from *Alice's Adventures in Wonderland* and *Through the Looking-Glass* an appearance that is "distinctive and original" that avoids relying on earlier versions of the story: "They're grotesques, as they should be, from the hydrocephalic forehead of the Red Queen to Tweedledee and Tweedledum, who seem to have been stepped on." David Edelstein similarly observes, "Burton indulges in his penchant for disproportion," fusing "the circus and the sarcophagus, the magic kingdom and the mausoleum." Edelstein points to the numerous ways in which Burton marries these poles of the beautiful and the terrible, from the topography and gnarled plant life of Wonderland to the post-apocalyptic tea party scene with the Mad Hatter and friends in a desolate, "bombed out" region of Wonderland, from the ghostly pallor and black-red lips of the White Queen to the elongated card-body of the Knave of Hearts. Edelstein concludes that, for Burton, "there can be no true beauty without a touch or a ton of decay."

Wonderland, or for Burton's film, "Underland," again provides a spectacle that fuses Bakhtinian and Kayserian grotesque in opposition to Alice's "real world" Victorian London, where the film begins. Burton's film reimagines Alice's trip down the rabbit hole as an escape from a surprise engagement ceremony that her mother has arranged in order to marry the nineteen-year-old Alice to a young lord. And in some ways, Underland seems to be Alice's imagined Bakhtinian parody of her own real world situation: she identifies certain parallels between a few of the characters she knows in London and a few she meets in Underland, and the opposing poles of femininity in Underland, signified by the infantile Red Queen and her sister, the White Queen, who represents near enslavement to social decorum and propriety, provide Alice with almost equally stifling, grotesque parodies of the only models of femininity that her own London offers: her options are to remain the narcissistic girl who lives in the fantasies of her own mind (as Alice's Aunt does) or be enslaved to Aristocratic sensibility in a marriage of convenience. But, ultimately, there is no satisfying or exact, one-to-one correlation between the two worlds — London and Underland. Underland is the "estranged" world, one with enough parallels to hint at the familiar, but the recognition of the familiar in such a context proves alienating (Kayser 184–85). Even Alice's friends in Underland prove to be difficult, sometimes infuriating, companions for her. At several points in the film, Alice seems perplexed as to why her imagination would produce such a weird and disorienting place, but as the film continues, she becomes less certain that Underland is her construction. Burton leaves ambiguous whether or not Alice has imagined Underland — that it is a dream or hallucination — or whether it is her imagination and spunk that make her suited for heroism in such an actual, existent Underland.

Alice's closest companion in Underland is the Mad Hatter, whose madness shifts from clownish buffoonery (for which he uses a lilting British accent) to rather menacing and violent rage (delivered in a thick Scottish brogue). The make-up, wig, and costume for the Mad Hatter are particularly clownish — white face, bright pastel touches around the eyes, red-orange Bozo-style wig, and a slightly undersized purplish suit, reminiscent of Joker's and Wonka's. The Hatter leads a gang of freaks — the March Hare; White Rabbit; Dormouse; Cheshire Cat; and Absolem, the hookah-smoking oracle — who serve as friends and protectors to Alice, though sometimes their help and guidance rings of antagonism. These freaks, who throng around the White Queen and her benevolent rule of liberation within the bounds of kindness, find parallels in the false freaks who cling to the Red Queen, donning prosthetic noses, ears, bellies, breasts, and goiters to gain her favor, apparently, by keeping her insecurities about her own bulbous head at bay. Again, then, Burton's themes of the mad clown and the gang of freaks, both of which ultimately represent a kind of dangerous freedom and liberating social aesthetic through appeals to the carnival spirit of the grotesque, subvert the ruling powers of Underland but also of London, for, as Alice reveals in the first act of the film, the aristocracy's attraction to corsets and stockings are unnatural falsities that ultimately betray her own body and identity, while her wild imagination makes her something of a freak among the youth of polite society. And it is as such a freak that Alice strikes out on her own upon her return to London, after defeating the evils of Underland, into the uncharted territories of her own world.

Part 2. Interpolarity: Binaries of the Grotesque

Like in *Alice in Wonderland*, then, Tim Burton's films generally tend to envision the world as divided, as split between two realities. They imagine worlds in which the official rule of the status quo is upset, degraded, judged, derided, and dethroned by the unruly, raucous menace of the carnival spirit — through the terrible freedom of mad clowns, by visions of the dead and ghoulish that outstrip normal life in vibrancy and texture, in the comradery and liberation that these oddballs and freaks find in each other's company, and in the strange propensity Burton's protagonists have to materialize their outrageous imaginations in the world around them. But Burton's films also give credence to the overwhelming nature of the normal world of official power and ideology that impinges itself on those who do not fit comfortably within its order, giving rise to alienation and/or sending such outsiders to seek the necessary isolation in which they can dream. Burton's movies nearly always sympathize or identify with the outsiders, weirdoes, and freaks, but his interest in and ability to depict the overbearing nature of the "established truths" of "the way things are" in conventional normalcy do not necessarily take a backseat: his tendency is to reverse the relationship, to reset the terms, to undermine the official side of his perennial duality by giving the spirit of carnival a permanent foothold through the grotesquery of his films (Bakhtin, *Rabelais* 34).

IV. Terry Gilliam's Mythic Madness

The hypothesis before us is simple: the grotesque consists of the manifest, visible, or unmediated presence of mythic or primitive elements *in* a nonmythic or modern context.

–Geoffrey Galt Harpham, *On the Grotesque*

Men are so necessarily mad that not to be mad would amount to another form of madness.

— Blaise Pascal, *Thoughts*

Conflict at the Borderlines

Terry Gilliam plays with a revealing theme in his 2009 film, *The Imaginarium of Doctor Parnassus*: in its purest visual form, it is the image of a stream, some kind of river that appears on screen as Parnassus is telling his daughter the story of how he made a deal with the devil, Mr. Nick, in order to regain his youth. After cashing in, Parnassus rides in a gondola with his young wife through a pale pastel paradise of oversized vegetation, dazzling color, haze, and mist — something out of Monet — a place of impossible vibrancy and serenity — propelled along by Parnassus' gentlemanly-looking dwarf friend, Percy. As they float along in apparent bliss, the gondola bumps into something that jars it to a stop. Parnassus looks and finds that they have run into a bloated cow corpse floating, half-submerged, in the water. The camera pulls back for a wider shot of the scene to reveal a distinct line in the water where the translucent blue meets the murky brown-red of blood and dirt and water. Gilliam offers a glimpse downstream: the river is filled with corpses; the sky is smoky and red; the trees blackened by fire and skeletal; and there smolders the remains of some recent apocalypse in the distance. Mr. Nick sits on some stairs leading up from the water in this depeopled, anti-paradise, his pant-legs rolled up, splashing his feet in the bloody water, sunning his face with a reflective fan, as he eats fruit from a pile next to him: "What's up, Doc?" he barks, laughing.

Images such as this one occur all over Gilliam's movies, representing intertwined polarities, each extreme of which seeming to rely upon and insinuate the other.[1] Each is married to the other, as in this scene, where the opulence and rejuvenation of one side is only possible *because of* the ruination and violence of the other. Gilliam's films are particularly interested in finding the places where the poles meet. These are fields of cosmic, metaphysical conflict, but just as much, they are sites of interpersonal, aesthetic, cultural, historical, and political conflict. His films find their centers in the connections and disruptions of the relationships between reality and fantasy, reason and mystery, rationality and imagination — between any number of related conceptual bifurcations. But, in Gilliam's worlds, these relationships are never easily defined or settled. He imagines worlds in which characters' lives are thrown into the territory of the mythic, in a manner not dissimilar to the mythic visions of Yeats or Blake, visions fixated on the necessity of imagining as immensely as possible; visions that, in highlighting imagination, imply the myths of the past along with a hope for real meaning in the mythic realm of the imagination. Northrop Frye writes about the imagination of the visionary in *Fearful Symmetry: A Study of William Blake*; he offers the reflection that, as children, most people feel that if they can conceive of something in their imagination, then it either is or could potentially become reality:

> All of us have to learn that this almost never happens, or happens only in very limited ways; but the visionary, like the child, continues to believe that it always ought to happen.... That is why Blake is so full of aphorisms like "If the fool would persist in his folly he would become wise." Such wisdom is based on the fact that imagination creates reality, and as desire is a part of imagination, the world we desire is more real than the world we passively accept [27].

All of Gilliam's films in one way or another deal with the tensions that Frye points out: the tensions between the reality of the world of imagination and of "the world we passively accept" (27). The imaginative in his films is connected with the mythic and the paradoxical, just as assuredly as passive acceptance is associated with rationality and pat answers to difficult questions. A number of Gilliam's films, most notably *Time Bandits,*

82

The Adventures of Baron Munchausen, The Brothers Grimm, and *The Imaginarium of Doctor Parnassus,* are concerned with the reality of the mythic world and the kind of imagination required to see it, but in or against a cultural context that has forgotten, dismissed, or maligned it or has explained it away. In other films, like *Brazil, The Fisher King, Twelve Monkeys, Fear and Loathing in Las Vegas,* and *Tideland,* Gilliam is more concerned with the crippling effect of characters' attempts at navigating the world of the imagination within the context of a troubling "real" world. These films meditate on variations of the madnesses in which Gilliam's characters lose themselves, to varying degrees, as their circumstances drive them into the mythic, mad worlds of their own imaginations. So, in either of these two directions — the thrust of the imaginative (the mythic) into the "real" world or of the retreat back into the imaginative, away from the "real" world — the films rely on the grotesque to mediate this conflict. In this chapter, then, I will demonstrate Gilliam's use of the grotesque by arguing that two particularly prominent manifestations of the grotesque in his films are visible in his explorations of the mythic and of madness, for him, both topics married to the imagination and its interface with the "real" and metaphysical world.

The Mythic, the Primitive and the Grotesque

Citing some overlap with Nietzsche's theory of the Apollonian and the Dionysian impulses in aesthetics, David K. Danow observes in *The Carnival Spirit,* following Bakhtin, that the concerns of the carnivalesque and the grotesque are, in a way, parallel to the German philosopher's but that the relationship between contraries in grotesque theory ultimately maintains a more volatile equilibrium between its two principal elements than does Nietzsche's dualism (141). Further, Danow argues, relying on Jung and Bakhtin, that Nietzsche's theory is, in the end, "stuck in aesthetics" (Jung's phrase), ignoring any prospect for a valid religious viewpoint as well as anything like the carnival spirit, in which any number of related dualisms or bifurcations (official/unofficial, lawful/unlawful, rational/irrational, etc.) are implied but jumbled up, reversed, played with (142). For Bakhtin and Jung, Danow argues, this level of thinking goes well beyond aesthetics: it is prehistorical, epistemological, anthropological: it relates a deep, existential reality that affords a novel relation to and inspiration of the aesthetic, but ultimately must be attributed to "cultural archetypes" (142–43). Danow concludes that the carnivalesque grotesque assumes a category analogous to archetypal images, mythologems, and motifs, which he characterizes as constructive principles of instinctive potency: the grotesque relates forms emptied of their content, signs whose signifiers do not readily provide compatible signifieds, that is, until artists imbue them with meaning (153).

The theory turned this way may account for some of the formal principles of the grotesque referred to in Part 1. Phillip Thomson discusses the grotesque's "gratuitous mixing together of incompatible elements for its own sake," which may also be implied in Kayser's variations on the grotesque as a "comprehensive structural principle," for example, in animal monstrosities, fusions of mechanical and organic elements, human forms diminished to inanimate objects, and even encounters with madness (Thomson 3; Kayser 181–84). Danow's theory may, too, contribute to a deeper understanding of the varying experiences of the grotesque in the acts of production and reception.[2] This makes some interpretive sense of how the grotesque can function comically in Gilliam's *Jabberwocky* in the 20th century and in some religious mode in the paintings of Breughel and Bosch in the 16th, but also how Gilliam could think of his *Jabberwocky* "as an homage to Breughel and Bosch" (Christie 72). If the grotesque represents a form waiting for its content, then that content is capable of quite a range of variation and value ascription, depending not only on the artist who attempts to imbue it with meaning, as Danow remarks, but also on those who "receive" it, interpret it, which, in turn, depends on the critical toolbox and cultural values according to which they make their judgments.

Harpham's quote above, the epigram that begins this chapter, posits the copresence of what he calls "mythic" and "primitive" elements similarly to how Danow discusses Jung's concepts of archetypal images and mythologems, each invoking Jung and Bakhtin to make his case (Harpham 51; Danow 153). Harpham claims that the grotesque consists in the mismatch of such phenomena within a context that seems incapable of understanding it according to its defining qualities but instead interprets through a "nonmythic," "modern" lens (Harpham 51). He argues that whereas logic in the modern era is predicated on a standard of avoiding contradictions, myth not only tolerates it, but pursues it and creates narratives to facilitate it (53). Harpham, invoking Levi-Strauss and Edmund Leach, contends that myth serves the purpose of mediating oppositions, reconciling conflict through subtle inducements toward the acceptance of opposing propositions (53). Whereas modern thinking attempts to sidestep contradiction by installing hierarchical systems for ordering meaning, mythic thinking protests against the notion of meaninglessness itself: everything, especially corporeal experience, must retain some kind of significance (Harpham 54). In rejecting nothing, then, myths are soiled with the material stuff of which the world is made: its solids, liquids, and gases: primitive narratives are distinguishable by their tendency "to treat everything — even the gods, even the dead — as a palpable and living presence" (Harpham 54). Modern thinking, Harpham goes on, has trouble seeing the sacred in what seems to qualify as filth because it has severed itself from its role in the life of a world that functions according to organic patterns of life, death, renewal (56). In the primitive or mythic mind, though, the life force expresses itself through the fertility that death and corruption make possible, just as the death of winter gives way to spring and buds sprout from fecund heaps of shit (56).

Harpham's analysis of the mythic has obvious reverberations with Bakhtin's theory of the grotesque, and Harpham recognizes this but is careful to delineate his critique of Bakhtin's theory of the carnival spirit. He warns that Bakhtin's grotesque entails a persuasive temptation to feel that, could we simply embrace the grotesque, we could thereby put ourselves to rights with the world — we could obtain a lost wealth of meaning, a purified ontology, and a reborn sense of innocence before nature: Bakhtin's grotesque invites us to snuggle (as it were) with our fellow creatures and cuddle up to the warm bosom of the cosmos itself (72). Apprehending the grotesque as grotesque, however, Harpham claims, "stands like a flaming sword barring any return to Paradise," and this is what Rabelais realized in his own day: his culture already required the concept; the mythic mind was already in decay (72). For Harpham, then, Bakhtin's hopefulness is misplaced. He argues that the fate of the mythic world is set by the time of the discovery of the Domus Aurea. By then, the mythic was on the threshold of metamorphosing into the "grotesque," on the verge of cultural alienation into a kind of sacramental interval offering participation in a world that had already departed (72). The mythic, which Harpham sees everywhere in *Rabelais and His World*, even if it is not often explicitly referred to, quite literally, becomes the "grotesque" as modernity takes a firm hold of western culture and as that culture fails to understand itself any longer in mythic terms (74). And now, out of context, the mythic becomes more associated with something like Kayser's attempt "to invoke and subdue the demonic aspects of the world" (Harpham 74; Kayser 188). The grotesque consists in primitive, mythic elements that are necessarily out of joint with nonmythic modernity, which can only understand them as alien, other, monstrous: grotesque (Harpham 51).

Dueling Fairy Tales in Jabberwocky

Gilliam's *Jabberwocky* provides an interesting anomaly to the pattern that besets the rest of the films in his career, for, as John Ashbrook observes in his book, *Terry Gilliam*, the film's protagonist, Dennis, "is that rarest of creatures in a Gilliam film, a protagonist with no imagination. His dreams are small and delusional" (26). Gilliam himself sees the film as a clash of fairy tales, as he says in an interview with Bob McCabe in the latter's *Dark Knights and Holy Fools: The Art and Films of Terry Gilliam*:

> In the one fairy tale you've got the little guy who slays the monster and gets the princess and half the kingdom, and that's what we're supposed to all want. The other one is what he really wanted, which is the fat girl next door, not this other stuff. So he doesn't get what he wants and that's what intrigued me about it. The other thing that intrigued me ... [was that] [h]is dreams are so small and yet he's caught in a world where fairy tale endings are possible, but he doesn't get the happy ending he wants, he gets the fairy tale ending we're all told we all want [McCabe 69–70].

Gilliam points to the conflict in the film between Dennis' rather modern (American?) dream of mild success through hard work and a dedication to efficiency and convenient (and similarly efficient) love with the "girl next door" and the late medieval world of the film, in which the popular imagination is still "mythic" enough to force its unwilling hero into the fairy tale ending. This conflict is nicely confirmed in the last shots of the film, as Gilliam tracks Dennis and his new bride as they ride out of King Bruno's city to the half of the kingdom Dennis has inadvertently earned, passing Griselda (the "fat girl" next door), who is now dressed in a nun's habit, screaming her frustration, and a street full of well-wishers; Dennis' protestations are heard as the film concludes with an iris shot and the sound of a prison door clinking shut. The world imprisons him in a mythic tale that he is too modern to dream for himself. But Gilliam also refers to the seeds of the burgeoning modernity that Dennis represents but which the popular culture of *Jabberwocky* has not yet fully embraced.

Jabberwocky is set perhaps on the cusp of the late medieval and early modern periods — medieval enough for the staples of medievalism — the king, the castle, the joust, the dragon — to be prominent and important in the narrative of the film, but modern enough for them to bear a heavy dose of filmic irony. King Bruno, "the Questionable," is ancient, and he spends much of his screen time hacking; he is dressed in moth-eaten royal rags; his castle is literally crumbling more and more as the movie's narrative moves forward, the entire east tower collapsing just after Bruno promises it to his daughter and her future husband. In the king's first appearance on screen, Gilliam robs him of any shred of royal dignity: Bruno is in bed, writhing in a nightmare, comically alternating between screams and snores, his ass in the air, his belly hanging out. Later in the film, when his daughter and advisor begin to find the joust too brutal — after nearly every knight in the kingdom has been extravagantly maimed by the Black Knight, their blood sprayed all over the court — Bruno decides to finish the competition by having the surviving knights play hide and seek, but then when this competition is settled no one can find the winner to tell him of his victory. The modern figures, besides Dennis, are the aristocrats, who are young, silver-tongued, efficient, and costumed in rather dashing Renaissance attire. They are also willing to use the fear and piety of the popular mythic mind as a tool to better subjugate the people. But, in the end, in the world of *Jabberwocky*, the myth wins; the popular imagination dreams up a fairy tale success for those who do not want or deserve it.

Perhaps the most prominent element in *Jabberwocky*, beyond but related to the conflict between the medieval and the modern, the mythic and the efficient or politically expedient, are the scatographic elements of the film, another layer in the overall texture of what Alan Brien of the *Sunday Times* calls "an uncannily persuasive Breughelesque portrait of the Middle Ages," adding some comparisons between Gilliam and Fellini and Bergman (qtd. in Thompson 6). The modern peasant dreamer, Dennis, is urinated on a number of times by those in roles representative of the primitive world. There are also a few defecation scenes: in the first, Mr. Fishfinger shits out of an open window into the river below, all the while talking to Dennis, who is attempting to woo Griselda, Fishfinger's daughter. All of the scatography, when taken together with the ways in which bodies, their excess solids, gases, and fluids, their amputated parts and pieces, are all welcome and integrated as part of the organic, primitive life in the film, becomes involved in Gilliam's overall vision of the mythic past of the medieval world, whose imagination was such that it could integrate the body and its functions into culture, and it is precisely this that modern-minded efficiency wants to displace, hide away, within ducts, pipes, and drains, perhaps, as in *Brazil,* pinched between walls, for those well-connected or rich enough not to have to be faced with their own excrement. The mythic past in *Jabberwocky* is still alive in the popular mind, and it has a certain liberating affiliation with the body and with the world, and while that mythic story prevails, Gilliam images it as crumbling, sick, and dying. And it is the contours of this demise that will concern him for the rest of his career in filmmaking.

Rupturing the Now: Myth, Modernity and Meaning

In Gilliam's cinematic world since *Jabberwocky,* modernity is ensconced in the historical setting of the films, but, more importantly, it has largely taken hold within the minds of characters in his worlds. Those with the imaginations capable of conceiving of mythic significance in the world are alienated by their various modern contexts, whether it is Kevin in *Time Bandits,* Baron Munchausen in *The Adventures of Baron Munchausen,* Jacob Grimm in *The Brothers Grimm,* or Parnassus in *The Imaginarium of Doctor Parnassus.* They have tapped in to a certain depth of mythic reality, but their worlds have little place for such visionaries. These worlds mock such depth as childishness, madness, dreaminess, or as an empty mysticism in a traveling sideshow. But Gilliam, in these four films, focuses in on the validation of such imaginativeness, and in each film he discloses the in-breaking of the mythic into the modern.

In *Time Bandits,* Gilliam conceives of a contemporary London, obsessed with paltry television game-shows and dedicated to the application of technology to banal bourgeois suburban life. The film figures these themes in the show "Your Money or Your Life" on the TV in Kevin's home (with its own form of piratical banditry) and in the obsession (shared by personified Evil) with mechanized appliances. All the while, Kevin is lost in books of ancient history and mythology. And this world, quite literally, breaks into his London, first as a knight on horseback that violently emerges from his closet, then as a rag-tag gang of pirate dwarves, rogue worker-angels from the heavenly realm, armed with God's map of all of the mistakes — the time holes — in the fabric of creation. What ensues is a romp through time — Kevin meets Napoleon on the warpath in 1796; Robin Hood and his band of merry thieves in the Middle Ages; and Agamemnon in ancient Greece; they arrive on the Titanic just in time for it to sink; and they drop through the bottom of the world into the "Time of Legends," before finally battling Evil himself, and eventually meeting the Supreme Being. *Time Bandits* is, at least to some degree, a children's movie, but Gilliam seems to withhold very little in envisioning his depictions of history. Further, since our guide is the contemporary Londoner, Kevin, we are given a point of identification whose perspective is entrenched in a modern context (even if he has an appreciation for the ancient and legendary), as well as a frame-narrative that bookends the film with a departure from and return to the modern, "real" world. This context influences the view we get of much of the history and legend through which Kevin passes on his travels, and Gilliam's grotesquery provides a kind of textural or tonal continuity that laces together these otherwise unrelated destinations.

With each stop through time, Kevin's travels reveal scenes which are apparently commonplace in each historical/mythical context in which he finds himself, but which to Harpham's "modern mind" would be greeted with disgust, shock, laughter, uneasiness, or some combination of them. In Napoleon's world, a city burns in ruins; people are being executed in the streets by the dozen. And all of this culminates with a scene in the midst of the destruction, in which Napoleon himself is entranced in a particularly violent puppet show, admitting when the drama concludes that his real love is watching "little things hitting each other." In Sherwood Forest, the brutality of the middle ages is signified in a trudge through the thieves' encampment, where ensues an arm-wrestling competition in which the reigning champion is seen, not only trouncing his opponents, but completely ripping their arms from their bodies and tossing them nonchalantly into a large basket of the severed limbs of past losers. All manner of raucous behavior persists, and Gilliam withholds Robin Hood until the last moment possible. Just when Kevin and the bandits are expecting the worst rogue yet, Robin emerges and proceeds to greet everyone as politely as a schoolteacher, taking the bandits' treasure by polite subterfuge. Kevin goes alone to Agamemnon's Greece, where the battle with the Minotaur is blazing, and after the snorting hybrid is dead and decapitated, Agamemnon offers no explanation for the beast, but instead carries its head back to the city and throws it into the street as a sign of victory. In the Time of Legends, there seem to be no precedents or rules whatsoever. An inept and befuddled ogre attempts to eat the time-travelers; they are carried off by a giant; and they reach the end of creation, the invisible barrier between the Time of Legend and the Fortress of Ultimate Darkness where Evil lives.

Along with Kevin's astonishment, wonder, and fear as his modern perspective is struck by the mismatch of the mythic material, there are also moments of recognition: his imagination has prepared him for interfacing with the mythic, and, by the end of the film, he has entered the mythic realm himself and lives there but also in his "real" world simultaneously, not unlike the vision of the imaginative adventurer we see in *The Adventures of Baron Munchausen*. If the mediation of contradiction is a central characteristic of the mythic, then, Kevin can enter the mythic as a mythic character, even as he continues on in the "real" world, without the one canceling out the other, again, just as Munchausen (Harpham 53). But also like the Baron, Kevin must, to some degree, kill his heroes in order to join them, as Ashbrook also notices (30). And this is the purpose of Kevin's experience of each epoch in history or legend — he is always to some degree disappointed. When the thrill wears off, he is able to see Napoleon as a violent, insecure nitwit; he is able to see Robin Hood hiding behind the brutality of his backwoods toughs; Agamemnon using his status as warrior-king to whitewash his rather pathetic marital problems; the ogre attempting to obscure his pitiable ridiculousness by inhabiting the role of the monster. Kevin discovers that ultimate Evil is silly, selfish, and petty, and that The Supreme Being is disingenuous, distant, and seems to know surprisingly little about his own creation.

Time Bandits also develops another of Gilliam's themes, barely hinted at in *Jabberwocky* in the appearance of the absurdly outfitted, one-man puppet show, and which *The Adventures of Baron Munchausen*, *The Brothers Grimm*, and *The Imaginarium of Doctor Parnassus* extend to a considerable degree: this is popular entertainment, often figured as some kind of stage or sideshow, as the last bastion of the mythic imagination. A similar theory is also suggested by the likes of Samuel Johnson in his famous *Preface to Shakespeare* and by Bakhtin in *Rabelais and His World* and in *Speech Genres and Other Late Essays*. Johnson avers that Shakespeare's experiments in "mingled drama" — a more ambiguous development of the tragicomedy in which the dramatist pushes the comic and tragic together to such a degree that one is indistinguishable from the other in certain plays, notable among these is *King Lear*—reach back to a primeval "chaos of mingled purposes and causalities," a veritable pool of contradictions, which, by the time of the Greeks and Romans, would be bifurcated into the poles of the comic and the tragic. Bakhtin, focusing more closely on Shakespeare's language itself, writes:

> The semantic treasures Shakespeare embedded in his works were created and collected through the centuries and even millennia: they lay hidden in the language, and not only in the literary language, but also in those strata of the popular language that before Shakespeare's time had not entered literature ... in plots whose roots go back to prehistoric antiquity and ... forms of thinking [qtd. in Danow 144].

This idea that popular entertainment can function as kind of a repository of mythic imagination (or, indeed, Bakhtin's "carnival spirit") is also one of the central theses of *Rabelais and His World*. And Gilliam, too, recognizes the quintessential importance of such entertainments and their potential as a means of transport for the mythic and as a temporally transcendent cultural apparatus.

In *Time Bandits*, the rogue angels, the band of dwarves, themselves become the show, giving stage performances for Napoleon and Agamemnon, and it is no accident that these performers serve as Kevin's link to the reality of myth, at least until he is sufficiently prepared to go his own way on a God-ordained mission back into his "real" world to "fight evil." In *The Adventures of Baron Munchausen*, Henry Salt's players perform rather poorly and ultimately require a good straightening out by the baron himself, but they play on nonetheless, even while the city crumbles down around them. Further, they are, after little Sally, among the first believers in the baron's mythic significance, Henry even leading the people against the Rite Ordinary Horatio Jackson's brutal common sense. In *The Brothers Grimm*, the stage show consists of the Grimm's elaborately falsified hauntings, aimed at extorting provincial communities by fabricating a supernatural event that is meticulously integrated into local lore and then charging them a fee to rid them of it. But the theme functions still, for it is Jacob who is responsible for tailoring these scares to the local myths with which he is truly fascinated, and it is also Jacob who has the imagination required to deal with the mythic when it breaks violently into the "real" world. Finally, in *The Imaginarium of Doctor Parnassus*, Parnassus' traveling sideshow is ever mistaken for a mere carnival attraction, seemingly torn from some circus in the distant past and starkly contrastive with its contemporary surroundings, as Roger Ebert observes in his review of the film. But the ancient mystic does indeed deliver on his promise to facilitate new discovery and enlightenment within one's own imagination, and, even if he gambles on the souls of those who enter in, the imaginarium is not a mere playground for the mind. As he tells an inquiring police officer at one point, "What we do here is deadly serious."

Both *The Adventures of Baron Munchausen* and *The Brothers Grimm* rely on a setting in the late 18th century, "The Age of Reason," *Munchausen*'s title sequence reports, and then, for good measure it would seem, it adds, "Wednesday." Both films find their dramatic centers in the rupture of mythic reality into a world that is circumscribed by the ideology of the "Age of Reason" and the brutal reaction of the "reasonable" French rulers to those whose imaginations conceive of worlds beyond what can be "analyzed, quantified, measured, rationalized," as the Munchausen character remarks in Gilliam's first draft of the screenplay (qtd. in McCabe, *Dark Knights* 132). The films explore this theme from different angles though. In *Munchausen*, the baron represents a fearless imagineer whose wild adventure story functions, again, through the device of a frame-narrative. But it manipulates the frame function in cleverly murky ways, ultimately disclosing that Munchausen has, merely by telling his story, defeated the Sultan's army, a "real" threat in the "real" world, by fighting, and even dying, but by doing so on some mythic or legendary, "other" level of reality. In *The Brothers Grimm*, the threat comes at the Grimms from both directions: the "rational" French overseers and the mysterious, ancient world of myth, which here is a rather complicated meta-folktale that incorporates aspects of the tales of Little Red Riding Hood, Hansel and Gretel, Snow-White,

Rapunzel, the Gingerbread Man, and I am sure others, and exploits the legends of the wolfman, the vampire, the golem, etc. In both films, the intrusion of the mythic into the "age of reason" is signified with fantastic grotesquery, while the threats and violence done in the name of reason are shockingly brutal and grimly realistic, ranging from the threat of the firing squad in *Munchausen* to *The Brothers Grimm*'s beheadings and elaborately structured torture devices.

The signifiers of the mythic in *The Brothers Grimm* include images of the enchanted forest coming to life: tree roots slithering about like snakes, then becoming tentacles that grab at unsuspecting passersby, or trees that creep around the forest, changing formation, taking on agency in their attempts to entrap the characters within their flanks. The film includes a number of transformations: the wolf into trapper, splattered mud into a golem, the golem (after ingesting a child) into an absurdly literal gingerbread man, and the Mirror Queen into shattered shards of glassy flesh. More images of bodily grotesquery are the living corpse — the Mirror Queen, who has won eternal life but not eternal youth (a theme Gilliam plays with again in *The Imaginarium of Doctor Parnassus*) — and the putty-faced child who attempts to wipe magic mud from her face and inadvertently wipes her mouth and nose smooth.

The mythic mediates the oppositions and contradictions on which the grotesque thrives, and none of it fits within the bounds of the explainable in the reasonable terms offered as the dominant truth in the prevailing modern minds in the film. The film plays with associations to a number of generic forms, including fantasy, horror, and suspense thriller, but, in the end, this seems to make it less recognizable as a Gilliam film. Gilliam's reliance on "state-of-the-art" computer generated graphics for much of its hallucinatory richness, as Ebert points out in his review, is impressive in its detail, but rings of the same kind of thing in Tim Burton's *Sleepy Hollow*, and so many other installments in the same visual vein. *Munchausen* is much more textured and nuanced; it is a far wilder visual treat, and, further, Gilliam seems more capable in this earlier film of realizing his off-beat vision. As Gilliam admits in *Gilliam on Gilliam*, and as Ashbrook points out as well, "One of Gilliam's stated aims ... [in *Munchausen*] was to bring to life the dark and broody illustrations Gustave Dore provided for the book," most fully realized in the casting of John Neville as the baron, in the scene in which Death (with sickle and hourglass) hovers over the baron to take his soul, and in shots of the "landscape of wrecked, skeletal galleons" in the belly of the sea beast (Ashbrook 55). Gilliam reports that in *Munchausen* his goal was to trap "the Age of Enlightenment between the baroque and the romantic," since the film is both baroquely "flamboyant and fabulously over the top" but also relies upon "nineteenth century stuff, such as the morbid romantic image of death" (Gilliam qtd. in Christie 176–177).

Steven Rea observes, in his article on the film for the *Philadelphia Inquirer*, that Gilliam worked with Fellini collaborators on *Munchausen*: cinematographer Giuseppe Rotunno, production designer Dante Ferretti, and costume designer Gabriella Pescucci, and the film bears resemblance in color, texture, and style to films like *Juliet of the Spirits* and *Satyricon* (49). The Turkish Sultan's harem, in particular, alludes to *Satyricon*'s unruly, excessive bodies: here, the variation of the human form is on display, filling the frame with portly nudes who pace circles around a pool and recline in hammocks above the action, as the Sultan's execution team, a turbaned dwarf with elfin features and an enormous hatchet-man, whose eyes have been scorched shut (a parody of blind justice perhaps), stand by and await their orders. After the Baron and Sultan make their absurdly silly bet, a testament to the Baron's unwillingness to be outdone by the Sultan and his weird world, the sultan brings out his musical invention, the torture organ (which is not unlike the human doorbell of *Jabberwocky* or the Monty Python "mouse organ"), a commingling of man and machine composed of pipes and prods that enclose a number of prisoners behind the bars of an elaborately designed pipe organ (Ashbrook 55). He plays excerpts from his opera, "The Torturer's Apprentice" (a vague parody of De Sade), to pass the hour that elapses while the bet's winner is still unknown. The Baron nearly loses the bet (and his head), but his cartoonishly quick (à la the Roadrunner) servant rises to the occasion, and the Baron wins the wager, which is, he claims, returning to the frame narrative, what began the war with the Turks under which the French city currently suffers. But to what end? What is the purpose of the sensual splendor in a film that simply seems to leave it all behind?

An answer to this question provides an explanation for this problem, but will no doubt create others; even so, it will give testament to Gilliam's overall statement of the imagination. After he relates the story of his wager with the Sultan, the Baron's narration is cut short as cannon fire rains down on the theater, and from this point forward, the distinction between the "real" world and the baron's mythic fantasy is blurred. And only within such a blur can the movie end as it does. The Turkish harem, in the world of the film, may or may not be embellished by the baron's imagination, but either way the grotesquely fleshy sensuality of the place is only one episode in Munchausen's systematic experience of the physical and the metaphysical: he experiences the poles of violent rage (Vulcan) and serene beauty (Venus) available in the mythological world; he travels in a pink balloon made of ladies underskirts to the moon (an obvious reference to Meleis's *A Trip to the Moon*) to visit its king, the comically Cartesian Ray/Roger[3], and queen, with whom Munchausen had an affair on a previous journey; he is swallowed by a leviathan in the depths of the sea; and he even experiences death (contra Wittgenstein), as the hooded, skeletal ghoul extracts the baron's soul through his mouth.

Munchausen, not unlike the works of Rabelais, is about the breadth, depth, and scale of the experience of the world, and the central role imagination plays in experiencing as widely and wildly as possible. The baron's adventures are, for him, based in his experience — a catchword for Gilliam's "Age of Reason" — but the possibilities of experience seem nearly limitless under the liberating tutelage of the mythic imagination. Further, Munchausen is never surprised, never shocked with wonder, at any of his experiences. He does not become "lost" in fantasy, as little Sally Salt seems to think at certain points in the film: he becomes carried away in the depth of his experience of the worlds of fantasy-reality, but he is on a parallel with this world. He is as much a part of the pantheon of mythic existence as the Moon King, Vulcan, or Venus, and these characters seem to acknowledge this fact as well. The "real" world of the late 18th century, though, has lost the imagination to conceive of leviathans, moon kings, gods and goddesses, or of anything that exists beyond the logical, and it has lost the mythic thinking required to make any sense out of Baron Munchausen, as his exchange with the Rite Ordinary Horatio Jackson depicts: Jackson: "We cannot fly to the moon, we cannot defy death. We must face the facts, not the folly of fantasists like you, who do not live in the real world." Baron: "Your reality, sir, is lies and balderdash, and I am delighted to say that I have no grasp of it whatsoever." Gilliam relates the baron's adventures through images and sequences that are grotesque because they work according to the rules of myth rather than the logic of modernity. These images of excessive bodies, human and otherwise, divided, enormous, tiny, but all very much alive — too alive in some cases[4] — and of contradictions of physical and metaphysical space and time are out of place in the modern reality of the "Age of Reason." Not only does Gilliam rely on the mythic in these films in order to impinge its grotesque otherness on the viewers, but he also seems to do so as a critique of the "modern mind" and its loss of vision and lack of imagination, its failure to experience the limitless worlds that a Baron Munchausen can live in. Such imaginativeness, in *Munchausen*, reignites the popular imagination, delivers the people from their fears, and threatens and overcomes official power and order.

But the mythic imagination is not only a place of liberation, of realizable fantasy, and impossible experience too often sidelined, forgotten, or defused by "modern" thinking; it is also revealed to be a dangerous place in Gilliam's films. *The Imaginarium of Doctor Parnassus* provides a meditation that extends in both directions. In *Parnassus*, the modern mind is short-circuited: few in the film's version of contemporary London have an imagination of proportions vast enough to dream with the mythic mind, but when they step through his mirror, Parnassus facilitates by magnifying to mythic scale and rendering in mythic terms the content of their own pathetic imaginations. Gilliam depicts these inward journeys, and the content is rarely surprising, but the scale and quality is, as Mark Jenkins puts it in his review, a "crystalline fantasy."

Parnassus, who takes his name from one of the "Muses' mountains," the highest peak of which also serves the function of providing the means for the salvation of mankind in the myth of Zeus's Deluge, is like Baron Munchausen in that he represents a mythic presence in a world that seems to have no place for such anomalies (Hamilton 40, 93–94). Also, as is the case in *Time Bandits* and *The Adventures of Baron Munchausen*, the world of the imagination in *Parnassus* has overlaps with the "real" world: what happens to people in the realm of imagination, whether bliss or death, has real consequences in the "real" world. Likewise, both Parnassus and his dark, slithery counterpart, Mr. Nick, each with his own vices, powers, and attractions in both dimensions, occupy the "real" world as much as they stand for opposite poles of good and evil in the realm of the imagination.

In Mr. Nick, Gilliam again redefines evil. In *Time Bandits*, embodied evil is locked away in a gothic fortress outside of light, time, and creation.

His master plan is to learn and exploit human technology, which his finale in the film shows him quite capable of, as he easily manipulates the machines of destruction that Kevin and the bandits have brought from the distant corners of time to use against him, even revealing himself capable of grotesque mechanical transformation. Human apathy and laziness and self-abstraction — human attraction to technology — are painted as vestiges of evil. This notion carries over in some ways to *Brazil*. Technology in this film, though, is imaged most prominently in the form of ductwork, wire, and pipes; in elaborately crafted information (gathering and disseminating) devices; and in the ever-present televisions and computer monitors, all of which are signifiers of the reach and influence of the state and of the popular desire for an easy and thoughtless existence. The state reaches out through technology with the promise of making life comfortable, more organized, and predictable by incorporating every part of society in its centralizing processes. But it fails frequently, and these failures are embarrassing for the state and require explanation and exculpation, and this becomes central to the narrative of the film (Christie 144). So, evil is technology here, but it is also politely bureaucratic, benevolently totalitarian politics, along with the obscene, clandestine structures of brutality and torture at its core. In *Munchausen* and *The Brothers Grimm*, images of evil come, again, from the ruling ideology, figured in government officials, and, also like *Brazil*, in the ruthlessness with which they wish to maintain the status quo. *The Brothers Grimm* involves a threat of evil from the mythical past as well, but it too is involved with the selfish wishes of a tyrant from a former age, one whose world and ideology have disappeared but whose powers have not. *Fear and Loathing in Las Vegas* figures a brand of evil as banal in the pathetically trivial excesses the American imagination offers in Las Vegas, the experience of which Duke and Gonzo supplement with drugs, as well as in the complete inhibition of even the especially dark reaches of the imagination.

Parnassus extends Gilliam's conception of evil to a strange marriage of some objective (or at least intersubjective) and subjective realities. Mr. Nick is an objective embodiment of evil, as "real" in the "real" world as Parnassus himself. But his appeals to people are through temptations of vice, selfishness, fear, security, and laziness. He tempts them with invitations to yield to their weaknesses: he offers a drink to a drunk, a sexual escapade to an uptight bourgeois lady, the security of their old-world Russian mother to some mobsters. It is interesting that within the world of the imaginarium, the polarity does not consist of the Devil and God, but Mr. Nick, a personalization of the Devil, and Parnassus himself. Parnassus represents salvation, and within the imaginarium his most frequent appearance is as a darkened mountain; just as in the Greek myth, Parnassus as mountain represents the realm of inspiration, imagination, liberation, of salvation. But one must choose between evil and imagination, between easy answers and cheap dreams and the mythic "story without which the universe would cease to exist," but he or she makes this decision from within the world of imagination. When people enter into the mirror, Parnassus facilitates the modern-minded by providing them with enough imagination to occasion the choice. Otherwise, it seems, they are Mr. Nick's as a foregone conclusion, since most in the street scenes in London have only enough of a mind to see the troupe as a mad gang of sideshow freaks, a Ship of Fools, if they notice them at all.

Dislocating Madness: The Cultural Experience of the Mad in Gilliam's Films

Gilliam's films provide deeper insight for the notion of madness as well. In all of the films I have been discussing, the characters associated with the mythic imagination are alienated in their social milieu, and most of them (Munchausen, Jacob Grimm, and Parnassus) are accused of madness. The worlds of these films, though, validate such "madness," proving that these characters are attuned to a world that the rest do not have the eyes to see, that is, until the worlds collide, and the modern-minded are struck with the mysteriously inexplicable or they are thrown headlong into an unpredictable fantasyland that is, perhaps, illogical and unanalyzable but unmistakably real. But there is another variation of madness that Gilliam's films are preoccupied with. There is a scene in *Jabberwocky* that prefigures this. A troupe of mad, zealous flagellants (quite obviously borrowed from Bergman's *The Seventh Seal*), who haunt the streets of the city and preach of the apocalypse the Jabberwocky represents, perform oddly violent acts of asceticism, evidencing both their madness and their piety. At one point, well into the film, they find Dennis and decide to offer him up as a sacrifice to appease the bloodlust of the beast and as a sign of their measureless faithfulness. Their leader waxes on and on about the terrible ordeal Dennis will undergo as his bones are cracked and he is incinerated by the Jabberwocky. One of the mad ones, obviously deeply affected by this description, takes Dennis' place and willingly undergoes the ritual sacrifice himself. Madness in this scene is depicted not only in the wild behavior of the mad, but also in its peculiar relationship to the unruly imagination, one prone to reveries, visions, and delusions, one prone to driving its bearer to the edge of himself. And it is by portraying this strain of madness that this scene prefigures the madnesses of characters in *Brazil, The Fisher King, Twelve Monkeys, Fear and Loathing in Las Vegas*, and *Tideland*. Further, most of these films resonate with this scene's depiction of the relationship that subsists among suffering (often self-imposed or voluntary), escape, and madness (though in various ways) and between madness and the mythic.

In *Madness and Civilization: A History of Insanity in the Age of Reason*, Michel Foucault discusses the shifts in the cultural "experience of madness" in the West from the Middle Ages and Renaissance to our contemporary experience in which the insane are confined within the conceptual clinical (and material) space of "mental illness" (xii). He summarizes his thesis in this excerpt from the preface:

> In the Middle Ages and Renaissance, man's dispute with madness was a dramatic debate in which he confronted the secret powers of the world; the experience of madness was clouded by images of the Fall and the Will of God, of the Beast and the Metamorphosis, and of all the marvelous secrets of Knowledge. In our era, the experience of madness remains silent in the composure of a knowledge which, knowing too much about madness, forgets it [xii].

Foucault's claim is that before the classical conception of madness emerges, just as modernity takes a firm hold of western culture around the arrival of the seventeenth century, madness is invested with a troubling significance — it is an eschatological figuration of life at its own limits: in the world, in humanity, in death (37, 35). Medieval madness accesses the prohibited wisdom concerning the Fall as well as the Apocalyptic fantasies of the age (22–23). As time moves on, madness migrates from the ominous threats of the world and its subterranean counterpart into human being itself and becomes linked to human dreams, illusions, and weaknesses, and in this specious attachment to itself, humanity generates the mirage of its own madness, projecting it on the mad as a mirror of the unsettling aspects it finds in itself (26–27). Foucault discusses the liminal location of the madman on the cultural horizon of the middle ages: he is confined within the city gates or upon the ships of fools, external to all, yet trapped within a means of exclusion that also encloses him; he is inside and outside at once; madness is a ritualized form of division, a sacramental absence (10–11).

In this notion of sacramental absence or exclusionary rituals, Foucault refers to the social and ecclesiastical structures that were created to deal with the threat of lepers in the Middle Ages. They were special cases, left to work out their salvation through their exclusion from others, from the physical spaces of the church. Measures were taken to reward lepers with eternal graces for their worldly experience of abandonment, for which their cultures ratified certain formulas for its ritual significance, thus conceptualizing their communion as one enacted through their exclusion (7). But when the disease and its victims vanished from cultural memory, these structures persisted without them, showing up two or three centuries later in the same places, except in these instances with the mad, who would take the leper's part in the drama, though with a new meaning and culture significantly changed by time (7). The mad roamed about the countryside, danced around in his fantasies, enveloped in the ideological husk of the leper, and the culture began infusing that hollowed-out role with new meanings.

Foucault observes that in medieval and early Renaissance conception, the voyage of the madman is doubly significant: the geographical expanse across which he travels is both real and imaginary; he is at once rigorously divided from society but also liberated to embark upon an "absolute passage" to another world (11). Each embarkation upon the waters of this murky ambiguity could be the last. When he sets sail, Foucault writes, his fool's ship is trained upon the other world, and it is back from that other place that the madman arrives when he returns to shore (11).

It is this freighted mysteriousness at the fringes of conscious reality that disappears from the modern, scientific experience of madness. By the time Shakespeare and Cervantes are working their ironic turns on tragic madness, the affliction itself is shifting its colors: Madness is becoming what Foucault calls "Unreason" within the "monologue of reason" (31–32, xi). In the "Age of Reason," madness signifies only reason's "other"; it occupies a silence; it has lost its rich, symbolic ambiguity (xi). Madness moves from the borderlands of the taboo and the terrible in the liminal spaces in the medieval and Renaissance mind and culture to the specifically delineated, concrete places of the madhouse and the hospital for madmen by the seventeenth century, and this orderly confinement serves to protect the latter epoch from the vast tragic threats madness represented in the earlier one: madness as such in the Age of Reason is the domain of the "disturbed" rather than the "disturbing" (35–37). Such a modern experience of madness as sheer "Unreason," then, divests it of its primitive, mythic otherworldliness. Foucault discovers the earlier experience of madness to entail a number of interesting ambiguities: madness as epistemological contradiction, or knowing by not knowing, or the "wisdom of fools" (22); madness as a repository of moral significance, the darkened mirror of the common man's pride and presumption (27); and madness as an ontological opposition to the status quo, that is, the association with the mad grin of death in/on the face of the living (15–16) and the ritual exclusion madness necessitates in church polity (10). Such variety in madness in the Middle Ages and Renaissance, Foucault suggests, represents a notably mythic approach to the experience of madness, which, as he demonstrates, is very much alive in the substantial empire of images collected in the works of Bosch and Brueghel, among others (15).

The loss of such consciousness, all but complete by the seventeenth century, and its displacement by "reason" not only mutes the mad within the monologue of medical science, but also robs the art of the past age of the mythical coherence represented in its images of threat and violence (35). This situation, this shift from mythic to modern thinking, renders the paintings of artists like Bosch and Brueghel artifacts, bastard accidents of a primitive age. And if Harpham is right, and "the grotesque consists of the manifest, visible, or unmediated presence of mythic or primitive elements in a nonmythic or modern context," then the modern experience of such works is likely an occasion in which the grotesque factors quite prominently (51). The other side of the coin is that, if Foucault's theory holds, images of madness reinvested with its mythic significance, images such as Gilliam's, also offer potentially grotesque, modern experiences of madness. Gilliam is interested in madness on both sides of Foucault's divide, and, not only this, but some of his films (*Brazil* to some degree, but more particularly *The Fisher King* and *Twelve Monkeys*) even seem to center in on the tensions between the two sides of Foucault's archeology as married counterparts that lend drama to his renditions of the mad in the movies. Others, like *Fear and Loathing in Las Vegas* and *Tideland*, play one form of madness against another: the madness of innocents against the imposition of the madness of a threatening world.

Gilliam signals madness in his films in at least two ways. The first is by the sympathetic organization of much of the narrative and perspective of a given film from within the subjective experience of its mad characters. This aspect of his style of filmmaking can have rather disconcerting, disorienting effects because, as is the case in *Brazil, The Fisher King, Twelve Monkeys, Fear and Loathing in Las Vegas,* and *Tideland,* the films' subjective perspective invites spectators to share in the delusions, hallucinations, and inner dialogue of mad characters, all while withholding a foothold of objectivity from a "real" world perspective for some time. Gilliam relates internal experiences of madness, often without them necessarily seeming mad, precisely by exploiting this exploded sense of ambiguity about what is objective and what is subjective, what is "real" and what is not.

Brazil and *Twelve Monkeys* implicitly rely on this ambiguity. Both films feature protagonists whose dreams viewers see with relative frequency, and these dreams are cued as dream sequences by the character waking up afterwards, by repeated images that are coded in the narrative as related to the dream world (such as Sam's winged warrior alter-ego in *Brazil* and Cole's dream-memory of the airport scene in *Twelve Monkeys*), and by manipulated sound and motion (the slowed motion and sound in *Twelve Monkey's* airport scene as well as in Sam's dreams of Jill in *Brazil*). But both films, after establishing the codes and cues for dream sequences, provide information that demands reinterpretation of earlier moments in the films. As Matthew Conley observes of *Brazil* in his thesis on Gilliam, when Sam "drifts off into his last fantasy without any of the clues which previously informed the viewer that Sam's real world experience ends and his fantasy one begins," the film moves into its penultimate twenty minutes, which provide climactic action and a happy ending (35). All of this is then undercut by a pull away from Sam's perspective to reveal that he has indeed gone mad, and, while this is a definite end to our view of his fantasy, as Katrina Boyd claims, in "Pastiche and Postmodernism in *Brazil,*" "the disorientation arises from the impossibility of determining when the dream began" because all of the cues have vanished (40). Sam's dream world has been overtaken by the signifiers of the "real" world. He has, through an escape into madness, "realized" his fantasy because his "real" world life has become, quite literally, unbelievable to him.

In *Twelve Monkeys* the generic conventions of the film's beginnings disclose that it would be well placed as a science fiction film, but when Cole is revealed to be schizophrenic, spectators are offered a rational explanation for the science fiction aspects of Cole's experiences in the future: that they are sequences in which Gilliam is showing viewers the contents of Cole's delusional reality. But, as Gilliam reminds us in an interview for *Gilliam on Gilliam*, the film offers subjective points of view from both the position of science or psychiatry but also from a position of the subject or his madness and allows the ambiguity that arises in their conflicting explanations to hang over most of the film (230). When information from both time settings begins to line up for Dr. Railly (a character who serves to mediate the reason and madness of *Twelve Monkeys* by verifying Cole's seemingly paranoid claims about the future, while also sharing in parts of his madness), viewers must again reinterpret the sequences in the future as "real." But aspects of the future Cole experiences become more and more absurd as the film continues, which may be because of Cole's subjective experience of madness, since excessive time travel, we are told from early on in the movie, is associated with driving people mad. As one level of narrative ambiguity related to an attribution of madness associated with the past setting lifts, then, and as Cole's predictions are confirmed, a new charge of insanity from the future setting is leveled against the protagonist, and the film ends without completely settling these out.

The second way in which Gilliam signals madness in his films is through the ways in which his actors physically manifest attributes associated with the madness of their characters. In most of Gilliam's films, exaggerated or excessive physical movement, often used for comic purposes, are rather prominent features of the director's style, as Dennis in *Jabberwocky*; the dwarves and Robin Hood's thieves in *Time Bandits*; and Berthold, Vulcan, and King Ray/Roger (among others) in *The Adventures of Baron Munchausen* all demonstrate. But with his mad characters in *The Fisher King, Twelve Monkeys,* and *Tideland*, the excesses of physical movement, along with exaggerated speech patterns and general bodily anomaly, become part of the repertoires of characterizing the mad. Parry, along with many of the supporting characters that people the two mad worlds in which he figures, that of the homeless and that of the institutionalized; Jeffrey in *Twelve Monkeys* and the institutionalized insane in that film; and Dickens in *Tideland*—all fill their time on screen with wild gesticulation, frequent nervous tics, and lot of rocking back and forth, evidencing not only a preponderance of nervous/internal energy seeking physical/external outlet, but also the alienation these mad characters from the ones who do not share their affliction, whose behavior is normally rather subdued. Along the same lines, these characters exhibit speech patterns that usually consist of loud, fast-paced, rambling rants and bodily anomalies, such as the Gay Bum's skeletal figure and Sid's leglessness in *The Fisher King*; Jeffrey's lazy eye and, as Ashbrook observes, Cole's conspicuous amount of "leaking" (drooling, crying, bleeding, sweating) in *Twelve Monkeys*; and Dickens's overly prominent gum-line, cranial scars, and general contortedness in *Tideland* (Ashbrook 74).

Wardrobe for Gilliam's mad ones reinforces their physical oddity: Parry as a homeless man is outfitted in exceptionally dirty clothes, along with some Quixotic accommodations for battling knights and as an institutionalized catatonic in weirdly colorful pajamas; *Twelve Monkeys* features the mental patients in bathrobes and hospital gowns, Cole in a see-through plastic raincoat (and nothing else), and Jeffrey in a tuxedo at one point; *Tideland* displays Dickens in a dress, blonde wig, and poorly applied, clownish makeup. Gilliam seems to allow those characters who may be on the fringe of madness to exhibit similar excesses in order to refer to their relationship with madness at given points in the narrative, even if it is only a flirtation that they are not wholly consumed by, as seen with Jack donning Parry's clothes and demeanor in *The Fisher King* and in Dr Railly's increasingly physical fits of hysterics in *Twelve Monkeys*. Beyond merely signaling the mad as "other" with these markedly visceral, visual, and auditory strategies for the purpose of establishing dynamics between characters, Gilliam also strips them of the baggage of modern normality as the movies present it in order for them to fulfill a purpose more akin to the mythic function of the mad that Foucault refers to.

Brazil, The Fisher King, and *Twelve Monkeys* figure madness as mythic on at least two levels: the mythic formal structure and content of characters' madness and the mythic functions of madness within the worlds of the films (in terms close to Foucault's description of the symbolically freighted cultural function of madness in the medieval and Renaissance eras). On the first level, each of the films' presentations of the delusions, dreams, fantasies, etc. associated with the madness of characters involves some reference to mythic thinking via a mythic formal structure, one that seeks to mediate contradictions in an overarching narrative (usually an all encompassing dualism) that thrives on their opposition and attaches meaning to almost everything (Harpham 53–54). Gilliam's penchant for archetypes and mythology, which he openly admits to in a number of interviews, is unleashed in intertwined myth references in each of the films: Sam in *Brazil* images himself in his dreams as an Icarus figure that fights monsters to protect an idealized (perhaps mythic) version of a real-world woman; Parry quests for the grail in *The Fisher King*; Cole attempts to save the world from certain destruction in *Twelve Monkeys*.[5] In all of the films, the mad characters' delusions depend on a good/evil dualism from within which they, on the side of good, must fight evil for the sake of some innocent other(s). As the mad/mythic narrative plays out, especially in *The Fisher King* and *Twelve Monkeys*, characters ascribe significance to objects that, outside the narrative of their delusions or fantasies, would be meaningless. Parry totemizes various objects to use as weapons and for defensive measures; his grail quest is centered on a wealthy stranger's trophy that he saw in the background of a photograph in a magazine. Cole is obsessed with collecting information, which leads him to eat a spider and interpret radio commercials as special messages for him, and when he becomes convinced that the scientists from the future are tracking him, he performs an effective but rather artless emergency tooth extraction with a pocket knife over a wounded pimp in a bathtub. *Twelve Monkeys* also features Jeffrey's paranoid rant about credit cards, consumerism, animal rights, and madness, in which heightened meaning is attached to any corner of human behavior and can be integrated into his systematic, paranoid critique of everything. In these films, Gilliam's use of mythic narrative as paranoid delusion of the mad, then, reaffirms Harpham's and Foucault's observations about the alienatedness of mythic patterns of thinking in the modern world as well as about loss of a meaningful context for the narratives of the mad to function.

On the second level, Gilliam's films center on the tensions between the modern experience of madness as stripped of any significance beyond the need to get well through treatment in confinement and the rich meaning attributed to the mad in the medieval and Renaissance experience of madness, which, though it frequently depended on their "ritual division" from society, culturally invested the affliction with an empire of images associated with the terrible, the tempting, and the unknowns of human existence (Foucault 10,15). *Brazil* highlights madness as an escape from the suffocating confinement of modernity. Sam's mythic daydreams and night-mares are as impossible to realize as it would be for him to escape from the Kafkaesque world in which he lives, and when he attempts to bring both dreams to fruition, he fails pathetically and falls so deeply into his delusions that he cannot be retrieved. The film establishes a relationship between the ideologies of social control and madness as escape, but it focuses more attention on characterizing the state and dramatizing the ten-sions between its hegemonic methods of incorporating subjects through civil and political measures in order to control them and the bald threat of violence as a tool of social control. Indeed, while this may not be the appropriate place to construct such a thesis, a Gramscian and/or Althusser-ian interpretation of *Brazil* built around Gramsci's conception of "hege-mony" from *The Prison Notebooks* and Althusser's development of it, especially, perhaps in the first fifty pages of *On Ideology*, would almost seem to write itself (if indeed someone has not already written an article along these lines).[6]

The Fisher King and *Twelve Monkeys* rely in a more centralized way on the plight of the mad in a modern context, and both films ride Fou-cault's dividing line between locating them alternatively in society's liminal spaces or in confinement in its institutions under medical care for their afflictions. Though the mad as homeless in both films reveals something more along the lines of the former model (of the ship of fools and the confinement within the gates of the city) in which they are free to wander but kept away (exclusion through a type of liberation), as patients, these characters waste away in institutions, which Gilliam depicts as dilapidated structures in which the insane take pills, watch television, and drive each other crazier. The implied *general* social function of the mad in these modern contexts, in either locale, is evacuated of meaning, with the possible exception of the scapegoat role the homeless play in *The Fisher King*, though this seems to be aimed more directly at their homeless-ness than their madness. The *specific* function the mad play within this more general silence, though — Gilliam's function for them — is closely related to their mythic significance to the middle ages and Renaissance.

106

In *The Fisher King*, Parry's symbolic significance to Jack is precisely related to Jack's own guilt about the effects of his pride and selfishness: Parry becomes an embodiment of these things. Jack attempts to alleviate his guilt through his attempts to alleviate Parry's suffering, but when this fails, Jack, in a sense, joins in Parry's madness by carrying out the latter's grail quest as a last-ditch attempt at a selfless act. And when all of the reason and science modern psychiatry have to offer fail Parry, Jack's victorious act within the ludicrous logic of the world of the mad/mythic narrative of Parry's delusions delivers Parry from his catatonia and from much of the debilitation of his madness. So, it is from within a context in which madness is freighted with man's projections of his own weaknesses that he is able to overcome those weaknesses, and help the madman overcome his as well.

Gilliam uses madness in *Twelve Monkeys* as representative of the secret knowledge of the world, and here the secret or forbidden knowledge involves many of the themes that Foucault claims to find associations with madness in the medieval and Renaissance era, including the Fall, fate or determinism (Foucault's "the Will of God"), and of any number of apocalyptic themes and images (Foucault xii). Again, to repeat this formulation of the last paragraph: the *general* function of madness that is implied in this film, too, is classically modern — the homeless/institutionalized insane occupy a silence, and they fill the geographical places that others rarely or never go; but, Gilliam's *specific* function for madness within the general ignorance and avoidance of the mad is implicitly connected to the apocalyptic and epistemological themes Foucault discusses as prominent in the medieval and Renaissance experience of madness. And even while these aspects of Cole's delusions are taken by the representatives of psychiatry as evidence of Cole's madness, eventually his apocalyptic predictions are validated — his "secret knowledge" actually *is* knowledge rather than delusion, lending some credence to Cole's discussion in the film of the human tendency to overextend their rightful bounds in pursuit of scientific knowledge, for, after all, the Beast in *Twelve Monkeys* turns out to be something of a "mad scientist" himself.

Fear and Loathing in Las Vegas and *Tideland* demonstrate Gilliam's employment of the madness, or perhaps the flirtation with madness, of the protagonists with similar functions in opposing contexts. Both films depict their protagonists as different kinds of innocents, innocents who are driven towards madness in response to a certain madness they experience in the world. In *Fear and Loathing*, the madness of the world is represented in Las Vegas, and the city represents the farthest reaches of what is possible to experience or of what is even imaginable in the context of American culture. The film makes for little guesswork as to its political theme: Duke's voice-over narration refers to the purpose of the trip to Las Vegas as a thoroughgoing exploration of the freedoms available in this country, a true American experience for those with enough grit to withstand it. Further, to reinforce this theme, the film features images of American flags almost everywhere, start to finish. And, as the film progresses through Las Vegas' bars, circuses, and casinos, Duke's commentary is usually pointed at how pathetic it all is, even on drugs. By the final episodes of the film, Duke and Gonzo have given up on Vegas and have turned the corner on their road to excess and experience back towards themselves, leaving them locked within hotel rooms traversing the crooked paths of the excesses of their own psyches with the help of their well-stocked pharmacopia. Interestingly, the largest image of an American flag comes onto the screen after Duke awakens some days after his dose of adrenachrome; the enormous flag has been painted across almost an entire wall in what looks like garbage, feces, food, and paint, as if the two themes of the true "American experience" and the search for excesses far exceeding those the country can offer have finally converged.

These "wake-up" scenes, which occur a few times in the film, are obvious sites of grotesquery, though perhaps not along the lines of the mythic/madness that I am arguing most directly in this chapter, or perhaps only tangentially so. These scenes and many of those featuring Gonzo are nearly suffused with evidence of Gilliam's interest in the lower bodily stratum, scatology/scatography, and the grotesque body (again, in this film, mostly Gonzo's). The film also contains Gilliam's signature of cartoonishly physical characterization: Duke creeps about exaggeratedly, and his movements become more extreme and less natural and his demeanor more paranoiac, the more drugs he takes.

Gilliam claims to have conceived of the adaptation of Hunter S. Thompson's book of the same name as "like Dante's *Inferno*, with Gonzo as a kind of Virgil, a pagan, primal thing that is out of control half the time. Then you have Duke/Dante watching and being guided" (qtd. in McCabe, "Chemical" 137). And it is the tension between Duke's role as observer, recorder, and commentator and his role as Gonzo's protégé that serves to establish a certain prophetic stance in his madness. All of the ridiculousness of the romp around the city is juxtaposed with frequent narration from Duke that, with an almost philosophical detachment, analyzes the meaning and development of the drug culture, the falsity of the American dream, the political failures of the 1960's, and so on. The disparity between the two is reminiscent of madman as the wise fool, who unknowingly speaks "love to lovers, the truth of life to the young, the middling reality of things to the proud and insolent, and to liars," but some of the hallucinatory visions Duke experiences reveal his connection to knowledge of another kind, the knowledge of the poles of metaphysical existence and human experience: Satan and the Apocalypse, absolute bliss and its corollary in suffering, earthly omnipotence and the banishment of the Fall (Foucault 14, 22).

Tideland's protagonist, the nine-year-old Jeliza-Rose, is nearly driven to madness by the grisly experiences she undergoes when she is isolated in the open spaces and picturesque country prairies of her father's childhood home. But Gilliam rides a fine line in the film between identifying Jeliza-Rose with imaginative naiveté and childish playfulness and with the threat of full fledged madness in response to her increasingly unsettling experiences. When her father dies unexpectedly the first night after their arrival to the house, she is unable to process it and continues, day after day, to attempt to rouse him; then, becoming bored and repelled by the early stages of his decomposition, she puts a wig on him, make-up, perfume, and sunglasses. Jeliza-Rose meets and befriends a mentally disabled man, Dickens, and the two have a number of intimately affectionate kissing scenes. Dickens's sister, Dell, an amateur taxidermist and former flame of the corpse/father, Noah, also enters into a tenuous friendship with Jeliza-Rose for a time. The young girl observes as Dell expels the intestinal gas from her dead father's bowls, pumps his fluids out, and cuts into his flesh. She wakes up hours later and gives her newly preserved father two doll heads, popping them into his hollow belly to take with him to his "next life," before Dell stitches him closed. His leathery corpse heads the table at Sunday dinner and cuddles the young girl at night.

Gilliam is unrelenting as to how far into the disturbingly grotesque he will go in *Tideland*, but he remarks in an interview with Paul Fischer that it is "one of the most sweet, tender films I've ever made." Gilliam reports in another interview, with Phil Stubbs, that his wife described the film as being "shocking because it was innocent." The tenderness and innocence in the film is tied to the half-mad, imaginative, and playful point of view of the little girl. *Tideland* is firmly situated within her perspective, and almost none of the horrifying images come into the film in a horrifying context, or *as horrifying*; she takes them as they come, one after the other, sending her deeper and deeper within this isolated world that gets weirder and weirder by the day. But Jeliza-Rose, since she is a nine-year-old girl with an already troubled past, a dark sense of playfulness, and two dead parents, has no context for the weird — she treats everything as of equal importance, and this is how Gilliam gives viewers her experiences in the film. The score is unobtrusive; most of the horrifying aspects of the film occur in full daylight against a beautiful landscape; he relies on mostly wide lenses and resists manipulating viewers' attention in the shots by drawing it towards the most horrible aspect in the frame. When she comes to the brink of madness, the film depicts these moments as exaggerated play within the imaginary world the little girl has created for herself: the doll heads she plays with and speaks for begin talking in voices she can hear — still in the voices that she had used for them earlier — but now they do so without her actually speaking for them; she is losing control, splintering. But she is resilient, and Jeliza-Rose is delivered from her mad-haunted voyage across the vast, grassy nowhere-lands through an apocalyptic train crash, "the end of the world," as Dickens prophesizes it when he shows Jeliza-Rose his stolen sticks of dynamite.

Tideland depicts Jeliza-Rose's navigation of her own madness "across a half real, half imaginary geography" that is peopled with mad ones whose return to sanity seems impossible; mad ones who create real worlds out of dead things and dead people to avoid the pain of losing them (Foucault 11). Their imaginations have figuratively and literally carried them away; they are isolated in the weird worlds of their own invention. And Jeliza-Rose's journey into those worlds seems to have granted a new knowledge, perhaps a forbidden one, as the closing scene seems to suggest, as the young girl bites into an apple, while apocalyptic fire blazes and the wounded lurch about all around her, and the glimmer of the blaze and its reflection in her eyes coalesce as that shimmering separates and flutters away as fireflies born of the incandescence of the moment.

The Politics of the Mythic

My interpretation of the film-worlds of Terry Gilliam has focused on elements of the mythic and the role it plays in Foucault's construction of madness (before and after the dawn and reign of "reason" in the Western mind), and the ways in which both the mythic and madness contribute to interpreting the grotesquery in Gilliam's films. As I pointed out earlier, the dynamics of these functions in Gilliam's films, as in Harpham's discussion, rely on a distinction between any number of related dualisms, many of which lead back to the relationship between "mythic," "primitive," "archetypal" thinking and patterns of thought that are conceived of as "nonmythic," "modern," "rational," etc. And the concept of thinking, in whatever guise, when Gilliam is concerned, must lead back to imagination, which for philosopher Markus Gabriel, implies the notion of reflection, the act of thinking.

In Gabriel's chapter on Schelling's theory of mythology in his and Slavoj Žižek's book, *Mythology, Madness, and Laughter: Subjectivity in German Idealism*, he argues that mythology is, in fact, alive and well in our own age but that it conceals itself behind a mask of rationality. He terms this turn on mythic thinking "the mythology of de-mythologization":

> This story is one of the cornerstones of our mythology that believes in scientific, manipulatory rationality's capacity to transcend historicity. It does blind itself to the possibility that the very era of the world as picture ready to be manipulated might itself be a world-picture, namely the world-picture of the world-picture. As Schelling, Heidegger, and Wittgenstein agree, reflection is inevitably bound to a set of finite, discursive expressions of itself generating imaginary frameworks, mythologies. *Those frameworks are usually not reflected and cannot be fully reflected: any attempt to achieve such a totalizing reflection simply generates another myth, a different imaginary* [18–19, ital. orig.].

If Gabriel (along with Schelling et al.) is right, then, all of the dualisms, the competing worldviews, etc. must find their center in reflection, in imagination, which provides the only real context we have for thinking. Further, if mythologies reveal necessarily imaginative forms of thinking, then what Harpham's theory is missing is a treatment of the disjuncture between mythic thinking and its modern counterpart as rival mythologies. For if reason is as much a construction of mythic thinking as any of the primitive narratives, just one that has made its own superiority part of its mythology, then the rivalry between mythologies for dominance in a culture must be markedly political because ideology (a form of mythmaking itself) plays a distinct role in what mythology will lead a culture's patterns of thought. In the context of the grotesque in Gilliam's films, then, such a conception of myth suggests that the relationship between the themes I have been concerned with here and the more political themes present in the films, and perhaps most prominently in *Brazil*, is a close one. Thus, my study of the mythic, madness, and the grotesque would benefit from a parallel study concerned with interpretations of Gilliam's political themes.

PART 3

Menacing Invasions: The Hazards of Time and Subjectivity

There was no longer even a murky daylight; black night had set it.
— Franz Kafka, *The Trial*

If Part 2 addresses the workings of the grotesque insofar as it can be identified as an effect of the interpolar dynamics between and among various sets of binary, albeit nearly identical or analogous, oppositions — or at least if such a theoretical approach to such oppositions can interpret them as being conducive to the kind of art the grotesque is — then Part 3 is concerned with moving into the core of such contradiction. My aim here is to engage the films of the Coen Brothers and David Lynch from a critical-theoretical perspective that attempts to penetrate the parallax gap, to enter the coiling geometry of the Moebius strip. Chapter V explores the charged moments in the Coen Brothers' films that seem to swallow up the future as they negate the past and force characters to react blindly to extreme situations that extend beyond their control, as their otherwise mundane lives intersect the catastrophic. These moments of the absurd contradiction between humans and their world occasion liminal spaces, moments of threatening and oppressive stasis, to which the Coens' characters often respond with aberrant physicality and in which the grotesque seems to thrive.

Chapter VI follows this trajectory inward with the films of David Lynch. Here, the grotesque helps bring to life Lynch's own "sick man's dreams" in films that dramatize the obliteration of the individual as this (anti)logic invades human perception, imposing its paradoxes towards the construction of menacing alternate subjectivities (achieved by appeals to the abhuman and to doubling), elaborate fantasies, and metaphysical substrates, which seem aimed at enacting a cancellation of individual subjectivity altogether. Lynch's films employ the grotesque in service to the uncanny. They imagine dark worlds rent by confusion, worlds that bespeak the heart of a paradox the core of which is contamination. And, as if against their wills, Lynch's characters unite with these dark worlds; they give in to them; they surrender to the dreadful impulses and desires that these worlds seem to arouse within them. The grotesque, indeed, becomes the measure of the ominously spiritual and its often abhorrent physical correlate in Lynch's films.

V. The Mundane and the Catastrophic in the Films of Joel and Ethan Coen

A man, being what he is, finds out *who* he is in moments of extremis: when he's got to jump left, jump right — when he can't stay where he's at.

— Harry Crews, *Searching for the Wrong-Eyed Jesus*

[T]he Absurd is not in man ... nor in the world, but in their presence together. For the moment it is the only bond uniting them.

— Albert Camus, *The Myth of Sisyphus*

Impaled on the Present: The Grotesque and the Crucifixion of Temporality

The films of Joel and Ethan Coen, if one could reach, perhaps, in what seems, initially, a critically unhelpful manner, for an overarching motif, a kind of spine to hold all of the ribs together, are about characters in crisis (like every other movie). Or, better, to borrow from the Harry Crews quotation above, their films are about characters in "moments of extremis," for the crises of a Coen brothers film extend beyond the dramatic or the tragic: they are catastrophic rifts in the characters' experiences of the world. Further, in keeping with Crews' line of thought, these moments of crisis demand actions and decisions, which the Coens' characters almost always make without foreseeing the consequences and which they either engage in without much reflection (as do Abby and Ray in *Blood Simple,* Hi and Ed in *Raising Arizona*, Jerry in *Fargo*, Miles in *Intolerable Cruelty,* Chad and Linda in *Burn After Reading*), or, alternatively, they get lost in their ruminations (as do Tom in *Miller's Crossing*, Barton in *Barton Fink,*

115

and Larry in *A Serious Man*), or both (as do the Dude and his crew in *The Big Lebowski*; Everett in *O Brother, Where Art Thou?*; Ed in *The Man Who Wasn't There*; Professor Dorr in *The Ladykillers*; and Llewelyn in *No Country for Old Men*). Whichever tendency predominates, the result is that the initial crisis spins out, centrifugally expanding the original crisis into others that become correlates of it.

This tendency is not unlike the one that overtakes Meursault in Albert Camus's *The Stranger*. Camus presents Meursault's offences against social and filial conventions early on in the novel as correlates of the murder of the Arab at the end of the first book, and his "moments of extremis" are exploded, just as they are for the Coens' characters. In those passages in which Meursault suffers under the blazing gaze of the sun, the passage of time seems to slow down or even lapse into the past or both: "It was the same sun, the same light still shining as before. For two hours the day had stood still; for two hours it had been anchored in a sea of molten lead.... The sun was the same as it had been the day I'd buried Maman" (58). Meursault's catastrophe too, then, begins in the mundane banalities of a few social indiscretions at the old folks home where his mother had died, and through some absurd logic, these "sins" implicate him in the gaze of the sun. It seems to be this sense of implicatedness that sets out the trajectory before him that leads him to murder, imprisonment, and the guillotine.

The Coen brothers' variations on such "moments of extremis" are often so absurdly stretched temporally that the Coens' dramatic films, even when (or especially when) it seems inappropriate, breach into the realm of comedy. In this way, the dramatic absurdity of Camus's existential "moment," the present, the right now, in a sense, gets exploded, and the ludicrousness of the copresence of "man" and "world" becomes, as with Camus's own theory of the absurd, a universal, applicable to the entire diegetic reality of the film (*The Myth of Sisyphus* 23). And as the films situate human beings in ever-expanding "moments of extremis," they sometimes find out *who* they are. But when the Coen brothers' characters make this leap to self-discovery, they frequently reflect Camus's maceration of the Socratic imperative to "know thyself": they know themselves only as strangers, outsiders whom they cannot understand and do not know (Camus, *The Myth of Sisyphus* 15). In such moments of enlightenment, they finally glimpse who they are, and they fail to recognize the image, or the weight of the knowledge is more than they can bear.

V. The Mundane and the Catastrophic

Geoffrey Galt Harpham's analysis of "The Grotesque as Interval," in *On the Grotesque: Strategies of Contradiction in Art and Literature*, situates such exploded moments as fertile sites for grotesquery (14). The grotesque inhabits an interval or gap, Harpham argues; it resides within the midmost moment of a narrative of the development of comprehension (15). Harpham, relying on Santayana, argues that the latter's theorization of the "interval" between apprehension and comprehension of phenomena provides a space for the confusion that the grotesque impinges upon those who behold it (15). Santayana suggests that when struck by the grotesque, interpreters essentially have two options: consider it as a warped instantiation of an ideal type, in which people meet the object with a notable sense of confusion that repels them from the it, though with the consolation that they may, without qualification, retain their previous categories of judgment, or consider the grotesque object for its "inward possibility," a path which embraces and extends confusion for the hope of discovery, ultimately culminating in allowing that which had initially seemed incredible, dreadful, or ludicrous to take "its place among recognized ideals" (Santayana qtd. in Harpham 15). Harpham claims that the grotesque's liminality, its situation within the interval, precludes us from developing a clear sense of how it functions, of its dominant principles, and of its organizational elements (16). In the interval, we are stuck between an awareness of significance and an inability to decipher the codes in which it is expressed: we are temporally impaled upon the present; the past is voided, and the future is halted (16). It is the same force that sustains what is to be known and we who seek to know (16). Harpham argues that within this space is where the grotesque lives — that it may be conceived as sharing the attributes and effects of this liminality — but also that this model of the anguished nascence of comprehension may be understood as analogous to the relationship between the seething energy we perceive in the grotesque and its obstructed or obscured formal structure (16). But, for Harpham, this confusion, into which the experience of the grotesque forces those who take the philosopher's path of "inward possibility," leads to new ways of thinking, leads to new knowledge, because it eventually generates intellectual movement toward the telos of arriving at an interpretation, some thoughtful discovery or explanation, even if the experience of the grotesque in the interval threatens those who attempt to brave it with agony, madness, and despair (18).

Harpham's theory has certain potentially fruitful parallels with the sketch of the Coen brothers leitmotif above, with the exception, perhaps, of the last move, that of seeking closure through interpretation, by which one arrives at some satisfactory theory or explanation. Some of their films provide a kind of closure, but not in a way that allows characters or viewers to effectively move past the confusion or the mystery of the grotesque in absurd collisions of humans with their "world." Their characters certainly reach the moments of new knowledge, but these moments are more likely to be signaled with a bout of nausea or a vacant stare than they are with a look of intellectual satisfaction at finally figuring out a way to codify a heretofore inexplicable experience because knowledge in Coen films is often the kind that wounds. Much of the critical work on the Coen brothers seems more aligned with Santayana's first path, as many critics attempt to circumscribe the weirdness or quirkiness of a Coen film by merely cataloging its precedents, allusions, and associations with earlier films, other filmmakers, and works of literature, which is, perhaps, why the brothers have gained a reputation among many critics as postmodern pastiche-artists.[1] Their films envision worlds in which humans are locked within Harpham's "purgatorial stage of understanding during which the object appears as 'a jumble and distortion of other forms,'" a stage analogous to Camus's exploded "moment" and Crews' "moments of extremis" (Harpham 15; Camus, *The Myth of Sisyphus* 23). Their most prescient characters are the ones who discover that what Harpham calls the "interval" is really the universal and that even if they try to invent ways to live amid the confusion — the absurd grotesquery — of the world, their questions will never find adequate answers, and the explanations they seek will forever fall short of satisfying them: things will never adequately "make sense" (this notion is the thematic core of their 2009 film, *A Serious Man*). Even in the films that offer a kind of closure or an "answer" (for example, *Raising Arizona; The Hudsucker Proxy; Fargo; Intolerable Cruelty; O Brother, Where Art Thou?;* or *The Ladykillers*), it is usually so obviously false, overly simple, or utterly ludicrous to the viewers — even if the characters have convinced themselves of its validity — that the tension between what the film tells its viewers and what it allows the characters to know or think sends those who attempt to interpret the film right back to Harpham's epistemological purgatory.

Harpham argues that grotesque art problematizes the idea of a center because it implies that coherence is always just beyond our grasp through metaphors or analogies the meaning of which is just out of reach (43). The grotesque at once *seems* "deep" or "profound," but it is also often so caught up in surfaces and initially so symbolically illegible that this promise of depth and substance seems a cruel tease (43). He grounds his theory historically in citing the transition from Renaissance *grottesche* style, a decorative style imitative of the images found in Nero's palace in 1480, which is literally restricted to the margins, the borders in *grottesche*, to the grotesque, as such, in which the threat of unwieldy meaning on the margins is more fully realized, and as it swaps places with the center, synthesis itself becomes its guiding aesthetic principle as it enacts reconciliations of aspects of the world that, before, seemed incompatible (47, 45). And a similar "swapping" of periphery and center can be seen in the Coens brothers' tendency to focus the subject matter of their films on characters who are, in Andy Lowe's words, "either moronic or mad," a charge to which Joel Coen responded, "[M]ost of our characters are pretty unpleasant.... But we're also very fond of those characters, because you don't often see movies based around those kinds of people" (Lowe 164).

In a way, the Coen brothers' film corpus can be read on a parallel to this aspect of Harpham's theory, especially in their pilfering of outdated acting styles from early cinema, now generally used in films only marginally here and there for comic effect (Comentale 238–239). In the works of the Coens such acting styles are synthesized and centralized in films that marry incompatible generic references to one another, as Ronald Bergan notices in his biography of the brothers, published in 2000:

> All their movies are comedies, and all of them, excepting *The Hudsucker Proxy*, are fundamentally *films noir*, disguised as horror movie (*Blood Simple*), farce (*Raising Arizona*), gangster movie (*Miller's Crossing*), psychological drama (*Barton Fink*), police thriller (*Fargo*), comedy (*The Big Lebowski*), social drama (*O Brother, Where Art Thou?*). Yet, however different they are on the surface, each of the films contains elements of the other, horror edging into comic-strip farce, violence into slapstick and vice versa [26–27].

The synthesizing tendency — the move to knit together the margins of film history — rarely "passes for 'realism,'" as Bergan also observes (27). The Coen brothers' films are thus highly stylized, as are most grotesques, and it is this aspect of their films that has proven to be the primary complaint among critics, going back to Pauline Kael and Jim Hoberman: that their films, as R. Barton Palmer summarizes, are all flash and no substance.... They are merely pointless deconstructions or hybridizations of familiar generic categories, art objects that become, in Hoberman's phrase, "lost in a hall of mirrors." They offer no engagement with the "real" or with "history" [45].

The distance between this complaint and Harpham's characterization of the threat of the grotesque to the "notion of a center," implying meaning or coherence just beyond one's grasp, seems negligible (Harpham 43).

Besides, as I have been trying to point out, the Coen brothers' films do engage a certain version of the "real," or at least the existential; they just tend to concentrate it within exploded "moments of extremis" (Crews in *Searching*). And to return one more time to the Crews quote to extrapolate another morsel of meaning: the Coens engage "Man, being what he is," in ways that I have already alluded to and that the rest of this chapter will focus on — that is, humans in their world as embodied creatures within but alienated from dramatically charged time and space — bodies that must act, react, or be acted upon in extreme situations (Crews' "jump left, jump right — when he can't stay where he's at"). And in the remainder of this chapter, I will, in effect, be chasing bodies through the films of the Coen brothers, attempting to tease out the theories above by locating what Philip Thomson refers to as the *physical* nature of the grotesque (8). But this central feature of the grotesque is never without issue. Thomson argues that we often laugh at obscene or abnormal renditions of physical cruelty or torment, but just as often this laughter is mixed with its opposite — responses of horror or disgust or repulsion (8–9). So, Thomson's idea that the grotesque's markedly physical nature simultaneously elicits impulsive but contrary responses in us — one civilized, one sadistic and barbaric; one horrified by violence, the other gleefully attracted to it — will also inform my discussion of this thread in the Coens' films (8–9).

The grotesque liminal space of the existential moment of extremis (to finally bring some synthesis to these matters) — this purgatorial crucifixion of time and space, of body and soul, of desire and fate, of revulsion and delight — is also the literary domain associated with the work of Flannery O'Connor, to whom both Harry Crews and the Coen brothers owe serious debts of inspiration and influence. I want to limit my comments here mostly to a particularly insightful moment in O'Connor's nonfiction prose, among the compilation of occasional pieces gathered under the title "On Her Own Work" in *Mystery and Manners*, in order to bring this introductory discussion to a point (rather than to open a whole other can of prover-bial worms). O'Connor writes that violence in her stories "is strangely capable of returning my characters to reality and preparing them to accept their moment of grace" (112). She goes on to state that her characters are so stubborn that only violence can do the work of stripping away from them all that is inessential, forcing them, "at considerable cost," to return to the reality they actually are or that they actually inhabit, as all that to which they have clung or by which they have identified themselves is vio-lently pared away (112–13). In a sentence very close to the way Crews speaks about these issues, O'Connor writes that it is the "extreme situation," the "violent situation," that "reveals those qualities least dispensable" in a char-acter's personality, "those qualities which are all he will have to take into eternity with him" (114). And it is precisely these situations in which O'Connor's "freaks" can be apprehended as figures for "our essential dis-placement" (as human beings) in the world and from wholeness, so it is in such a way that these freaks may accordingly attain a kind of prophetic status and be attributed a certain sense of depth in or as art ("The Grotesque in Southern Fiction" 44–45).

The contribution that an inclusion of an O'Connorian view of vio-lence provides to the discussion so far is one that both focuses the previous theories surrounding the "moment" and anticipates the engagement of Coen brothers characters to follow. Harry Crews' words approximately paraphrase O'Connor's, but without the theological or metaphysical over-tones, but if we give this dimension in O'Connor its due consideration, we cannot help but notice that, for her, such violently "extreme situations" are intended to provide ruptures in the lives of her characters that function according to an undeniably purgatorial (in the theological, Catholic sense) process. For O'Connor, violence can purify characters, ridding them of all that is not *really, essentially,* them. It reveals who they are. Thus, can we not weave a metaphysical dimension into Harpham's more strictly the-oretical invocation of the term to mean a liminal nonspace, gap, intersession between apprehension and comprehension? If we can, then the grotesque as interval, indeed as a kind of purgatory, may function to distill characters to their essential selves (and perhaps readers/viewers along with them). Turned this way, such purgatorial moments of extremis, of violence, can only be existential for characters, even if from the outside (as it were) we can identify their metaphysical workings. Accordingly, those scenes of ridiculously ludicrous but brutally barbaric violence, those in which Coen brothers characters are *reduced* to bumbling idiots, cartoonish caricatures of themselves — those scenes that are now regarded as "classic Coen brothers" moments — such scenes are also deadly serious: for caricature works according to a logic of distillation, of capturing essences. Coen freaks, too, may thus be seen as O'Connorian prophets of human displacement in the rupture of existence.

Figuring the Crossroads: Blood Simple *and* The Big Lebowski

Most of the Coens' films revolve thematically around crises in exploded moments, as I outlined above. All of the films are, in essence, about painfully mundane characters, "losers or lunkheads, or both," as Joel Coen puts it in an interview with Andy Lowe, whose lives are spinning out into confusion as they are struck with the catastrophic, as "man" and "world" collide in a crisis that refuses to die (164). Brief analyses of this theme as a narrative tactic in *Blood Simple* and *The Big Lebowski* will provide a vantage point from which to see this thematic tendency in the Coen brothers' other films. While *Blood Simple* treats the catastrophic as the consequence of a character action/decision in response to a crisis that takes place before the film even begins, *The Big Lebowski* depicts the world's intrusion upon its central character, which ignites catastrophe and, likewise, calls for decisive action.

The first shots of *Blood Simple* are of Texas landscapes — barren, desolate, bleak — with a voiceover narration supplied by the film's villain, Visser, about how alone one is in Texas, how "something can always go wrong," and how no one will help when it does. The second sequence depicts Ray driving Abby to Houston at night. She is fleeing her husband, Marty, whom she is afraid of and whom she fears she will kill if she does not leave. Already, then, in the first moments of the film, the scene is set: Abby, as Crews would put it, has jumped left. A crisis has interrupted her otherwise mundane Texas life, and she has reacted. The first two sequences lay this out very neatly, though, as not only a clash between Abby and her husband, but also a clash between individuals, really any of the main characters, and "the world," the ambiguously barren realm of everything that is "out there," which the establishing landscape shots, and particularly the one of the blank billboard in the equally blank desert, signify. Interestingly, the billboard is an object specifically intended for the communication of something, and yet it is blank. Like the landscape, or together with it, the billboard communicates not "nothing," but rather that there is nothing more to communicate than sheer desolation. The accidents remain, but the message is gone. Within this void, nearly every action that a character takes in *Blood Simple* is a reaction built around Abby's original crisis moment, and nearly every move turns out to be the wrong one, as that initial move — having Ray drive her away — explodes, eventually costing every character's life (the primary ones: Marty, Visser, Ray) except for Abby's, which is preserved by sheer accident.

Cathleen Falsani claims that "*Blood Simple* is a meditation on free will" in her book, *The Dude Abides: The Gospel According to the Coen Brothers.* She writes, "No one in the film is coerced into making mistakes. Their undoing is entirely their own" (32). But such an argument would have to assume a concept of free will in an existential vacuum, which fails to account for the core problem of the film. James Mottram writes, in *The Coen Brothers: The Life of the Mind,* that "the film's central theme is communication breakdown" (20). He continues, "The characters only ever see part of the whole picture. This is a world where nothing is as it seems" (21). This gets closer to the point: the "world" for the Coen brothers in this and many of their other films is everything outside of the individual subject — time and space, but also other people, who, especially in their attempts to communicate, display the meaninglessness that characterizes the absurd in their ridiculous pantomime of the humanity the subject shares (Camus, *The Myth of Sisyphus* 10–11). The absurdity and grim comedy of the film turn on the hinge of this tension: the "moments of extremis" demand immediate responses, but no one in the film has enough perspective to make the right move or an informed decision about what to do or how to act. They do not really have the "free will" Falsani ascribes to them because their clash with the world suspends them in a purgatorial phase of understanding where everything is a jumbled confusion in which they are already implicated in some way and which also demands that they act now (Harpham 15).

On the opposite end of the spectrum for this theme in the Coens' films is *The Big Lebowski.* Here, the world quite literally intrudes upon

123

the Dude shortly after he is introduced as the protagonist of the film by the Stranger. A victim of mistaken identity, the Dude is thrust into a world of kidnapping, avant-garde art, high society, the pornography industry, intrigue, and violence, all through force but completely by accident: the impingement of the interval is an intrusion. But the upshot is the same. Even though the catastrophic engages him and his world, which is, again, a painfully mundane mélange of bowling, drinking, driving around, smoking pot, and bickering with those in his small circle (mostly just Walter and Donny), when he is hailed by the world in a moment of crisis, he must act; he must respond, even if the response is called for by an ambiguous outside world that quite literally comes out of the darkness from every direction (most of those scenes in which his "moment" reduplicates and becomes more complex are shot at night). Further, every move he makes throughout the film (or every move that is made for him or forced upon him) hinges upon the initial intrusion by the Treehorn thugs, who are looking for another Jeffrey Lebowski with whom the Dude, quite by chance, happens to share a name. Most of the other Coen brothers' films work with one or the other or some elements of both of these narrative scenarios to some degree. So, whether the mundane lives of their "congress of misfits" (as Ethan Coen puts it) collide with the catastrophic through some fault of their own — that is, through some short-sighted act or decision engaged in to deal with a crisis — or through a mere accident or impingement of fate, which then demands action or decision anyway, the conclusion is the same: the characters are caught at a crossroads-moment with the catastrophic, and no matter what they do, that moment seems inescapable, and it multiplies, explodes into a dizzying swirl of extensions and unexpected ramifications (qtd. in Ciment and Niogret 167). And, if Harpham is correct, such exploded moments of crisis or extremis are charged with potential for the grotesque, which impales characters or viewers on the moment at hand, obliterating the past and arresting the future (16). They are moments buzzing with chaotic energy, and they leave people anxiously grasping for some way to make sense of the confusion.

Both *Blood Simple* and *The Big Lebowski* offer scenes that provide visual metaphors for this theme that are stitched into the narrative. In *Blood Simple*, it is the scene in which Ray, assuming Abbie has killed Marty, attempts to dispose of his body. Marty, in a sense, becomes the bodily signifier of crisis that continues to multiply. The whole sequence refers back to this theme. At first discovering Marty's body, Ray attempts to clean up the blood with a thin jacket, and the blood pool just smears everywhere; it actually seems to increase in volume with his repeated attempts to soak it up, even soaking through the bed sheets Ray puts in the back seat of his car long after Marty is in the ground. Ray transports the body to a field in the middle of nowhere, and when he returns to the car after scouting out the landscape, Marty is missing. He discovers that Marty is still alive, worming an escape attempt on the ground. The scene continues for nearly twenty minutes without music or dialog, only Ray's grunting, sighing, and labored breathing and Marty's groaned attempts to threaten Ray. This aspect heightens the tension, but the scene is mercilessly comical for its baroque extension of the theme it metaphorizes: Ray has already responded to the crisis moment of finding the body; now he is implicated, but when he discovers Marty to be alive, he is struck with a new crisis, one more extreme than the last but linked to it, and he hesitates, weighs his options, but will have to respond again. After realizing he cannot muster the will to run the dying man over with his car, or whack him with a crowbar or a shovel, he decides just to bury him, letting Marty squirm and moan unintelligibly as Ray digs the hole, rolls him in, disarms his impotent attempt to shoot him, and begins shoveling dirt on him.

In *The Big Lebowski*, aspects of the Dude's first dream sequence serve a similar purpose in becoming metaphoric of the version of the crossroads of the mundane and the catastrophic that this film offers. After establishing the mistaken identity plotline and introducing the interruption of the catastrophic into the Dude's otherwise mellow existence, the Dude is knocked unconscious by Maude and her crew. The narrative follows him into unconsciousness and viewers share his dream, which effectively symbolically recapitulates the Dude's take on what has happened to him so far in the film: He was gliding along peacefully until he was sucked into the world. The dream depicts this with a shot of the Dude flying over Los Angeles, guided by his bowling ball, and then suddenly he is careening towards the ground. The next scene finds the Dude miniaturized in a bowling lane, where he is sucked into the finger-hole of a rolling bowling ball. The camera then issues a shot from the Dude's disoriented perspective inside the bowling ball looking out as it rolls and, finally, crashes into a set of pins. This scene refers back to the rolling tumbleweed in the desert, used to signify the Dude's independence and suitability for his place and time in the first shots of the film, as well as to the stylized shots of bowlers in their own brief crisis moments when the ball is their world — those seconds between releasing the ball and watching it strike the pins — which serve as the backdrop for the credits and title.

Whether one is discussing the crisis that won't lie down and die in *Blood Simple* or the one that forcibly imposes itself on the subject in *The Big Lebowski*, as these visual metaphors for the alternative ways in which the Coen brothers tend to integrate the catastrophic clash of their characters and the world demonstrate, there is something ludicrous or absurd about such collisions, but also something disorienting, violent, and anxiety-producing. Further, as both of these examples also demonstrate, the most poignant aspect of the character at the crossroads with the world is that all of the internal conflict, confusion, anxiety, and disorientation has to be represented physically — through the body, by or in actions or inaction, by or in expressions or moments when characters look expressionless: the goofy smile of the Dude as he flies over LA in his dream or his Shaggy and Scoobie Doo screaming when something goes wrong; Ray's stoic attempts not to show the internal despair outwardly and its manifestation in his body in sickness, insomnia, and loss of appetite or his dull, sinking gaze, and near speechlessness in the scene at the pay phone when Abby seems to know nothing of Marty's death. To return to the montage of bowlers that introduces *The Big Lebowski* for a moment: the men are shown rolling the ball, the shots often slowing their motion to isolate and extend those seconds when they are not in control, when the result of their action is undetermined; these shots capture physical responses to the anxiety and investment of what the bowlers have riding on the roll — their implication in the outcome. And this sequence is weirdly funny, repulsive, even tragic in a way, as these men uncontrollably fall into physically performed rituals for exorcizing their internal tensions in "moments of extremis." And the film portrays these moments as if they were the key moments of their lives. But, then again, this is the kind of irony the Coen brothers are known for depicting. It may be the peculiarity of the outward expressions of the inward machinations associated with the themes I have been discussing so far that give the Coens' films their characteristic quirkiness that make them recognizable as Coen brothers films.

126

Acting Codes, Violence and the Moment

In a revealing comment in his article, "The Joel and Ethan Story,"
John H. Richardson observes that the Coens' *Miller's Crossing* "is a movie
teeming with caricatures that keep revealing real characters underneath."
He cites a few pieces of evidence: "We see a buffoonish gangster, then
meet his child, we see a tough guy, then meet his male lover. Even a dead
man still has a toupee between him and the bald truth. It's an unsettling
combination of the grotesque and the touching" (81). James Mottram, in
his book, observes the similar point about the seeming disjuncture between
the caricatural tone established through the stylized acting in the film and
the human depth that the characters turn out to have, noting that, though
the film "rollicks in the silliness of the [gangster] genre, [it] still somehow
plumbs the depths of human emotion" (61). Similar appraisals of the Coen
brothers' characters abound in the critical work on the films. Whether it
is *Raising Arizona's* characters, which a review in *Variety* paints as "so
strange ... that they seem to have stepped out of late-night television,
tabloid newspapers, talk radio" in the film's display of "the surrealism of
everyday life," or Eddie Robson's consideration of the heightened sense of
banality of the characters in *Fargo* in his book *Coen Brothers*, Coen characters reflect a certain affinity with cartoon characters, as George Seesslen,
among others, discusses briefly in "Crimewave" (Rev. of *Raising Arizona*
45; Robson 165; Seesslen 30–32). But within or underneath their exaggerated, cartoonish physicality are fully conceived, round characters.

This quality in the Coens' films, and particularly in *The Big Lebowski*,
is the focus of Edward P. Comentale's essay, "'I'll Keep Rolling Along':
Some Notes on Singing Cowboys and Bowling Alleys in *The Big Lebowski*.
Comentale unearths an earlier, more "gestural mode" of acting, which has
slowly diminished in the cinema, that markedly departs from the attempts
at "psychological realism" in character portrayals that have become the
cinematic norm (239). The Coen brothers, in exhuming this "gestic mode,"
Comentale argues, resuscitate melodramatic forms of characterization and
action as well as "the jerky histrionics" of an earlier age of filmmaking
(239). He points to Hi McDonnough's round up of the Arizona quintuplets
in *Raising Arizona* and to Everett McGill's boxing scene in the Woolworth's
in *O Brother, Where Art Thou?* as performances that are overtly gestural,
cartoonishly plastic, and pervasively externalized (239). Comentale appeals

127

to Roberta E. Pearson's study, *Eloquent Gestures,* to argue that the primary difference between the acting styles, or codes, which Pearson refers to as the "histrionic code" and the "verisimilitude code" is predicated on the degree of physicality, as Comentale summarizes:

> With the histrionic code, each gesture was magnified, intensified, and accelerated, performed broadly on the physical body for the common body. The verisimilitude code, by contrast, works to establish the individuality of the character and the existential isolation of the moment [241].

Comentale remarks that the view of the Coens as postmodern geek-aesthetes may effectively be challenged by recontextualizing their films within an extensive film tradition of "popular gesturalism," noting that their exhibition of spastic, dystonic, and/ or ataxic bodies is not unlike the stylized distinctiveness and reflexivity of the popular singing cowboy westerns (240). In these films, he observes, quoting Peter Stanfield, the "focus was on the act of performance": "horse chases, fistfights, courtship, slapstick comedy..., and the music. Rather than understand performance as an act of illusion where the trick is to convince viewers that they are not watching actors, the series western celebrated performance as an act of value in and of itself," and these representations responded to the desires and fears of the lower and working classes (Stanfield qtd. in Comentale 240). This tendency in the work of the Coen brothers, Comentale continues, *seems* to tap into Miriam Hansen's notion of "vernacular modernism," a corpus of slackly stitched-together popular forms that tend to "register, respond to, and reflect upon processes of modernization and the experience of modernity" and may reflect an attempt to explore a "universal language of mimetic behavior" that speaks to the common crises of people living their lives in the perplexing space of modernity (Hansen qtd. in Comentale 241).

Well, yes and no, for there *is* something markedly postmodern to the aesthetics within which the Coens make their films, and, while the appeals to the "gestic code" may reflect the problems of modernism, though through a postmodern lens, they do not do so as optimistically as an ascription of Hansen's "vernacular modernism" would entail. The extreme use of gesture in their films is too extravagant to be explained as an attempt to explore a "universal language of mimetic behavior" (Hansen qtd. in Comentale 241). In fact, physicality (or the gestic code) in the Coen brothers' films is so often employed with such grotesque gratuitousness that it

seems to communicate very little beyond itself. Consider the sheer physicality of the baroquely over-wrought chase scene in *Raising Arizona* or
any scene in which Gale and Evelle figure: the belching, screaming,
whooping, eating, drinking, smoking, excessive speaking (sometimes all
at once)—the sheer excess of movement—it all goes well beyond an
attempt to develop characters or serve the purposes of plot. The same
excess of physical gesture is present in *Miller's Crossing* when Leo defends
himself against a mob hit from the Italians: After methodically killing one
of the men as succinctly as possible, he machine-guns the other repeatedly
from a distance, sending the man's body into a kind of grimly comic dance,
donned the "Thomson Jitterbug" by the Coens, and as he flails his arms
and shuffles his feet as he continues to fire his own Tommy gun, the man
shoots off his own toes, as "Oh Danny Boy" climaxes ironically on the
soundtrack (Robson 85). In the same film, in the hit on the Sons of Erin
Social Club, when an old man emerges from the door waving a white flag,
he is shot by a man from the Italian gang, after which his body convulses
for a number of seconds on the ground as the men look on laughing to
each other. The list goes on, and one could point to Barton's excessive tics
in *Barton Fink*; or Jerry's frequent fits of ineffectual hysterics, or his wife's
comedic attempts to escape her kidnappers, or nearly any scene with the
seething Carl, or those in which Gaear erupts into violence in *Fargo*; or
even Rooster Cogburn's attempts to prove his masculinity and marksman-
ship in *True Grit* by shooting bottles and cornbread that he hurls into the
sky, causing him to get lost in his long duster and fall sputtering to the
ground. Comentale points to the frantic hostility of the "gestic body" in
The Big Lebowski, and one could point to similar qualities in most any
other of their films. In some sense, the histrionic code is about a self-
referential focus of attention on bodies as means of performance, an exhibition of sheer physicality. But in addition to the Coens' excessive rendition
of this code, there is another aspect to which I have alluded in the examples
listed above: its astonishing negativity (Comentale 241).

David Sterritt argues, in "*Fargo* in Context," that the Coens work
"carnivalism and grotesquerie" into their films through distorting normative body language to signify the various incapacities their characters
demonstrate for living harmoniously among the encroaching social structures that surrounds them (20). And Comentale similarly ties their reval-
idation of gesture in succession with the modernist bourgeois concern with

129

a remarkable malfunction of communication (242). Following Giorgio Agamben, Comentale argues that the gestic codes of acting in early cinema are the exemplifications of the final public efforts made by bourgeois culture to scientifically record the language of gestural expression, even as it slipped from their grasp; these codes of acting represent the last spasms that that culture could muster up before becoming completely irrelevant, for their catalog of gestures no longer performed their intended social function (242). And this theory, he claims, is closer to how the Coens brothers use the gestic code in their films. He observes that in the Coens' work gesture is frequently born out of frustration and then endlessly and obsessively recurs, as with Bernie in *Miller's Crossing*; Barton in *Barton Fink*; Jerry and Carl in *Fargo*; Walter and the Dude in *The Big Lebowski*; Ozzie and Harry in *Burn After Reading*; Larry and Arthur in *A Serious Man* (242). Further, gestures seem to emerge as communication breaks down — when words fail, when meaning falls flat. In such instances, the gestures become oppressive and monstrous, rather than shrinking in disappointment: during moments when language is frustrated or stalling, Coen characters have a tendency to completely lose their composure and often engage in gesture reminiscent of those of characters and acting styles of the silent film era (243). Paul Caughlin, in "Acting for Real: Performing Characters in *Miller's Crossing* and *Fargo*," suggests that such physical exhibitions of reaction or loss of control, especially those that take place when the characters are "diegetically alone," reveal their "true" selves (235–36).

There are other characters who are nearly catatonic or seem to refuse communication or have some inability to gesture. In the case of characters like the Dane in *Miller's Crossing*, Gaear and Shep in *Fargo*, and Chigurh in *No Country for Old Men*, the general woodenness of their physicality, flatness of affect, and lack of expression seems to indicate an antisocial disdain for communication, and when they do break into gesture and movement — when they do express themselves — it is almost always with shocking and sudden violence. Others, like Ray in *Blood Simple*, Pete (the elevator operator) in *Barton Fink*, Smokey and little Larry Sellers in *The Big Lebowski*, Ed in *The Man Who Wasn't There*, the General and Lump in *The Ladykillers*, and Rabbi Minda in *A Serious Man,* seem to have given up on communication (Ray and Ed), are too old, too burned out, or too dumb to communicate aptly (Pete, Rabbi Minda, Smokey, Lump), or they simply refuse for undisclosed reasons (Larry Sellars and the General).

Coughlin points to Tom's constant poker face and minimal communication style in *Miller's Crossing* as an act of performance, an intentional projection of a flat, tough guy personality, which Tom hides within and uses to manipulate the impressions others have of him; such a theory could apply (at least to some degree) to a character like Chigurh in *No Country for Old Men,* as well as in Rooster's deadpanned testimony in the courtroom scene near the beginning of *True Grit* (229). Regardless of the reasons, the "communicative dysfunction" represented in the flatly uncommunicative is the other side of the coin of the gestic code that Comentale is interested in. He concludes that, for the Coen brothers, gesture is conceived as existing externally to mundane systems of normative communication and as such it effects a relinquishment of its responsibility to social utility (245). In consequence, gesture is liberated to reveal bodily human existence as a performance of "mediality": it exhibits the process of the human body itself becoming a means of its own expression through the veiled reality of the cinematic medium (245).

It is through exaggerated bodily gesture or its nearly comatose, though equally odd, inversion, then, that the Coens signify the interiorized anxieties, frustrations — the inner turmoil — that characters experience as the result of their clash with the world. And it is precisely the excessively gestural physicality of the bodies of characters expressing this inner turmoil, even if nothing is effectively communicated to anyone else, which ties the peculiarity of the acting styles in the Coen brothers' films to the markedly physical nature of the grotesque that Thomson describes. In a rather interesting manner, then, the Coens revise the histrionic or gestic code in light of the meaning that Pearson associates with the verisimilitude code. By making the bodily histrionics grotesque through sheer and gratuitous excessiveness, as well as through the unrelenting negativity and violence that frequently accompany it, and by utilizing this revised code in largely modernist narratives that rely on the tensions of exploded moments of extremis for their punch, the Coen brothers merge the "common body" with "the existential isolation of the moment," resulting in films that are as much about the "exhibition of performance" as they are about the emergence of that frantic exhibition at points when all other meaning fails (Comentale 239–40). The gestures are, perhaps, still performed "on the physical body for the common body"; the difference is just that the "common body" for the worlds of the Coens' films is inextricably trapped in the absurd tragicomedy of the existential moment. Their images are not unlike the one Camus invokes towards a similar purpose in *The Myth of Sysiphus*:

> Men, too, secrete the inhuman. At certain moments of lucidity, the mechanical aspect of their gestures, their meaningless pantomime makes silly everything that surrounds them. A man is talking on the telephone behind a glass partition; you cannot hear him, but you see his incomprehensible dumb show: you wonder why he is alive. This discomfort in the face of man's own humanity, this incalculable tumble before the image of what we are, this "nausea," as a writer of today calls it, is also the absurd [11].

The Carnivalized Body, Laughter and the Grotesque

The body in the Coen brothers' films is an unruly object. Very few of their characters reflect anything like the dominant Hollywood norm for attractiveness, as Makita Brottman observes with reference to *Fargo*, though the point could be applied to any of their films: There are almost no "conventionally handsome" faces or traditionally attractive bodies among film's weird characters, whose "corporeality often verges on the grotesque" (77). Those characters whose bodies are, perhaps, closer to the "dominant cinematic aesthetic," seem always about to be betrayed by bodies over which they seem unable to assert much control (78). She refers here to Jerry and Wade from *Fargo*, whose escalating anxiety finds release in violent little tantrums and frequent bouts of flailing, in the case of the former, while the latter's "thickness" is so thoroughly represented in his physicality that his body hardly registers being shot by Carl before he falls to the ground. Further, in the cases of those actors whose characters would initially seem to be exceptions to the rule, like George Clooney or Brad Pitt, the overbearing use of the gestic code in acting paints their characters as increasingly and ridiculously comical. In Clooney's roles as Everrett, Miles, and Harry in *O Brother, Where Art Thou?; Intolerable Cruelty;* and *Burn After Reading* (respectively), he demonstrates his knack for the exaggeratedly cartoonish movement and register of emotion associated with the gestic code in Coen brothers films. And in *Burn After Reading*, Chad's (Pitt's) good looks are part of the comic aspects of his character: a mixture of "dumb blonde" and "fitness junky" associations come to bear on a man whose funniest moments in the film are when he attempts to play serious for the sake of blackmailing a CIA analyst. Further, when the Pitt and Clooney characters share a scene in *Burn After Reading*, Harry immediately shoots Chad in the head and then must dispose of his beautiful body, a scene in which the comic and violently negative aspects of the Coens' use of the gestic code come together with a number of other elements to situate the otherwise light-hearted spy movie knock-off in the vein of the blackly comic grotesque. Catherine Zeta Jones' role as Marilyn in *Intolerable Cruelty* is almost literally the "exception that proves the rule," for, though her character moves, speaks, and carries herself with grace, the film depends upon such attributes to establish the character of Marilyn as a duplicitous gold-digger. Moreover, her girlfriends in the film—presented as older, more experienced "types" of Marilyn herself—are all portrayed as fixated on their former beauty, and they frequently discuss their cosmetic surgeries, spa treatments, etc., all of which drive the theme of the frivolity and duplicity associated with such refined beauty in the film. All of this coalesces in effectively ironizing Marilyn's own beauty.

Enough with exceptions: the characters the Coen brothers are known for are either too fat or too skinny by the standards associated with the "dominant cinematic aesthetic": they are "kinda funny lookin'. More than most people even," as one of the prostitutes remarks of Carl when questioned by Marge in *Fargo* (Brottman 78). Even more than this, bodies in Coen brothers films are afflicted with uncontrollable giggles (Visser in *Blood Simple*, Nox in *The Big Lebowski*, the Hudsucker executives in *The Hudsucker Proxy*); menstrual cramps or reproductive problems (an oversized male prisoner and Edwina in *Raising Arizona*); uncontrollable appetite for food or drink/alcoholism (Gale and Evelle in *Raising Arizona*, Bill in *Barton Fink*, Marge in *Fargo*, the Dude in *The Big Lebowski*, Ozzie in *Burn After Reading*, Rooster in *True Grit*); unceasing verbosity (Mink in *Miller's Crossing*; Buzz in *The Hudsucker Proxy*; Carl in *Fargo*; Everett in *O Brother, Where Art Thou?*; Frank in *The Man Who Wasn't There*; LaBeouf in *True Grit*); chain smoking (Gaear in *Fargo*; Ed in *The Man Who Wasn't There*; the General in *The Ladykillers*); bouts of nausea/vomiting, or irritable bowel syndrome (Marty in *Blood Simple*, Tom in *Miller's Crossing*, Charlie and Bill in *Barton Fink*, Norville in *The Hudsucker Proxy*, Marge in *Fargo*, Mr. Pancake and Mountain Girl in *The Lakykillers*, Llewellyn in *No Country for Old Men*); serious (and audible) respiratory problems (Arthur Digby Sellers in *The Big Lebowski*, Herb, along with a number of other ailments, Wheezy Joe in *Intolerable Cruelty*, Rooster in *True Grit*), and continuing to live when, for all practical purposes, they should be dead (Marty in *Blood Simple*, Herb in *Intolerable Cruelty*, Reb Groshkover in *A Serious Man*), not to mention Arthur's sebaceous cyst in *A Serious Man*, which he is draining with a medical pump or blotting with a rag or simply clutching for most of the time his character is on screen. Bodies are also sights of ghastly acts of violence: they are beaten, shot, stabbed, exploded with hand grenades, buried alive, calculatedly dropped from bridges onto moving garbage barges, decapitated, dismembered, disemboweled, forced into woodchippers, bitten by snakes, choked, dragged by motorcycles, plugged with hydraulic cattle-killing devices, hanged, electrocuted, burned, scattered (in ashen form), and maimed or killed in car crashes. They are everywhere screaming, bleeding, oozing, convulsively weeping, laughing, farting, exaggeratedly breathing, making animal sounds, and engaging in intercourse with one another. One bites the ear off of another; another nearly bites his own tongue off and persists in talking; one ingests a prenuptial agreement with some barbecue sauce; another accidentally eats a cigarette; one fatally mistakes his pistol for his inhaler; another wears an obtuse bearskin and collects corpses for their teeth. The body in Coen brothers films is unruly, unpredictable, uncontrollable; it is pathetically fragile, and it is unbelievably tenacious. Whatever it is or does in a Coen film, the body signifies its physicality in ways that align with Bakhtin's theory of how the grotesque can "'carnivalize' the site of the body" by anatomizing and dismembering it, or, as Brottman puts it, drawing attention to the significance of topsy-turvy actions and movements that exhibit sequences of anatomical images that render the human body comically and ridiculously out of joint with itself (80–81).[2]

Brottman emphasizes, though, that the "site of laughter" for such instances of the ridiculous or comical grotesque achieved by the "carnivalized body" is not the film's characters, for whom the threats and circumstances are often anything but funny, but its spectators (82). Laughter at such grotesquery is "libidinal"; it is associated with the tensions produced in what is conceived as the crass derision of the body (82). This identifies the tension raised in us between the congruent but contradictory impulses that Thomson identifies: our surface-level, civilized horror or disgust and our deep-down, unconscious sadistic and barbaric glee (8–9). For Bakhtin, however, this conflicted response is more than just the result of opposing impulses, a notion through which Brottman aptly connects the theory to

Fargo: for the film brings to our consciousness our own inescapable situation of being embodied in similarly pathetic, disgusting, and unpredictable flesh through mortifying and parodying our powerlessness and incompetency and reminding us of the vanity and arrogance with which we dedicate ourselves to the pretentious effrontery of order and dignity (82). Given this dynamic tension and its relation to audience identification and laughter, our own embodiedness is signified in the tendency of the Coen brothers' characters to be ever at the mercy of their bodies, even when (or especially when) they or we make claims to "higher consciousness," a move, Brottman continues, borrowing from Henri Bergson's *Laughter*, that is representative of the very essence of comedy (83–84). Laughter and hostility are inextricably bound up together as an implication of human social life, Brottman suggests, and such uncomfortable laughter at the grotesque is mechanistic; it is a psychological response that performs the social function of mitigating anxieties about the unexpected and unfamiliar (84, 90). Such laughter is multivalent: we laugh impulsively as an outlet for the hostilities, tensions, and frustrations for which society, which attempts to dominate and subdue the aggressive impulses of its members, affords no other channels of release, and we laugh because we recognize ourselves in the characters, and our ridiculous bodies in theirs (90).

The body in the Coens' films, then, reflects what Terry Eagleton refers to as the "somatic root" of Bakhtin's theory of the carnival grotesque in his chapter on Bakhtin in *Walter Benjamin or Towards a Revolutionary Criticism*: carnival pluralizes and cathects the body; it dismantles its wholeness by forcing its transgression of its own limits through a concentration on images of the body's various parts and their interconnection with and openness to the outside world (150). Eagleton emphasizes Bakhtin's theme of investing the body with meaning precisely at the points of "erotic interchange" between the inside and outside, which always reveals an "inside" as well (150). Such aestheticized images of the body as the Coens'—bodies grotesquely mascerated or obliterated, bodies acted in or upon in odd ways, bodies seen devouring the world, bodies whose insides are leaking out in some way, bodies whose movements appear not to square with their reality—such bodies, then, reflect the carnival grotesque theorized by Bakhtin. And, frequently, their films also seem to reflect a humanity thoroughly situated in the festive realm, a kind of utopian vision of humanity's ultimate unity with the world or the possibility or dream of such unity, such as one could identify in *Raising Arizona;* perhaps *The Hudsucker Proxy; The Big Lebowski;* or *O Brother, Where Art Thou?* (Bakhtin, *Rabelais* 46). But there are as many or more films to which such a conclusion seems completely foreign or, at the very least, fraught with problems.

So even if the body as the site of humanity's erotic and existential interchange with the world — and the inescapable context of his "moments of extremis"— reflects a form of Bakhtinian liberation through decrowning and degrading "the civilized" as such, many of their films fixate on themes more akin to the sense of existentialism that Bakhtin seems to despise, but they do so by depicting the body in similar ways and circumstances (Bakhtin, *Rabelais* 49). *Blood Simple, Miller's Crossing, Barton Fink, The Man Who Wasn't There, No Country for Old Men, Burn After Reading,* and *A Serious Man* all exploit the grotesque in their treatment of bodies, and the conclusion of the crises in all of them ends rather tragically, even cynically in some cases (*Miller's Crossing, Burn After Reading,* and an argument of cynicism could probably be made for any of the others as well). The remainder, *Fargo, Intolerable Cruelty, The Ladykillers,* and *True Grit* close ambiguously, in ways that could be interpreted as ultimately "life-affirming," though one could just as easily make arguments for these films' conclusions as myopic toward a point of irony or as obvious attempts at drawing tensions between the overly simplistic attitudes with which the characters are willing to see the drama end and the extradiegetic perspective of viewers that have seen the action unfold and cannot possibly be pacified with the pay-off. In these more dismal, abysmal renditions of the crisis moment and the bodies implicated in it, civilization is judged, but so is "life as a whole" (as Bakhtin would have it), and both are found wanting (Bakhtin, *Rabelais* 50).

A Moment in Time: Tragic Determinism and Radical Contingency

In Cormac McCarthy's *No Country for Old Men*, there is an exchange between Chigurh and Carla Jean, just before Chigurh kills her, most of which is captured in the Coen brothers' film adaptation of the novel, in which Chigurh relates, with stunning acuteness, the philosophy according to which he understands the unfolding of events in the world, why he has to kill her, why it is nobody's fault, and why the coin toss is the most grace he can allot for her miserable situation. The coin toss, of course, does not go her way, and she responds, challenging Chigurh to explain himself. He does so by referring to the hidden determinism, the workings of fate, in the logic of coincidences: With every moment in life there is a choice, and everything depends upon that choice, every time. "The shape is drawn," he says, the accounting scrupulous, and to the one attuned to the underlying metaphysics of such rhythms, the outcomes are predictable (259). Carla Jean asks for a reprieve; she tries to appeal to Chigurh's capacity to choose not to follow the path that he perceives as a necessity. He replies by explaining his dedication to his singular purpose — the fatefulness of coincidence — and its effect of aligning him with an insurmountable force that people refuse to believe in (259–60). Finally, he comes to his conclusion:

> When I came into your life your life was over. It had a beginning, a middle, and an end. This is the end. You can say that things could have turned out differently. That they could have been some other way. But what does that mean? They are not some other way. They are this way. You're asking that I second say the world. Do you see? [260].

It is, perhaps, ironic that such a philosophy — one ambiguously caught somewhere between fate and accident, between free choice and determinism — should come into a Coen brothers film by way of their adaptation of someone else's work, for many of their films revolve around this ambiguity, which Chigurh states here so precisely, so confidently. Richard Gilmore sums it up this way, in his essay, "*No Country for Old Men*: The Coens' Tragic Western." There are at least two sides to Chigurh's philosophy, Gilmore states. One asserts a kind of cosmic detachment in the tragic inevitability of the world's circumscription of human desires and freedom of choice. The other turns on a radical contingency: that our every desire, choice, and action is implicated in the inevitability that governs the future (71). So, what is, perhaps, hardest to deal with is not the proposition that our fates are bound by the determination of a world that does not care about us but that the sense of inevitability linked to our lives at any given moment is in some way resultant from our own past actions and decisions, that we are somehow accidentally culpable for whatever happens because of our dimly lit navigation of our own lives (71). In this way, then, when characters face this reality in times of crisis in which their mundane lives are struck with the catastrophes toward which, according to such a philosophy, their lives have been heading all along, the past is sucked into the present moment, and the future is negated. They are stuck in the middle, in an exploded moment, an endless present. Further, if such an ambiguous relationship persists between human choice and its implications in the inevitability of fate; that is, if, as Chigurh suggests, "The shape is drawn," and "All follow[s] to this," then every decision anyone makes is somehow constitutive of "the world" that blindly governs fate for all (McCarthy 259). The world is everything outside the self, but also implicates the self because it requires actions/decisions from the self at every turn that inevitably lead to "moments of extremis," or death, or both at once. This is why Chigurh is such a chilling villain: he is the agent of such inevitability and interconnectedness in the world, for, as Dieter Meindl argues, the "existential dimension" (what Bakhtin refers to in positive terms in medieval and Renaissance culture as "life as a whole"), for the modernist grotesque, becomes terrifying because wholeness of existence—Being itself—wipes individual human consciousness away; total Being is the context in which the "individual" as such is annihilated (19). But Chigurh, though taken from McCarthy, is also a Coen brothers "type," a force of nature, so to speak, with certain parallels to the agents of destruction in their other films, such as Visser in *Blood Simple*, the Lone Biker of the Apocalypse (Leonard Smalls) in *Raising Arizona*, perhaps the Dane in *Miller's Crossing* or Charlie in *Barton Fink*, Gaear in *Fargo*, parodied in the nihilists of *The Big Lebowski*, and Sheriff Cooley in *O Brother, Where Art Thou?* And in *The Man Who Wasn't There* and *A Serious Man*, the nature of evil, fate, and human choice/action, etc.—in short, life, death, and meaning—as with *No Country for Old Men*, become thematic centerpieces.

Whether comedy or tragedy predominates in a Coen brothers film, both are always present. They achieve an ambiguity and tension in fusing the two poles and in appealing to the emotions in viewers associated with each at the same time. Many of their films rely on the intersection of the mundane and the catastrophic, and their characters never seem quite equipped to deal with it, and so the films are, in a way, tragic. But the exaggerated and excessive physicality in their films can make their grimmest scenes sites of comic grotesquery. Thematically, their films frequently focus on crisis moments in ways that seem to betray a kind of cynicism about meaning in human life, but therein is also the comedy, for, as Douglas

V. *The Mundane and the Catastrophic*

McFarland observes in an essay about the Coens' "philosophies of comedy," comedy for the Coens is not so far from how Kierkegaard conceives of it in the *Concluding Unscientific Postscript to Philosophical Fragments*, and it is closely aligned with the tragic. Kierkegaard states,

> If the reason for people's hustle-bustle is a possibility of avoiding danger, then busyness is not comic; but if, for example, it is on a ship that is sinking, there is something comic in all this running around, because the contradiction is that despite all this movement they are not moving away from the site of their downfall [46].

McFarland claims that the contradiction at the heart of Kierkegaard's discussion is implied not only in comedy but also in life. It entails a contradiction between our infinite ambitions and the existential finitude that threatens them, between our yearning to act on our own behalf and the essential meaninglessness of those actions (46). So, likewise, the Coen brothers' focus on excessively physical depictions of such crisis moments, their extension of these moments through philosophically informed thematic devices and narrative tactics, and the comic cynicism that seems to underlie their films — all of this speaks to the contradictions that thrive when human finitude is struck with "the world" — when the mundane and the catastrophic intersect, and when that intersection demands some decision and/or action through which one attempts to sidestep the inevitable, and such extended or suspended moments are fertile fields for grotesquery.

VI. Obliterating the Subject in the Cinematic World of David Lynch

Horace, in conceiving his hideous mermaid-beast, spoke of the inventions of a "sick man's dreams." In its shocking way, the modern grotesque appears to postulate that such a sick man's brain is possibly the lowest common denominator of the human condition itself.
— John R. Clark, *The Modern Satiric Grotesque and Its Traditions*

To those artists who are engaged not only in wresting signs and symbols from the chaos of action, but also in mocking the complacency, coarseness and banality of the environment, the contamination of life is the core of existence. The world is estranged, life is absurd, the grotesque is the measure of all things, spiritual or material.
— Robert Doty, *Human Concern/Personal Torment*

Lynch, Uncanny Grotesque and The Amputee

Two relatively recent studies of the uncanny in Lynch's films, Steven Jay Schneider's "The Essential Evil in/of *Eraserhead*" and the chapter entitled "'It is Happening Again': Experiencing the Lynchian Uncanny" in Allister MacTaggart's *The Film Paintings of David Lynch: Challenging Film Theory*, relate the concept in different ways. Schneider's essay attempts to demonstrate the ways in which *Eraserhead* utilizes thematic and formal techniques from the domain of horror in order to generate uncanny effects, while MacTaggart's broader thesis attempts to locate the uncanny — an "uneasy 'nonspecificity'" — as the haunting centerpiece of Lynch's film corpus by unearthing images of the home and the double (among others) (Schneider 5; MacTaggart 119). Anthony Vidler, Laura Mulvey, and Chris Rodley in essays published in the 1990s also make contributions in this vein of inquiry towards Lynch's films. But, while most invoke the grotesque in its adjectival sense, they are more concerned with theorizing or utilizing the uncanny with respect to Lynch's engagement with film history/genre (Vidler 10), his film rhetoric (Mulvey 150), or for introductory purposes (Rodley ix-xi) than they are in seriously examining Lynch's engagement with the grotesque and its overlaps with the uncanny. And in this chapter that is what I will attempt to do.

Lynch's short film, *The Amputee*, made for the purposes of testing filmstock in 1974 (Rodley 66), perhaps best introduces this topic and suggestively invites the sort of critical attention that I would like to extend to his other works as well. Rodley's summary of the film in the filmography section of *Lynch on Lynch* reads like this:

> A woman sits, reading and composing a letter in her head. The correspondence apparently concerns a tangled emotional web of various relationships and misunderstandings. A doctor enters. He sits down in front of her, quietly treating and dressing the stump ends of her legs, both severed at the knee. The woman continues to work on her letter, without acknowledging either the doctor or the treatment in progress [296].

The film is only five minutes long, but in the brief time that passes Lynch evokes both the grotesque and the uncanny, which I will discuss briefly and directly here, leaving the theoretical apparatus for the next section.

The disturbingly physical nature of the film is particularly evocative of the grotesque, and the stationary camera's depiction does not shy away from the scene: throughout the brief time span the camera captures the woman's seated body, stumps and all, even to the point that the blocking and camera position required for the scene seem to ensure that the viewer always sees the stumps and sees the grisly "treatment" by the doctor, even though he sits between the camera and the patient. Further, the doctor's treatment is not as cleanly "clinical" as it sounds in Rodley's description: the doctor unwraps the stumps, and while the camera stares on at the unhealed site of the amputations, he clips at them with a small surgical implement, blots them with some gauze, and then seems to be draining fluid (audibly as well as visually) from them (perhaps accidentally? Is she bleeding out?), and then gets up to leave hurriedly, as if something may have gone awry, and there the film ends. The contrast between what seems to be the doctor's restrained panic near the end (as the fluid drains or blood flows out) and the fact that not only does the woman seem undis-turbed, but that she seems not even to notice, as she goes on with the voiceover narration of the letter, is pronounced, absurd, and defies rational explanation. The visual content of the film makes the clinical treatment seem both barbaric (audibly pricking at the open-ended stumps until they bleed or run) and professionally medical (the doctor wears the white coat, has a special tool and gauze, and moves with a deliberate sense of confi-dence or professional decorum). Further, tension, both grotesque and uncanny, arises when one considers the extremely personal nature of the doctor to patient relationship — something familiar to most people — and the nearly complete refusal of each character to acknowledge the other that seems the central irony of the film. Perhaps more disconcerting still is the fact that the environment is ambiguous: the woman seems to be at home (she is in a rather plush "easy chair," and she has a notepad and appears to be in domestic surroundings), but the doctor is there performing a rather messy procedure. Another layer of mixed grotesque and uncanny has to do with the melodramatic or "soap opera-like" content of the letter the woman is composing, and in which she is completely lost, even as her insides literally drain out of her legs.

So, if the uncanny relies on the tension between the familiar made unfamiliar or of the unfamiliar in the familiar, it is certainly present here. How familiar is going to the doctor or composing a letter or explaining a complicated relationship? But how alien (to most anyway) is undergoing a stump treatment, or one (possibly) within one's own favorite chair at home ... that goes wrong? And how caught up in the emotional entangle-ments of the letter would one have to be not to acknowledge a medical professional scraping away at one's unhealed stumps? And if the grotesque similarly relies on tensions produced by nonrational circumstances and conflicts of opposites, what easy fodder there is for it here in *The Amputee*: any number of breeches of rationality or "normality," the oppositional conflict implied between the mind and the body, and the absurdity of the doctor to patient rapport all belong to the grotesque. The structural prin-ciples in *The Amputee* seem to ensure a heightened sense of grotesquery, and the uncanny effects of such grotesquery — the tensions between recog-nition and alienation, or an alienated familiarity — seem to marry the con-cepts, at least insofar as they find an uneasy home in this film. And this forms the thesis of this chapter: Lynch's films often rely on the grotesque in their evocations of the uncanny, and both are ultimately aimed at disclosing or enacting a rupture in the identity or "self" of the individual subject.

A Grim Metaphysics: Obliterating Subjectivity

In his book, *American Fiction and the Metaphysics of the Grotesque*, Dieter Meindl argues that, while the grotesque often subverts the natural arrangement of things, it also at times evokes the nonrational dimensions of life, dimensions which altogether oppose notions of order and pattern as a matter of course (15). As he unpacks this assertion as an attempt to enfold the disparate theories of the grotesque espoused by Kayser and Bakhtin, Meindl subtly revises their positions for his own purposes, carefully reading each in light of the other in order to construct a theory that functions satisfactorily when applied to art produced in a modern (romantic/post-romantic) context. Meindl demonstrates that Kayser's grotesque is an unfathomable sphere that inspires horror, insecurity, and revulsion; it represents a recognizable world in decay, a cosmos crumbling before us, a dismantlement of our normative experience, and it likewise imposes a disintegrative force upon our orientation toward symmetry, order, completeness, and proportion (15). Meindl identifies psychological alienation and madness among Kayser's central motifs. Such alienation functions through nightmarish or dreamlike images in which disparate realities are braided together and thrust at the false masks of all that is reasonable, normal, or certain (15).

In his shift to the carnivalesque grotesque, Meindl rightly centers in on "life as a whole," or "the totality of life," as the underlying concept of Bakhtin's semiotic reconstitution of bodily human being, which, as Harpham claims, in *On the Grotesque: Strategies of Contradiction in Art and Literature*, is one of the fundamental premises on which Kayser and Bakhtin utterly contradict one another (Meindl 17; Harpham xvii–xviii). For Bakhtin, the grotesque's reliance on "life as a whole" bars the horror and anxiety at the center of Kayser's theory (Bakhtin, *Rabelais* 50; Meindl 18). Bakhtin accuses Kayser and practitioners and theoreticians of the modern grotesque (if indeed it can be captured with the same signifier as its earlier manifestations in the medieval and Renaissance eras) of cultural amnesia, as remembering back only as far as the romantics and, as Meindl lays out the matter, disregarding the ancient origins of the grotesque, origins which find their roots in the recognition of the inherent duality of reality bifurcated into comic and tragic myth (Meindl 17–18).

After observing that the grotesque transcends this rift because it relies on and incorporates the tensions between opposites, since its central characteristic in both scholars' theories (and any number of others) is self-contradiction, Meindl concedes that the romantics effect an extensive, though not complete, displacement of the grotesque as Bakhtin conceives of it (19). The carnivalesque grotesque, while communicating an existential sense of joy, maintains its relation to fear, for, as Meindl argues, Bakhtinian grotesque is "related to fear" through its transformation and conquering of it in a way not completely unrelated to the aesthetic hopefulness of Kayser's grotesque as a means to invoke and subdue — to exorcize — the demonic. In transforming and conquering the fearful aspects of the world by making them silly or by mocking them — by "degrading" them — the carnivalesque grotesque is still implicitly "related" to fear (Meindl 19). Romantic expression of the grotesque reverses this relationship; the grotesque's bright pole and its affirmation and establishment of a participatory role in life as a whole largely falls away (19). Further, Bakhtin's rosy, carnivalized interpretation of death as implicitly threaded into life as a whole as the cosmic catalyst of rebirth and rejuvenation rather than as the negation of life, is out of joint with artistic expression in the modern era, beginning with the romantics (19). Relying on Ian Watt's study of the novel, Meindl claims that modern literature's artistic endeavor has more to do with the definition of the nature of individuals in its attempts to be truthful to their experience than it does with expressing the total wholeness of life (19). Further, to embrace such a conception (life as a whole) "spells the obliteration of the individual": life as a whole — absolute Being as such — undercuts and obliterates individual human consciousness, and with it any hope of identity, of individual subjectivity. Meindl agrees that the grotesque is still predicated upon the mediation of the existential totality of Being, even in the modern era. What has changed is the response: the grotesque, Meindl claims, gravitates toward its darker pole in its modern expression because the dimension of total existence horrifies the individuals qua individuals — it confronts them with the threat of dispersion back into a monolithic cosmos: Life itself. It confronts them, therefore, with obliteration (19). Meindl claims that the shift toward something more along Kayserian lines in romantic grotesque results from a shift in philosophical orientation towards an individualistic and subjective worldview from one more closely aligned with Bakhtin's carnivalesque grotesque and its world-affirming, life-embracing dynamism. And as history moves on, modern and contemporary turns on the grotesque provide even grimmer evolutions of the philosophical reorientation visible in the romantics (19–20, 16).

So, the grotesque, then, in this later extension, Meindl claims, is employed as a strategy to demonstrate the rupture in the subject no longer able to identify itself harmoniously with the world, with the O/other, or even with itself. Robert Van Boeschoten clarifies this rupture (though in another context), borrowing from Sartre and Artaud. He claims that the "other" is hell for Sartre in its potential nullification of the individual's capacity to "believe in oneself," whereas for Artaud the threat to the self emerges from within, in perceiving the "self" as "other" (271). Thus, the "self" can be overtaken and annihilated by "psychology, cliché, and the commonplace"; it is crushed by "repressive authority, distorted 'truths' and perverse assumptions" (271). One may also think of the various directions among Lacanian approaches to a central rupture in the subject, some of which will come up later in this discussion, since such approaches are relatively well represented in scholarship on the films of David Lynch. Meindl's contribution here is the way in which he subtly but thoroughly infuses an inverted interpretation of Bakhtin's central premise into Kayser's theory, and this move effectively transports Kayser's "aesthetic" approach to the grotesque into the "existential premise" on which Bakhtin's theory is based: Meindl thereby is able to universalize the Kayserian world of anxiety and horror by reconstituting it on an existential foundation (Meindl 18–19). In this way, to return to his initial characterization of the function of the concept, Meindl's grotesque emphasizes, like Kayser's, the "horror-provoking potential of the grotesque," but it equally thrives on the familiarity, universality, and ambiguity of the "nonrational dimension of life as such," which can be both captivating and menacing, harmless and devouring, etc. (15).[1] Thus, Meindl seems to be deepening the sense of the uncanny already present in Kayser's version of the theory by identifying his own revision as one that in some ways implicates the other concept, to which I now turn (Meindl 16).

The Uncanny Experience of the Grotesque

In his discussion of Edgar Allan Poe's "The Fall of the House of Usher," Meindl lists the prototypical features of the uncanny: isolation, silence, and blackness, but then he moves to more specific features of the uncanny in Poe's story: madness, intersections of the inanimate and animate, doppelgangers (or doubles), recurrence, the mechanical quality of nervous disorders (like seizures in epilepsy) (58). These latter features, Meindl observes, are characteristic features of the grotesque (58). Such features (and others) disclose a certain slippage in critical vocabulary — a possible overlap of concepts, and one that is central to the films of David Lynch. Andrew Bennett and Nicholas Royle, in their discussion of the uncanny in *Introduction to Literature, Criticism, and Theory,* invoke many of these same "forms that the uncanny takes," but they also broaden the term beyond Freud's psychoanalytic interrogation of the concept in his essay, "The Uncanny" (37). They observe that the uncanny's function is "making things *uncertain*: it has to do with the sense that things are not as they have come to appear through habit and familiarity, that they may challenge all rationality and logic" (37 ital. orig.). While this conception of the term relieves it to some extent of its inscription within the psychoanalytic system, that is, as Steven Jay Schneider comments in an essay on *Eraserhead,* via the concept of the return of the repressed, or through validations in reality of beliefs that one had "previously 'surmounted,'" it may also be slightly theoretically vague, as David Punter and Glennis Byron seem to indicate in their book, *The Gothic* (Schneider 10; Punter and Byron 283–84). But Bennett and Royle's suggestion that the uncanny's challenge to rationality and logic — its fundamental sense of uncertainty — identifies it with Meindl's notion that the grotesque privileges and evokes the "non-rational dimension of life as such" (15).

Further, Schneider points to Noel Carroll's discussion of the uncanny in the latter's *Philosophy of Horror, or Paradoxes of the Heart* for a more specific outline of the uncanny. Carroll, Schneider remarks, demonstrates how feelings of uncanniness and horror can be associated with apparent violations and transgressions of the cultural and conceptual categories associated with a particular society: some of these can include "mutually exclusive dyads" like me and not me, the living and the dead, inside and outside, human and machine, etc. (Schneider 10; Carroll 32). Carroll extends this notion later in his study into a discussion of the role of the uncanny in the overlap between horror and fantasy: the uncanny names the experience of knowing something that has been hidden but is at the same time familiar — the experience of something at "the limits of a culture's definitional scheme of what is" (176). "The objects of horror, in my account, are impure," Carroll continues, "and this impurity is to be understood in terms of interstitiality, recombinative fusions of discrete categorical types, and so on" (176). Thus, for Carroll, horror and fantasy can evoke the uncanny because these genres strike viewers with images and ideas of what are often familiar objects that *become* "impure" because they transgress dominant boundaries (32, 175–76). Again, there is notable overlap here with respect to central aspects of grotesque theory: both rely on tensions between conflicting and opposing poles in cultural consciousness; both thrive in the subversion of the pantheon of dominant cultural values and images; both reveal or point to a rupture in the self. So, what is the difference?

I will attempt in the rest of this chapter to delineate the respective roles of the grotesque and the uncanny in Lynch's films by investigating the obliteration of the subject — both in terms of conceptual/ psychological identity and in terms of corporeal being and, of course, their overlap. My suggestion here is that the grotesque functions as a formal strategy in David Lynch's films toward an effect of something like an experience of the uncanny — that is, the two concepts, the grotesque and the uncanny, when they overlap in the various forms suggested above, do so to different ends, and this is why they can share the forms that they do. Uncanniness, then, is sometimes the effect of the grotesque's various formal or structural strategies of clashing contradictory images and concepts together in a way that allows the ambiguity and abnormality of their relationship within the image, but also within the overall structure or narrative of a film (or other work of art), to subsist, and often to subsist in excess of what would normally be expected, thus stressing or deepening the nonrational character of the numerous contradictory aspects associated with both terms. Turned another way, "uncanny" may describe one of the effects of the troubling recognition of the existential or universal aspects summoned up in the dark and menacing modern grotesque in the perceiver's response (Meindl 19), even if, or especially if, certain of the tropes associated with the grotesque draw out mixed responses. Such unresolved ambiguity in the relationship between incompatibles in the work and in the response thrives on the tensions between what is foreign and what is familiar — transforming them into cites of uncertainty, making what is normally "homely" (*heimlich*) "feel" "unhomely" (*unheimlich*) (Thomson 27; Punter and Byron 283).

Doubling, Subjectivity, Rupture and the Abhuman

In his analysis of the roles of Sandy and Dorothy in *Blue Velvet* in his book, *David Lynch*, Michel Chion invokes what is probably the most widely used metaphor in Lynch studies: the Moebius strip:

> Sandy and Dorothy incarnate two sides of one figure, each side endlessly leading to the other as in a Moebius strip. Their worlds are divided according to a traditional scheme: the blonde is associated with conventional life and daytime whereas the brunette belongs to the night and a world of shady, fearful characters [86].

Such doubling is everywhere in Lynch's films — both in terms of his frequent reliance on the double, a typical strategy of characterization in literature and film associated with gothic, grotesque, uncanny, and horror as well as in a deeper, more thoroughgoing structural or conceptual sense, one that Slavoj Žižek calls the "ridiculous sublime" in his book, *The Art of the Ridiculous Sublime: On David Lynch's Lost Highway* (22). For Žižek, this phrase describes the tendency for

> the most ridiculously pathetic scenes (angels' apparitions at the end of *Fire Walk With Me* and *Wild at Heart*, the dream of the robins in *Blue Velvet*) ... to be taken seriously. However..., one should also take seriously the ridiculously excessive violent "evil" figures (Frank in *Velvet*, Eddy in *Lost Highway*, Baron Harkonnen in *Dune*) [22].

After pointing out that this "enigma of the coincidence of opposites" (3) in Lynch's films is not sufficiently explained "along the lines of a Gnostic dualism," which effectively pushes each to one side of a cosmic continuum, Žižek suggests that what could be conceived as the "letting go" of "excessive phallic 'life power'" that Lynchian male characters enact in order to passively access "the subconscious maternal/feminine energy" with which they become who they are (with which, that is, the "sleeper awakens," to borrow a phrase from *Dune*), as seems evident in Paul's transformation in *Dune*

148

and in Sailor's tender lovemaking in *Wild at Heart*, is undercut by its opposite but ultimately identical function to the contrary: Paul's "proto-totalitarian warrior leadership" and Sailor's quasi-erotic satisfaction after "letting himself go" when he brutally murders Bobby Ray Lemon in the first scene in *Wild at Heart* (complete, I add here, with a post-coital smoke) (22–23). Žižek concludes the chapter, "the point is precisely that one *cannot* simply oppose this violent 'subconscious' to the good one.... Doesn't Lynch's ultimate message reside therein, as in *Twin Peaks*, where Bob (Evil itself) is identical to the 'good' family father?" (23 ital. orig.). Žižek, here, points to the same notion as Chion but reads it at a deeper structural level: Lynch's Moebius strip bars simple dualisms in character construction as well as in broader thematic motifs that operate across or between his films. To spell his point out a bit more clearly, Žižek's claim is that for Lynch's characters (Sailor and Paul but also Diane in *Mulholland Dr.*, Jeffrey in *Blue Velvet*, and Fred in *Lost Highway*) to "let go" — to let their passion carry them — has mixed effects: such "letting go" allows his characters to be "truer" to their passions, perhaps, but those passions lead to consequences that make simple dualistic psychoanalytic ascriptions untenable. In Lynch films there is always something lurking on the flipside of the strip that complicates, negates, or threatens a character's "positive" or "progressive" movement.

Punter and Byron point out similarly, relying on Robert Miles' work in an analogous vein, that the figure of the double, or *Doppelgänger*, in Gothic art and literature emphasizes the modern representation of the "self finding itself dispossessed in its own house, in a condition of rupture, disjunction, fragmentation" (Miles qtd. in Punter and Byron 40). But the construction of the double locates such anxiety within the subject — the alien double emerges from within (Punter and Byron 40). They go on to comment that "the real problem is not the existence of some more primitive and passionate internal self, but the force with which that self must be repressed in accordance with social conventions" (41). So, just as Žižek's analysis of Lynchian duality indicates, Punter and Byron agree that the double represents "not simply a split," which can easily be conceptually thrust to either side of a continuum of cultural values, social conventions, moral structures, etc.; the figure of the double has to do with "a more complex fragmentation of the subject" (41).

They also refer to the concept of the "abhuman" as related to the double. Punter and Byron observe that most "abhuman bodies" in Gothic literature "are the product not of supernatural forces but of scientifically explainable processes, and it is the scientist who becomes the pre-eminent figure in the Gothic fiction of the period," that is, the late 1800s (41). They go on to note, "Fears about the integrity of the self are forcefully articulated at this time through the emergence of what some critics call 'Darwinian Gothic'" (42). I am using the concept of the abhuman in this chapter to capture the term's connection to liminal bodies, those bodies that are "in the process of becoming" something else and/or as the indefinable "other" appropriating or mimicking the human form — either of which contains an implicit threat to human subjectivity and menaces conventional boundaries, forms, and certainties with the dissolution, ultimately, "of the human subject itself," as the Gothic moves into the Modernist world (Punter and Byron 41–43). I will be using the abhuman in this more modernistic context: Lynch's work has some overlap with scientific knowledge, Darwinian thought, and the like, but his films integrate these themes within a complex of ideas that also invite speculation concerning metaphysics, psychology/psychoanalysis, etc.

Interpreted this way, one can see a clear comparison between the abhuman and Noel Carroll's discussion (above) of the uncanniness of the "impure" in horror (Carroll 176):

> The abhuman may be a body that retains traces of human identity but has become, or is in the process of becoming, something quite different. Alternatively, it may be some indefinable "thing" that is mimicking the human, appropriating the human form. Either way, it is the integrity of human identity that is threatened; these are liminal bodies, occupying the space between the terms of such oppositions as human and beast, male and female, civilized and primitive [Punter and Byron 41].

In both cases, then, with the double and with the abhuman, the obliterating effect of multiplying the subject — of finding an alien other in the self or of finding the self in an other — has certain potential for engaging the grotesque in its representation. Ambiguously bringing together opposing identities and/or bodies in especially disconcerting ways that invite both some degree of familiarity with the fusion and an alienating sense of distance or repulsion aligns these theories with a thumbnail sketch of the formal structure and function of the grotesque. Further, it is perhaps the degree to which one identifies with the familiar here that influences the degree to which the perceiver experiences the uncanny in response.

Uncanny Doubling: Self, Other and the Trauma of the Real

Doubles abound in Lynch's work. On one level, Lynch constructs doubles that appeal to the same sorts of formal or structural strategies at work in the grotesque but ultimately seem more suitably described along the lines of Gothic uncanny. Among these are double identities constructed by doubling people whose outward appearances fall in line with current trends of attractiveness for their gender with other "attractive" people (and frequently Lynch uses the same actor for each). Examples of these kinds of character pairings include Laura and her cousin Madeline from *Twin Peaks*, Renee and Alice and Fred and Pete in *Lost Highway*, Betty and Diane and Rita and Camilla in *Mulholland Dr.*, and Nikki and Susan in *Inland Empire*. While these pairings may reach into the grotesque at certain points — the similarly weird murders of Laura and Madeline by Leland, as evidenced in the TV series and in the film; the dismemberment and reconstitution of Renee into Alice, as well as the brief scene in which her face is replaced with the Mystery Man's in *Lost Highway*; Fred's warped and distorted head and face as he seems to undergo the beginnings of a second transformation at the end of *Lost Highway* (deformations that Pete seems to bear some vague semblance of when he first enters the film with a protuberance on his forehead); Betty's confrontation with her own jelly-faced corpse (Diane) in *Mulholland Dr.*; and Susan's absurdly drawn out death scene and her defeat of the Phantom at the end of *Inland Empire* — for the most part, if there is deep-seated grotesquery among these doubles it is a moral one, which, while it may fail to fit within the grotesque's notably physical character, does cohere with the "metaphysics of the grotesque" that Meindl theorizes. Interestingly, though, many of these sets of doubles function as an inversion of the way the figure of the double conventionally works.

As Punter and Byron's analysis of doubles, which they extrapolate from Stevenson's *Dr. Jekyll and Mr. Hyde* and Wilde's *The Picture of Dorian Gray*, reveals, the double represents a "more primitive and passionate internal self" that needs to be re/suppressed so that their civilized counterpart can maintain an appearance that upholds an adherence to societal conventions (41). But Lynch's doubles are frequently constructed through fantasies by characters whose primitive passions have overtaken them and driven them to commit foul deeds, for which their doubles serve as temporary denouements. Or, put in the Lacanian terms through which Todd McGowan interprets Lynch's films in *The Impossible David Lynch*:

> Fantasy as such emerges in order to cover up a real gap [that is signaled by desire] within ideology or the symbolic order. Lacan uses the term "real"as a third category of experience (in addition to the imaginary and symbolic) to indicate the incompleteness of the symbolic structure, its failure to constitute itself as a coherent whole. Ideology uses fantasy to shore up its point of greatest weakness — the point at which its explanations of social phenomena break down [leaving unsatisfiable desire in the wake of the subject's inscription within the symbolic] — and this injects a potential radicality into every fantasy [10].

This "radicality" McGowan refers to is the bleeding through of the Lacanian "real" into fantasy as the "traumatic moment enacted within the fantasy" once it has fully played out (22). Interestingly, many of these moments of rupture are those in which Lynch appeals to the grotesque, as in Betty's confrontation with her own (Diane's) decomposing corpse, whose jellied face at this point has some resemblance to that of the molded or burned face of the Bum who seems to control her fantasy, or in her disconcerting experience at Club Silencio, which produces the glimpses through the bald falsity of the affecting performance there that kills the fantasy, not only of the impassioned singer and song at the center of this sequence, but also of the passionate mutual love between the Betty and her amnesiac friend. Or in *Inland Empire's* finale, when Nikki/Susan finds and kills the mysterious Phantom, her face distorts, seems to melt, and then becomes a smeared, dirty inanimate mask, which then merges with the Phantom's own visage in a disturbing utilization of the shot/reverse shot technique.

Other of Lynch's doubles in *The Elephant Man, Blue Velvet, Twin Peaks, Wild at Heart*, and *Twin Peaks: Fire Walk with Me*, rely more thoroughly on the grotesque to produce uncanny effects that are as haunting as the more Gothic variations in the absence of corporeal distortion and/or deformation. But these grotesque doublings bring with them an unnerving recognition or familiarity that works on a different level. In his book, *David Lynch: Beautiful Dark*, Greg Olson discusses doublings in Lynch's films and draws out similar functions between the pairings of Treves and Bytes in *The Elephant Man*, Bob and Leland in *Twin Peaks* and *Twin Peaks: Fire Walk with Me*, and Jeffrey and Frank in *Blue Velvet* (123–24). He draws attention to the ways in which the doubling of a character who sees himself as "good" and "innocent" with a "malevolent cinematic force" impinges a troubling sense of familiarity with the "bad" other onto the "good" character (124). This recognition of the other in the self is particularly troubling, as when at pivotal points in *The Elephant Man* and *Blue Velvet,* Bytes and Frank accuse Treves and Jeffrey of being "like me." It is troubling because, at least to some degree, it is obviously true: Treves, like Bytes before him, is accused of "freak hunting" on a number of occasions (and not just by Bytes), which forces him to question whether or not he is a "good man" (and Lynch cuts away before his interlocutor can answer); Jeffrey not only shares a woman with Frank, but begins to share in the latter's violent, abusive erotic style. One could also interpret Lula and Marietta as doubles of one another in *Wild at Heart.* Lula invertedly identifies with her mother in her attempts not to be like her and in her repressions of the murderous associations her mother draws out in her mind, and vice versa in Marietta's case: she overinvests her own identity in Lula's, which leads to her attempts to possess and control Lula and make love to and murder Sailor, Lula's lover.

Twin Peaks' and *Fire Walk with Me*'s Bob as double for Leland (and, later in the series, for Cooper) invites another avenue of interpretation more centrally located within the conventions of the grotesque precisely because Bob, as a character, is a particularly grotesque one. Whereas Bytes is reminiscent of the grotesque of a Dickensian variety and is certainly not someone with whom Treves wants to identify, Bob, Frank, and, to some extent Marietta (and women in *The Grandmother*), function on a wholly different level. Bob, as an "evil, extradimensional entity" (more on this aspect later) that craves the dark pleasures of "punishing sex and torturous death," as Olson puts it, bears certain resemblance to Frank, who shares similar appetites. And while both characters are imaged and acted in their respective roles as frightening, there is also an exaggerated sense of ridiculousness to them that makes the very real threats that they represent all the more unnerving because of its excessively physical clownishness. Lynch's camera frequently captures both characters in wide angle close-ups, head on, which allows the actors to render the scary ludicrousness of the characters in abnormally physical gestures and facial manipulations, such as Frank's frequent bouts of exaggerated gas-huffing and his wide-eyed glares and Bob's facial tics, lusty smiles, ogling eyes, all prominent features in the many mirror scenes in which he figures. Sound is another venue for the weird threat of these characters to emerge, as in Frank's orgasmic wheezing with the gas mask, his creepy whispers, and silently lip-synched singing and their contrast with his "normal" bark of a speaking voice, and in Bob's lascivious giggles and murmurs, which contrast with his violently physical deeds and primitive sexual roars. To recognize oneself or find familiarity in these grotesquely rendered doubles, as do Leland (and later even Agent Cooper) and Jeffrey, is to come undone, and Lynch gives us images of this as well: Consider Jeffrey's breakdown in his bedroom and the mingled sense of repulsion and obligation he seems to feel towards Dorothy near the end of *Blue Velvet* after Frank has broken her too, or Leland's complete emotional and existential obliteration after several episodes of finding pleasure (singing and dancing, even during the acts of murdering his niece and attempting to murder Donna) in his unification with Bob. In both scenarios, the uncanny recognition of the self in the grotesque other and vice versa, culminates in varying degrees of what Olson refers to as "the terror of depersonalization," a complex sundering within the self (115).

In *Wild at Heart*, Marietta is revealed as rather grotesque throughout the course of the film — as a murderous, conniving drunk, who almost seems a grotesque parody of the cliché "overprotective mother," and that seems to be how Lula sees her: "My mother just loves me too much," she says as an explanation for Marietta's attempts to keep her away from Sailor. But her most grotesque appearances in the film occur when she is alone — many of the martini-glass-in-hand drunken scenes in which she is visibly frazzled and almost cartoonishly out of sorts, and particularly the one in which she vomits after lipsticking her face completely red and symbolically "slashing" her wrists red with the makeup. In this way, the viewer sees her hide away the far reaches of her insanity (?) from Lula, which keeps Lula's anxieties about seeing herself doubled in Marietta at a relatively low level of grotesquery, even if this ascription is more pronounced and more disturbing for the viewer.

Lynch's short film *The Grandmother* also relies on markedly grotesque depictions of human beings: the mother and father figures are appetitive, atavistic creatures, who spend almost as much time on screen emulating dogs (initially, on their hands and knees barking, yelping, and whining at each other and at their son) as they do acting like human beings (a role for which they still seem to rely on appetitive and aggressive behavior, which is complemented with the intermittent sound of dog vocalizations in the sound design). The Grandmother herself is also a notably grotesque figure. She is born onto a bed in an upstairs room from an enormous seed pod planted and tended by the Boy, who serves as midwife to her birth from the pod, pulling her fully grown, fully clothed (shoes and all) body from the oozing canal of the plant. If there is a set of doubles here, it is the Mother and the Grandmother, and they can be seen as almost an inverted analog of the same dynamic that subsists between Lula and Marietta—each depicting opposite versions of femininity and maternity, but *The Grandmother*'s overall surrealist aesthetics paints both sides as grotesque. The Mother is slender and pretty, while the Grandmother is portly and wizened. Further, the Grandmother's affectionate, loving treatment of the Boy is juxtaposed with scenes in which the Mother stands by or laughs at the Father's abuse of the Boy or another in which she forcibly attempts to show her affection by violently grasping at him as he tries to escape her clutches. If they serve as doubles, then they do so as surrealistically stylized polar oppositions in the Boy's (and the spectator's) experience of maternal figures.

Among Lynch's numerous doubles, one particular set stands out, which bridges the discussions of the double and the abhuman (to come in the next part of the argument), and this is the doubling of Merrick in *The Elephant Man* with himself. Lynch describes Merrick as "what kept me going" on the project: "He was a strange, wonderful, innocent guy. That was it. That's what the whole thing's about" (qtd. in Rodley 103). It is in terms of this "wonderful" contrast, the contrast between the outside (the "strange") and the inside (the "innocent"), that Merrick can be conceived as functioning as his own double. The film presents Merrick's body as monstrously strange (even as it depicts him as an affable, intelligent man), and much has been made of the, possibly exploitative, structural strategy of delaying the audience's visual gratification of regarding him, as Joe Kember, relying on Sergei Eisenstein, points out in "David Lynch and the Mug Shot: Facework in *The Elephant Man* and *The Straight Story*": "Merrick's face is a fascination of the eye, inviting strategies of shock, defamiliarization and distanciation among the film's spectators" (25). Merrick as an "attraction," Kember states, is necessarily married to the "principle of objectification," which is arguably exploited in the film by Lynch as much as by anyone else before him (24). Merrick's body, in a certain sense, is his double, but, again, his doubling externalizes his physically ghastly and monstrous deformations, as do the doublings of Diane in *Mulholland Dr.* and Fred in *Lost Highway,* but in a way that morally or metaphysically aligns with theories of the grotesque rather than one that is predicated upon sheer physicality. But unlike those characters, Merrick has to take his external presence with him when he lives out his fantasy as a Victorian dandy, as a "normal" person. And as is demonstrated in the scene in which the night porter exploits and abuses Merrick, ultimately forcing him to look at his own reflection in a mirror, he regards his own deformed physicality with the horror of uncanny recognition: he screams just like everyone else does when they first encounter him, further verification that within he really is just "like everyone else" and that it is the burden of his own excessive flesh that keeps his fantasy from being complete.

Further, Lynch demonstrates this rift between the inside and outside, between the "normal" and the "monstrous" by appealing to the uncanny effects of the grotesque through the reactions of members of society high and low who cannot help but relate to Merrick as their social position seems to suggest they ought to relate to a freak (at least insofar as the film represents this). The scenes that revolve around images of Merrick's troubling form in fancy clothes, in a "homely" Victorian flat, or with his cigarette holder, perfumes, and hairbrush, talking romantically to a framed picture of a famous actress, are some of the most uncomfortable and contrastive moments of grotesquery in the film, and they intensify the rupturing doubling at work in Merrick's character. As McGowan observes, Merrick "has sustained the fantasy of becoming a normal subject, and when the film ends, he achieves this fantasy as he lies down to sleep the way that everyone else does" (65). McGowan continues by, again, reminding the reader that fantasy (as Lacan understands it) provides a traumatic kernel of the real: in this case that the steep price of such fantasies do not leave us the possibility of claiming that what we get is not what we want (65). In the end, for Merrick to fulfill his fantasy and slake his desire, he must kill his double, a notion Lynch also experiments with in different ways in the cases of Jeffrey, Paul, Diane/Betty, and Nikki/Susan.

In a discussion of *The Elephant Man*'s sound design, Chion refers to coalescence of the sounds of the thuds, hisses, and whistles of industry that evoke an aura of the London of the Industrial Revolution and "Merrick's laboured, asthmatic, terrorized breathing..., as if there were a continuum between the sensation (conveyed primarily by the sound)" of

Merrick's suffering, worn out bodily equipment and the film's analogous rendering of the machinery of industry (49). Such juxtaposition is apparently intentional, as Lynch's comments on the film denote:

> [The] pictures of explosions — big explosions — they always reminded me of these papillomatous growths on John Merrick's body. They were like slow explosions…. So the idea of these smokestacks and soot and industry next to his flesh was also a thing that got me going [qtd. in Rodley 103].

Lynch continues this line of thought as he shifts to a reflection on the human body in general:

> Human beings are like little factories. They turn out so many little products. The idea of something growing inside, and all these fluids, and timings and changes, and all these chemicals somehow capturing life, and coming out and splitting off and turning into another thing … it's unbelievable [qtd. in Rodley 103].

I do not think it is stretching too far to draw the conclusion from these remarks and from the structure of the film itself that the excesses of Merrick's body are analogous to the excesses of industrial energies released in the factory explosions and the channeling of pollutants, steam, and noise that Lynch refers to here and that find places in the montages of Merrick's troubled birth and of life in London. He functions as a kind of human harbinger of the threat of such excess: his "little factory" has overproduced; his body's "timings and changes" are out of sync; his body continues to produce life, but that life fails to split off and never becomes another thing and thus threatens and ruins his life. In a way, his haunting figure functions as the human epitome of the excesses of industrial power. He is Victorian London's double: diegetically, as a "freak" or a medical anomaly, he fascinates, challenges, and threatens the identities of spectators by the mere fact of his humanity, and as an individual subject, his "normal" character within fascinates, challenges, and threatens even more so because, in domestic contexts, his spectators are not afforded their comforting distance from the evidence of his mannered gentility because the context has shifted. Extradiegetically, Merrick functions as the human double of London's industrial excess and danger. In either stance, then, Merrick's presence evokes the abhuman. His is a multivalent, metamorphic body (Punter and Byron 41). Insofar as he functions as a human subject (an identity he is forced to proclaim to an angry mob amidst the public toilets late in the film) in a body that seems to have "become, or is in the process of becom-

157

ing, something quite different," he calls into question the distinction between man and beast ("elephant man") or even invites speculation about the disintegration of the subject from the outside in, a rupture that threatens to divide and obliterate the self through the "slow explosion" of the body (Punter and Byron 41; Lynch qtd. in Rodley 103). And insofar as his body functions as a troubling epitome of industrial London — that is, as a "depersonalized," deformed, exploding human body that emits excessive noise — he fills the role of something indefinable (a dangerous overabundance of energy or being, and a corporeal metaphor thereof?) that threatens human identity by "appropriating the human form" (41).

The Slippery Subject: Mysterious Evolutions and Metaphysical Entities in the Lynchian Cinemaverse

Eraserhead demonstrates an inversion of *The Elephant Man*'s approach to an abhuman figure. *The Elephant Man*'s melodramatic approach to Merrick's plight as mistreated and misunderstood gentle monster garners audience or viewer sympathies by supplying kind characters for audiences or viewers to identify with, like Treves, his wife, and Mrs. Kendall (and others who warm to Merrick) over against the more baldly exploitative characters of the likes of Bytes and the night porter. But, while there are glimpses of what may be pity (in Treves' shedding of a tear at first beholding Merrick), Merrick is exploited as monster (even by Treves) until he proves his humanity through speaking, learning, and getting on with others socially. In *Eraserhead*, the figure of the "baby" enters the film's world as a horrible, abortive little "thing" that is not recognizably human to the spectator (it resembles a large skinned rabbit with its ears and limbs severed, which is wrapped in gauze to prevent its insides coming out) but which is named as "human" (though "premature") and is treated by Henry and Mary as a human infant would be treated (Mary spoons it baby food; Henry gives it a fatherly "aw shucks" look when he enters the apartment in the scene where the baby makes its first appearance). And indeed the baby's behavior (resisting food, crying at night) has resemblances with those of human infants, but along with these come the mocking, sneering laughter at Henry's romantic failure with the woman who lives across the hall; its shifty eyes; and ghastly sores. This reversal of the more melodramatic approach to Merrick invites not pity, empathy, or sympathy, but because Lynch "intentionally primes only to violate" (the film announces a baby in order to repulse the viewer with its image of the "baby"), as Schneider observes, the director, with this figure and in other aspects of the film, invokes the familiar in order to alienate and disgust (11, 8).

Ken Kaleta, in his book, *David Lynch*, remarks, "*Eraserhead* is a film pervaded by a feeling of unreasonable horror" (22). The film tracks Henry through the familiar melodramatic narrative of a rocky relationship with a woman who gets pregnant, which forces new roles and responsibilities (and stresses) on the adults of the relationship, and then things begin to get worse and worse, and the child is the one who suffers most. Put this way, the film seems like a soap opera, and, to some degree, its plot overlaps with such sensationalizations of the banal in normative day-time television fare. And this is instrumental in establishing *Eraserhead's* "unreasonable horror," its uncanniness: because in relating a commonplace melodrama, *Eraserhead* backgrounds the beginnings of life as the result of the workings "in some cosmic control room" and supplies an epilogue in Henry's travel "after death to the galaxy behind [his] radiator," taking every opportunity along the way to bury his audience in its "avalanche of repugnant images" (Kaleta 18–19). Thus, *Eraserhead's* world is a world conducive to uncanny grotesquery in its play with abhuman figures, even though at its core it is a soap opera story. And just as the melodramatic narrative (the soap opera) at its center is exploded and undermined through the use of grotesque images and thematic figures that are shot for the full hyperbolic effect of their contrast with the commonplace, so Henry, the film's protagonist, who evokes the despairing stoic deliberateness of a Buster Keaton or of some character out of a Samuel Beckett play, is decapitated, his head replaced by the phallic head of the parasitic "baby" from within him. Whether this scene within the radiator world represents some metaphysical occurrence or Henry's nightmare vision about bearing the "baby's" burden, the abhuman images function all the same: the baby threatens Henry's human identity, his happiness, and kills his potential to grow or change (as is signified in the inclusion of a bleeding tree in the *mise en scene* of this sequence). This threat is objectified to some degree when Henry steps into the hallway and sees the neighbor woman, with whom he had previously shared his bed, with another man (effectively adding another strand to the soap opera thread). In another example of Lynch's play with the shot-reverse shot technique, the spectator first sees Henry peeking out his door; then the camera shifts to his perspective, depicting the woman and her new man, but the gaze shifts then to her perspective of Henry peeping out at her, and in this shot (from the woman's gaze), Henry's head has been replaced by the "baby's" phallic head. Lynch finishes the short sequence with another perspective shot from Henry's point of view to capture the horrified repulsion on the woman's face before she disappears through the door to her apartment (with the other man). The eraser factory scene that follows perpetuates the grotesque depersonalization of Henry's character (a drilled-out sample of his head is machined into erasers for pencils), but its upshot allows Henry the moral/metaphysical context by which he can "erase" the baby as well as the troubling world outside the radiator.

The concept of the abhuman can also facilitate the interpretation of the characters in Lynch's films who seem to exist on some metaphysical or mystical or "spiritual" plane beyond "real world" reality in a given film but who make appearances in or influence that reality in some way. Characters such as *Eraserhead*'s Man in the Planet and Lady in the Radiator; *Twin Peaks*' and *Fire Walk with Me*'s Bob, Mike/Gerard, Man from Another Place, and other Red Room/Black Lodge inhabitants; *Lost Highway*'s Mystery Man; and *Mulholland Dr.*'s Cowboy, Bum, and size-shifting elderly couple all present a certain sense of hope, confusion, threat, or help to other characters in the films in which they figure. They seem at certain points in Lynch's films to be the constructs of characters' fantasies; the fulfillments or their wishes; externalized or metastasized embodiments of forces from deep within the mind (superego, libido, death drive, etc.); and, at other times (and indeed sometimes simultaneously), they seem to function as incomprehensible "others," "shadows" to whom the "normal" rules of human existence seem not to apply, powers which they can at times lend to others through themselves or put to use for their own malevolent purposes.

While *Eraserhead* appeals to many horror conventions, as Schneider demonstrates, the film appropriates such aspects of the horror genre into a dynamic context that also relies on melodramatic, surrealistic, and absurdist techniques (5). As Lynch's career moves forward to *The Elephant Man*, one can still recognize aspects of these genres and aesthetics, but melodrama and horror have taken precedence, or, put more precisely, *The Elephant*

160

Man relates melodrama through the images of horror. But, in many ways, the horror aesthetic lightens as Lynch's career comes into its own from *Blue Velvet* forward. The abhuman figures in these films more precisely reflect Gothic aesthetics than those of horror, a distinction to which Kelly Hurley refers in an essay in *The Cambridge Companion to Gothic Fiction*, observing that horror is usually recognized by its tasteless lack of restraint in indulging in "graphic imagery and extreme scenarios as it depicts decomposing, deliquescing, and otherwise disgustingly metamorphic bodies" (192–93).[2] The metaphysical characters in his later films reflect similar positions to those in films like *Eraserhead* (the Man in the Planet and the Lady in the Radiator), and they reflect, also like these earlier manifestations, subtler approaches to evoking the uncanny through employing the grotesque in the films' presentations of abhuman characters. This is not to say that Lynch's tastes for depicting bodies emitting matter, being dismembered, decapitated, etc. have changed — they certainly have not. The point is that those aspects in the more recent body of films are integrated more realistically into the diegetic frame, which functions to pronounce more distinctly the weirdness, the otherness, of the presence of what I have been calling his "metaphysical" characters. And this is one way in which these characters function for the development of conditions favorable to the uncanny in the films in which they appear, for as Freud remarks in his essay on the concept, the writer evokes the uncanny if he

> has to all appearances taken up his stance on the ground of common reality. By doing so he adopts all the conditions that apply to the emergence of a sense of the uncanny in normal experience; ... But the writer can intensify and multiply this effect far beyond what is feasible in normal experience; in his stories he can make things happen that one would never, or only rarely, experience in real life.... [H]e tricks us by promising us everyday reality and then going beyond it ["The Uncanny" 156–57].

Lynch does Freud one better: his "everyday reality" is frequently hermetically "normal"—shiny, bright, hopeful (consider the ways in which Lynch establishes the "normal" worlds of *Blue Velvet, Twin Peaks,* or even the first thirty minutes with Betty in *Mulholland Dr.*)—which allows his transgressions of the "normal" to be particularly affecting. And even in *Wild at Heart* or *Lost Highway,* Lynch establishes an "everyday reality" that is grounded in a grotesque or grim sense of realism (respectively), which he then also transgresses, though to different ends, in

161

order to provide shocks that are hard for the viewer to prepare for. Lynch's "metaphysical" characters typically emerge with the transgression, or the transgression occasions their emergence, or vice versa. Whichever way one interprets the relationship, these characters add a wallop to the shock.

Beginning with *Eraserhead*'s Man in the Planet and the Lady in the Radiator, Lynch's metaphysical characters are associated with duality, the values or associations of which are difficult to decipher. They are connected with life in the "real" world, but they stand within and without at once. The Man in the Planet pulls the levers that seem to move life into being, and it is his disturbed face that reappears when the "baby" is wiped out, while the Lady in the Radiator engages in the death dance that squishes life out of the sperm-like creatures the Man in the Planet metaphysically thrusts into the world with his levers and machines. And yet the bodies of these two entities seem to contrast with their metaphysical vocations. The Man in the Planet's body is covered with sores or burns; his movements are jerky, machine-like; his countenance is ominously stern (and also covered in sores). The Lady in the Radiator's appearance is one that evokes purity, innocence, and virginal femininity, as signified in her 1950s-style blonde hairdo, her unceasing smile (emphasized by the enormously puffy prosthetic cheeks), girlish dance steps, and gestures of invitation (which center around her breasts/heart). In contrast to Henry's neurotic wife as well as to the seductive brunette who lives across the hall, the Lady in the Radiator brings associations of the ideal virgin/mother, whose love is comfortingly nonsexual and, as such, nonthreatening to the film's protagonist. Both she and the Man in the Planet resemble humanity, but they are marked as "other" by their bodies and by their positions within the world of the film. Their connection with Henry's "real" world is ambiguous but certain. Is the Man in the Planet some ill-formed demiurge responsible for creating life in his own image? The X family's involuntary seizures, the "baby's" sores, and the over-industrialized cityscape all point to images associated with the brief glimpses Lynch allows of him. Does the Lady in the Radiator represent the warm embrace of death, an escape from the Henry's miserable fate in such a world? Or is the image of the radiator (its pipes locking the Lady within) an inverted metaphor? Is the life within the radiator world the fullness of life? Is it Henry who is locked out from this fullness? Is his murder of his "baby" necessary for entry because it

162

entails killing the part of himself by which he is connected to the life produced by the Man in the Planet (this may explain the cataclysm that surrounds the death of the "baby" as a kind of personal apocalypse)? None of this is clear. What is clear is that these two metaphysical characters exist on a plane of existence behind, within, around the "real" one: they are "other" and their deformations inscribe their otherness into the bodies of their characters. In a way, their threat is similar to the one represented in Lynch's other characters from beyond or behind reality.

In *Blue Velvet*, after his initial observation of Frank with Dorothy, Jeffrey asks the unanswerable question of Sandy: "Why are there people like Frank in the world?" And this is a question that the film allows to float around in Jeffrey's mind but never attempts to answer in its construction of its two sides of aestheticized American fantasy, the dream and the nightmare (McGowan 91). But if the question is not answered in Lynch's later films, he at least seems to entertain it more openly, and the context for asking such a question leads Lynch back into the arena of *Eraserhead*'s metaphysical features. *Twin Peaks*, *Fire Walk with Me*, *Lost Highway*, and *Mulholland Dr.* all experiment with figures that lurk in the shadows of reality, influencing what people can know and do in the world — backgrounding good and evil with the mixed realities of abhuman characters who take various human forms, but who, again, seem to exist on a plane of existence different from but related to Lynch's "real" worlds.

In the world of *Twin Peaks*, the metaphysical realm is associated with what the series calls the Black Lodge and White Lodge, which may be the variations on the binary of good and evil — indeed variations on any number of binaries of value, proportion, behavior, emotion, etc., which Cooper (along with a few others) discovers in his dreams, visions, and entrance into Red Room in the series' final episode — and so the two lodges may, ultimately, be the one dynamic place. The multiplicity of subjectivity in this place, some of which bleeds over into the "real" world of Twin Peaks, is one of its dominant features. Most of the characters associated with the Red Room exhibit bodies that traverse any number of variations of the binaries associated with human beings. There is a dancing dwarf, a sluggish giant, a one-armed man, the atavistic Bob; then there are also those from among the living and the dead of human reality who appear in the Red Room. Some of the metaphysical figures bodily traverse the boundary between the Red Room and the human world, while also appearing in visions or dreams (Bob, Gerard/Mike, the Grandmother and Grandson). Others (the Giant and the Man from Another Place) seem not to leave the Red Room, though the Giant appears to Cooper in visions from there.

As "indefinable" beings that "mimic the human" by "appropriating the human form" these characters may be appropriately described as abhuman. Further, these characters inhabit bodies at the extremes of human corporeality, an aspect of their reality that relies on elements of grotesque extremes of contrast to reflect a certain balance or middling of reality that may be inferred among them: the giant and the dwarf, Mike/Gerard and Bob, the aged woman and the young boy. Further, some of these characters appear (most prominently in episode 29) in doubles of themselves, as the Man from Another Place and the Giant at one moment appear weird but friendly and the next as insanely evil (an aspect that carries over to shadow selves of Laura and Cooper). This extends further when the Man from Another Place and the Giant are revealed to be doubles or shadows of one another (as the Giant says as he sits down with the dwarf, "One and the same")—extending the multiplicity of their subjectivity beyond the bounds of their bodies. McGowan argues, again relying on Lacanian psychoanalytic theory, that the Man from Another Place, Mike/Gerard, and Bob are embodied representations of facets of the unconscious, concluding that they are both unified and divided against one another in an eternal struggle over possession and enjoyment, presence and absence, death drive and libido (144–49). While McGowan makes an interesting argument, the Lodge seems to supersede the unconscious as such, but McGowan's extension of the identities of these characters as both unified and severed provides yet another threat to subjectivity as such. All of the metaphysical Red Room occupants seem to merge, overlap, and converge, but, just as much, they occupy separate bodies (extreme bodies: excessive, diminutive, old, young, partial, beautiful, ghastly), and oppositional, conflicting identities: they are one and many at once, as the grotesque image of Mike/Gerard and the Man from Another Place figures visually when, in *Fire Walk with Me*, Mike/Gerard is seated in the Red Room, the dwarf at his side, where his missing arm should be ("Do you know who I am? I am the arm and I sound like this: wa wa wa wa"). One gets the sense that each of these characters fits with the others in some fashion or at some point in the Lodge's temporal scheme to present some metaphysical unity just as assuredly as their severance from one another ruptures that unity, leaving some grave wound that transcends worlds.

Not only do these multiplied metaphysical subjects threaten the concept of human identity merely in their corporeal existence in human bodies as identities that merge and separate and cooperate and conflict according to some otherworldly rhythm, but these metaphysical machinations are intimately connected with goings on in the "normal" human existence of Twin Peaks. These figures are responsible for, or related to, at least some of the acts of good and evil in the "real" world, and they feed on the extremes of human emotion, at human subjectivity pressed to the brink. Whatever the specifics of their connection to life in Twin Peaks (or the rest of the world), they influence what happens there; some live in the city; some speak to or through townspeople or inanimate objects; some inhabit its citizens and engage in evil with or through them. Not only does the uncanny world of *Twin Peaks/Fire Walk with Me* threaten human identity with respect to the degree to which the beastly animal is still alive in the civilized individual (in a psychoanalytic variation of Darwinian Gothic perhaps), for example, but it also shows that such beastly impulses are precisely the flip side of the strip, that one is not separate from the other, and that, somewhere, behind or within whatever it is that makes up the world, those two conflicting aspects (and many others) that struggle within the human subject emerge from an otherness that impinges itself on the human world, influencing people and events there, even as it withholds its secrets.

The same sense of mystery and threat pervades the metaphysical characters in *Lost Highway* and *Mulholland Dr.* The figures of the Mystery Man, the Cowboy, and the Bum (and his cartoonish, size-shifting elderly henchmen) all appear in concrete human form but all are associated with an otherness that makes their positions within their stories transgress the borders between the physical and the metaphysical, the worldly and the otherworldly, the possible and the impossible. The physical presence of Mystery Man and the Cowboy defies rational explanation: the Mystery Man can be two places at once, can appear and disappear at will, can enact a transferal of one man's subjectivity to another's and back again; the Cowboy can control the fate of a young film director, just as assuredly as he can control the electricity in a rodeo ring by his mere presence, and he can "wake up" a dead woman as he facilitates the reversal of time and the fading of a fantasy. Both characters also occupy bodies whose features seem to break down distinctions between genders: the Cowboy and the Mystery Man have hairless faces with feminine features, the latter's even bearing white powder makeup and deep red lipstick. While the Cowboy appears in the garb his name suggests (which in the history of film is usually a signifier of the tough, rugged masculinity evoked in numberless westerns), he speaks with a high, soft, effeminate drawl. Similarly contrastive is the image of the Mystery Man as an ill-tempered, paunchy, middle aged hermaphrodite documenter (or else as one of the weirder characters stolen from a Robert Wilson play) and the brutality he evokes in his threatening speech and actions on even the most menacing "real world" character in the film (Mr. Eddy/Dick Laurent). Lynch in these characters invokes and transgresses traditional distinctions between male and female and mixes associations with each to intensify the otherness these characters represent. And this otherness reaches a whole new level in the figure of the Bum, whose presence in *Mulholland Dr.* seems to be strictly confined to representing a dangerous, mysterious presence that is nearly impenetrable (as is visually represented in the obfuscation of his face by burns, mold, or grime and in his vagrant occupation of the "real world's" non-places) but that is ultimately behind the trouble at the center of the film.

Olson and McGowan argue convincingly that *Lost Highway* and *Mulholland Dr.* revolve around the dreams/fantasies that Fred and Diane construct for themselves in order to escape their despairing troubles, their guilt or desire, and their own subjectivities (Olson 437, 532; McGowan 164, 195–96). This argument entails that the "metaphysical" characters operate within the fantasies and so are not "real" in an objective sense; they are constructs within the fantasies. But Lynch, never being the kind of director that makes such conclusions easy ones to arrive at, does not supply the clues on which such interpretations are based until well into the films, after establishing the characters and their drama and relationships and throwing in these weirdly "other" metaphysical characters as well. Further, such conclusions require the interpreter to bridge the narrative gaps and structural distortions that have become characteristic Lynchian qualities: Lynch does not disclose that "by the way, this was all a fantasy." He simply breaks the narrative: Fred's cell is now occupied by Pete, who does not know how he got there, and his parents refuse to discuss it, indicating only that the Mystery Man was involved; Rita disappears, and Betty wakes up as Diane, whose relationship with Camilla (who looks like Rita) has apparently fallen apart, and it all has something to do with a Bum and a mysterious box. If some of what we see is fantasy, it is we as interpreters of the films who have to make the judgment. And in the case of *Inland Empire*, Lynch's experimental non-narrative approach goes even further, inviting Olson to defer to Lynch's belief in reincarnation and Hindu spirituality to attempt to make sense of the three hours of doublings within doublings and fantasies and dreams within and around one another — of characters interrupting other character's scenes (sometimes their own) because they have been or will be invoked through another character's narrative (which somehow makes them "real," brings them to life) or through some vague but powerful creative fiat (672–73).

Whether one finds these arguments convincing, though, for my present purposes, does not really matter because, whether the metaphysical characters "really" exist or not, or whether Fred can "really" turn into Pete or Diane into Betty, etc — none of these things matter for this argument. In fact, Lynch's tendency to intensify the ambiguous and paradoxical aspects of his films through experimentation with plot and narrative, camera work (blurring, metonymic close-ups, editing, etc.), or the inclusion and depiction of characters who seem both human and not (with whose bodies, faces, speech, and action he subtly subverts conventional delineations of human identity) — whether "real" or fantasy — these aspects converge to demonstrate the obliteration of the individual human subject (Jerslev 152–53). Moreover, the argument that some of these abhuman metaphysical forces represent externalized facets of the unconscious, as McGowan argues, may be the most disturbing rupture of selfhood yet (162). This argument effectively explodes the subject: its unconscious is spilling out, becoming "other" identities, multiplying the subject beyond the double (Fred as Pete but also as Mystery Man; Diane as Betty but also as the Cowboy and the Bum), doubling reality itself. Distinctions between inside and outside disappear; the subject and life as a whole coalesce. And the weirdest, scariest, most threatening otherness is a version of the self that marks and enacts its own obliteration, intensifying the use of the grotesque in producing the uncanny by ripping past the oppositions and recognitions of "homely" and "unhomely" into "the categorical oppositions such as me/not me, inside/outside, living/dead" that Carroll discusses (32).

Pervert on Parade: Modernist Grotesque, Being and Lynch's Sick Brain

David Lynch is often accused of having a sick mind, most famously, perhaps, in Roger Ebert's insinuation in his review of *Blue Velvet* that Lynch's pairing of "jokey, small-town satire" with the hypnotic, darkly exploitative sexual scenes in the film displays "behavior that is more sadistic than the Hopper character." But to return to the epigraph with which I began this chapter, John R. Clark's claim that "In its shocking way, the modern grotesque appears to postulate that such a sick man's brain is possibly the lowest common denominator of the human condition itself" may demonstrate that Lynch is up to more than Ebert assumes (Clark 25). Ebert's response to the film seems to touch precisely upon the uneasy feelings that the use of the uncanny grotesque can create: he recognizes the uncomfortably familiar aspects and the "almost hypnotic pull" of disturbing desires portrayed in the film as "born from the darkest and most despairing side of human nature," but then scolds Lynch for juxtaposing this with the "small-town idyll," and the "deadpan irony," platitudes, and corny dialog that go along with it. He writes that what annoyed him most was Lynch's repeated tendency to place "himself between me and the material." One could accuse Lynch of similar techniques in some of his other films: the weird Lynchisms that seem to interrupt the plot, structure, and relationships, but without which the film would be a very different work. Many such aspects are the ones that I have already discussed or alluded to: Lynch's fascination with excess and oddity in the appearances of most any of the "metaphysical" characters, in the death scenes in which dead bodies remain in positions that seem impossible for dead bodies to sustain (Andy in *Lost Highway* and Gordon in *Blue Velvet*, for instance), in scenes in which eroticism and violence merge (in *Blue Velvet, Twin Peaks, Wild at Heart, Fire Walk with Me,* and *Mulholland Dr.*), and in the many severed or missing or blown off body parts in Lynch films. And Lynch is nearly always "placing himself between" the viewer and the material, integrating the various, seemingly polar, associations and values into a grotesque aesthetic that seeks to present them as not polar oppositions, but as identical opposites, the coincidence of which is, perhaps, necessary — as necessary as it is for the subject (often a protagonist) to fragment, fall apart, and (often) die.

These qualities in Lynch's films — and those related qualities I have spent this chapter discussing along the lines of his use of the concepts of the double and the abhuman — fit well with Meindl's theory of the grotesque, outlined in the first part of this chapter, and also overlap significantly with the uncanny. But, further, Lynch's aesthetics and Meindl's metaphysics of the grotesque seem to insinuate one another. Meindl's Heidegger-based existentialism grounds his theory that the dark, modernist grotesque seeks to dig into human "existential depths," thinking beyond the binaries of subject and object (good and evil, beauty and ugliness, etc.) and scouring the depths of "primitive thinking" (perhaps not unlike the grotesque as Clark's "common denominator") for the visions of madness, terror, myths, and dreams, which the grotesque can reignite and reconstruct in the present moment for reimagined aesthetic conceptualizations of the dark existence (Meindl 31–32). Moreover, Lynch's penchant for experimentation in the film medium that attempts to remind the viewer of the presence and character of the medium (in precisely the way that Ebert finds annoying) also aligns him with Meindl's and Kayser's observations that the grotesque in art intensifies its inclusion of signs of its own "createdness" as art, highlighting the "work" art is and does (Meindl 135; Kayser 184). And Lynch's experimentations with the *mort vivant*, the depiction of the arrested lives of his often delusional characters also aligns him closely with Meindl's explication of the same form of representation of the flux of "life itself," of Being as such, that he identifies as an important venue of grotesquery in modernist literature (210).

PART 4

Into the World and Back Again: From Politics to Paradox

Angel of gaiety, have you tasted grief?
Shame and remorse and sobs and weary spite,
And the vague terrors of the fearful night
That crush the heart up like a crumpled leaf?
— Charles Baudelaire, "Reversibility"

As a gesture to marry the form of my argument to its content, I am concluding this study with a contradiction, or better, a paradox. Baudelaire reproaches the "angel of gaiety" with the irrefutable and potent despair that she forgets or ignores or is not made for, for she (as "angel" perhaps) does not know that what it means to be human is to suffer in the face of gaiety (among his other "reversibles"), simultaneously, as it were. This is approximately where I am aiming this last installment: the grotesque is located, most appropriately, I claim, in the human. The problem, of course, is that this does little to clarify anything about anything. Instead of making clarifications and drawing clear, objective conclusions, however, I am more interested in complicating things further. Chapter VII attempts to address this central "human" aspect of the grotesque in terms of culture, politics, and the family by teasing out how the grotesque might function as an implement of social critique. Chapter VIII is a continuation of this journey outward, but it also entails a return: here, I follow Herman Melville in a contemplative journey out into the world, beyond it, and back — a journey which adheres, almost disturbingly, to the formal coordinates of the grotesque. It is a journey that goes in circles, but it is one that also offers the wisdom of Baudelaire's crumpled leaf: it suggests a certain critical "posture."

VII. Politics, Culture and the Grotesque Family in Hippie-Slasher-Horror

> Only what does not fit into this world is true. What is requisite of the artistic act no longer converges with the historical situation, which is not to say that they ever harmonized. This incongruity is not to be eliminated by adaptation: The truth, rather, is in carrying through their conflict.
>
> — Theodor Adorno, *Aesthetic Theory*

> They are us.
>
> — *Night of the Living Dead*

Born of Corrosion: Truth, Aesthetics and the Grotesque

One could point to the grotesque as the context for the kind of truth to which Adorno refers above. In *Aesthetic Theory*, he discusses the dialectical conflict between the beautiful and the ugly. The ugly's retention of a certain degree of ambiguousness, he posits, arises from the subjective tendency to subsume all that is condemned by art ("polymorphous sexuality," the "violently mutilated and lethal," etc.) under the "abstract and formal category of the ugly" (47). The ugly becomes a perpetually recurrent, "antithetical other" to art, but it is an other without which, Adorno claims, art, according to its own principles, would cease to exist: art appropriates this other, which is beauty's antithesis (and vice versa), via a relationship based on mutual negation, and this other "gnaws away correctively on the affirmativeness of spiritualizing art" (47). The "ugly," here, and its relation to beauty, seems to have obvious overlap with both "light" and "dark" grotesque and their respective emphases on life, the body, and death. But more to the point, it is precisely this conflict that Adorno gestures towards — a conflict between any number of dialectically opposed sets of concepts that he discusses in the passage: unformed and formed, harmonious and dissonant, beautiful and ugly, world and subject, rational and primitive, repressed and conscious, etc.— which grotesque art takes as its raw materials (46–47). The grotesque is, of course, concerned with the ugly, but it is more precisely involved with capturing the way in which the ugly (and each of the other "negative" concepts) "gnaws away" at the beautiful (and each of the other "positive" concepts): the grotesque is the paradox born out of such dialectical conflict, but it does not represent a synthesis in which conflict can recede or disappear. No, quite the opposite: grotesque art thrives on and heightens tensions by pronouncing them, by imaging opposites as one. The grotesque is also associated with the quality of the "new" that Adorno identifies, which emerges in "modern art" after ugliness is given its full dialectical power by being freed from "the harmonistic view" that reigned in earlier aesthetics (46). Just as assuredly as the grotesque entails this new, ambiguously paradoxical instantiation of opposites in conflict, it also manifests Adorno's "distintigrative impulse," the death of art, the rupture of expression (52–53). Such duality doubles again: the grotesque incorporates the birth of the living from conflict of opposites and the death of the dead from their overlap and/or division — both, as it were, almost identically, and simultaneously — uniting, dividing, integrating, fragmenting across or within the parallax gap of the two sides of Žižek's conceptual Moebius strip.

The analyses in this study of the paradoxes, conflicts, and ambiguities of the grotesque and its related thematic and theoretical corollaries have surfaced in a particular methodology that has been employed to discuss the films and directors treated in this work, and this methodology betrays a kind of "soft auteurism." However, as I briefly stated in the introduction, one should not therefore assume that my recognition of these directors' intersections with the grotesque is necessarily or implicitly related to identifying in their artistic intensions an attempt to "author" grotesque movies. The present book should not be read as a straightforwardly auteurist approach to film aimed at exposing the grotesque as a facet of a particular director's oeuvre. Indeed, something like an inversion of this is closer to my intention: this book represents an attempt to unwind the philosophy of the grotesque, and the particular directors' oeuvres are intended to help delineate and illustrate facets of how the grotesque can function aesthetically (existentially, metaphysically, etc.) from a variety of perspectives (production of art, reception of it, interpretation of art, etc.). So, one important move, as I draw this study to a close, is to glimpse the grotesque from the far side of auteurist theory, a move which is already under way in appealing to Adorno to resituate the concept and identify its social or political function in a form of criticism derived from another brand of modern aesthetics.

In the broader cultural terms Adorno uses to discuss the corrective power of ugly or "negative" art for the sake of a "new," "modern" conception of what art is, aesthetics as such, must also be understood as a vital site of renewal in culture (46). Such art takes for its own the ideological project of "what is proscribed as ugly" and relies on the energy that emerges when the "beautiful" intersects the "ugly" in art (48). An aesthetics that locates its heart within such contradictions or paradoxes necessarily abandons any kind of wider cultural or political naiveté, for this is art that "must denounce the world"; this is art that "creates and reproduces the ugly," perhaps in a way analogous to Bakhtin's concept of carnival's degradation (Adorno 48; Bakhtin, *Rabelais* 25). This means that if the grotesque is to function for a critical perspective in aesthetics, then it must also metastasize (as it were) and make its way into the rest of the cultural body of theories and loci of expression: an aesthetics of the grotesque assumes (or at least implies) a social, political dimension. Such an idea seems appropriate, especially considering some of Adorno's positions on film, a medium which he characterizes as ever at the center of a conflict between aesthetic and social concerns, a form almost constantly reduplicating itself in maintenance of the status quo but occasionally, almost accidentally, becoming art in some odd instances of its own self-transcendence (Adorno, *The Culture Industry* 182–85). So, in the next several pages, as an anti-auteurist critical intervention before my final reflections, I will demonstrate the usefulness of another approach to understanding the grotesque and its relation to films and filmmakers from a perspective more amenable to social and political theories, one less caught up in the problems and controversies of auteurism.

A Chainsaw to the System: The Bourgeois Family, Ideology, Transgressive Horror and the Grotesque

Tania Modleski writes that the "exploitation" or "slasher" film frequently engages in an "unprecedented assault on all that bourgeois culture is supposed to cherish," like the ideological apparatus of the family, which effectively makes this subgenre worthy of an exceptional status under the generally condemnatory judgments of Adorno, et al., concerning "popular" film (Modleski 288, 286; Adorno, *The Culture* 185). She points to films by slasher-horror directors like David Cronenberg, Tobe Hooper, George Romero, Brian De Palma, and others as proof that such instantiations of popular culture are capable of subversive and critical art that undermines and challenges the domination of status quo (288–93). Matt Becker, in his essay "A Point of Little Hope: Hippie Horror Films and the Politics of Ambivalence," argues, within a similar trajectory, that hippie era horror directors George Romero, Wes Craven, and Tobe Hooper present in their first "major" films a post-hippie political ambivalence that oscillates between featuring a "radical" politics that is broadly aligned with the peace-love antiestablishmentism of hippie ideology and one that is "reactionary" in its starkly depicted images of an America haunted by the palpable public failure of this progressivist politics — of the general bleakness concomitant with an American politics and culture caught up in the strife and upheavals of the late 1960s and early 70s (43).

Frederick Jameson's psychoanalytic–Marxist theory of the "political unconscious," which asserts that "even the most apparently apolitical" works "possess a political content" by virtue of necessarily being circumscribed within the historical "moment" of their production, may provide a helpful way to think through the political content submerged in Hooper's, Romero's, and Craven's breakout films (Childers 232; Becker 49). The argument here is, then, that the films address the politics of the times in which they were created through a kind of unconscious cultural "trickle down" effect, and this is a theory to which George Romero broadly assents: "It was 1968, man. *Everybody* had a 'message.' Maybe it crept in. I was just making a horror film, and I think the anger and the attitude and all that's there is just there because it was 1968" (qtd. in Becker 51). Becker supports his thesis with an outline of the tenants of hippie thought and then tracks those ideas and their counters in the films. He traces these ideological lines by gesturing at several topics of critique present in each of the films, but since his argument regards the wider issues of a suggestion that Romero's 1968 zombie film *Night of the Living Dead,* Craven's 1972 thriller *The Last House on the Left,* and Hooper's 1974 classic "slasher" *The Texas Chain Saw Massacre* emerged from the discontents of three disaffected hippies — whom he sees as representatives of a broader swath of an American subculture—Becker does not exhaust the topics he introduces. One of the motifs that surfaces in his essay is the "American family." I am picking up where Becker leaves off: here, I am sketching a reading of how these films deliver critiques of the family within the political and cultural contexts of the United States of the 1960s and 70s. I am trying to demonstrate that the films can be read as horror "symptoms," as reactions (containing implicit critiques) of the "body" (the cultural body) to certain oppressions and repressions associated with the apparatus or construct of the family within the ideological structures of American culture. My wager here, more specifically, is that the films criticize the ideological construct of the "traditional American family" by appealing to the grotesque mode, which the films employ toward a function similar to that for which Bertolt Brecht directed his "estrangement effects" (or V-effects).

In *Hollywood from Vietnam to Reagan*, Robin Wood articulates a theoretical framework for understanding the critical capabilities of horror films. This hermeneutical model relies on a distinction between "basic" and "surplus" repression. Basic repression is an inescapable, universal form of repression connected with the deferment of gratification, with the patterns according to which we develop memory and thought processes, with self-control, and with the ways in which we interact with other people (70–71). Surplus repression has more to do with the cultural ideologies engaged to oppress individuals, which result frequently in *re*pression of unwanted characteristics by individuals themselves: it names the procedures by which culture conditions people to inhabit prefabricated roles in their society (71). According to Wood's analysis, those things that individuals repress remain inaccessible (outside of an analyst-aided decoding of the work the mind does in dreams); but oppression is imposed from the culture outside the self, and whether, and to what degree, people recognize "its reign over them" differs from one person to another (71). Wood sums up by reconnecting the two terms: repression is what happens when we fully internalize oppression (71). For Wood, all of this is relevant to American horror films because the horror genre presents the most direct and clearest responses to these analytic categories at work in the individual's relation to culture by dramatizing the "dual concept of the repressed/the Other" in the Monster (75). He goes on to note that the veritable goal of the genre is to recognize and dramatize everything that civilization attempts to repress and oppress (75).

175

A political critique from such a perspective of a film as outwardly outrageous as *The Texas Chain Saw Massacre* may center on the social genesis of the film's "monsters": they emerge from the disturbing effects of violent and dehumanizing labor under an industrial form of capitalism on one hand (the position of the slaughterhouse "killer" as such) and of the loss of the context that makes that kind of labor relevant in society on the other (since the "killer's" had been replaced by mechanized processes). "They are victims too," Wood remarks, "of the slaughterhouse environment, of capitalism — our victims, in fact" (92). The fusion of the tensions associated with these circumstances with traditional, patriarchal value systems still extant in America produces the slasher family that wreaks havoc on the younger, more urban, "progressive" (the new age books and hippie attire) generation that inadvertently invades it in search of their own foggy memories and familial roots in that geographical area. Thus, the rural cannibal family has effectively internalized the oppressions imposed upon them by their culture — especially as that culture has begun to disintegrate around them. Their consequent repressions of those characteristics that threaten their "normal" way of life paint the norms of the traditional and the patriarchal — the "good old days" of what America used to be in general — with an uneasy, grotesque ambivalence. *Texas Chain Saw Massacre* presents the slasher family as, effectively, a repulsive specter of traditional American values scoured of the saccharine sentimentality with which the official culture approvingly reflects on its own past (in something like *The Andy Griffith Show*, for example). The drama of the film revolves around a kind of return of the repressed played out on the bodies of the young and attractive — and particularly on Sally, the focal victim and heroine of the film. On a certain level at least, behind or within the conflict between protagonists and antagonists is an implied conflict of ideologies associated with each group. But this aspect, too, requires a little more unpacking in order to do justice to the significance of the novel use of the horror genre employed at this particularly fraught cultural moment in American filmmaking.

Frederick Jameson's comments on what he calls "Gothic films" in *Postmodernism, or, The Cultural Logic of Late Capitalism* work well with the Marcusean framework that Robin Wood establishes in order to read these horror films with the political inflection necessary to tease out their transgressive critiques of the American family. Politically, Jameson asserts, Gothic films represent a "class fantasy (or nightmare) in which the dialectic of privilege and shelter is exercised": class privileges can isolate and protect at the same time; the flip-side of establishing the "protective wall" of privilege, though, is that it encourages the production of (often nightmare) fantasies in those that it protects: the other side of that wall may be teeming with "envious forces" who are organizing, plotting, and preparing to attack — but they are rendered invisible by the wall itself (289). Gothic films, then, establish a collective dream for the privileged class that dramatizes the double-bind built from their struggle to remain "on top" of the lower classes: thus, the same structures that they put in place to protect themselves from this "other" also blind the bourgeoisie to whatever burgeoning threats that they may imagine to be on the horizon, and this results in generating collective, or class, anxiety.

"The more formal leap," Jameson continues, comes when a political or social "collectivity" (like the "U.S. public") is substituted for the "victim" in the film fantasy (289). With this move, Gothic films become at least somewhat political, and it is through this kind of process of identification that such films may convey or encourage anxieties and fantasies of this class's economically privileged and sheltered exceptionalism — "under the threats of stereotypical madmen" (289). For my present concerns with these three horror films, I do not think it is stretching Jameson's intent here too far to suggest a theoretical jump to a space between the individual victim and the national public (or the class victim as a whole) to smaller collectivities that can be interpreted as representing both of these terms, and that can similarly be seen to function as victims in these films. It is important to note, too, that the victim collectivities in the three movies are arranged around bourgeois family units. In each film a middle class family (or part of one) functions as a core around which the drama of victimization plays out: the Coopers in *Night of the Living Dead*, the Collingwoods in *Last House on the Left*, and siblings Sally and Franklin in *Texas Chain Saw Massacre*.

Jameson concludes that "these collective fantasies" depend on the "reinflation and artificial reinvigorization" of the "binary opposition between virtue and vice" for their effects. Therefore, the construction of a concept of evil occupies a central position in the establishment of modern gothic films. Evil, so conceived, Jameson contends, is "the emptiest of sheer Otherness" (289–90). Horror depends on the good/evil binary as well, but the three films under consideration here (and the more interesting modern horror films in general) complicate the relationship between the terms of the binary. While these films do indeed function as collective nightmares (or dismal fantasies), their refashioning — or even politicization — of the valuation and contextualization of good and evil clears them of Jameson's condemnation of the brand of "evil" that he identifies in Gothic films: "the emptiest of sheer Otherness" (290). And while each of these three films casts the middle class as the victim of some form of evil, and thus plays on bourgeois anxieties for effect, the political and cultural scope of these films is wider than in Jameson's "Gothic films" and much of the horror corpus before the late 60s. Evil in these three films is not constructed by rash attribution of that valuation to an empty otherness, to an alien and therefore blank cultural signifier (as in something like Tim Burton's *Mars Attacks*), but instead to the familiar itself, to the very structures of normalcy that enable the privileged class to remain on top of the rest of the world. They depict a politically charged version of Kayser's alienated world. In these films the line that divides good and evil gets obscured. The victim often becomes the monster, and the monster becomes the victim, but each without giving up its initial status as monster or victim. The films make what is "normal" and "familiar" strange, unrecognizable, detestable, disgusting — it is as someone in *Night of the Living Dead* remarks of the zombies: "They are us."

The Last House on the Left, Night of the Living Dead and *The Texas Chain Saw Massacre* imply certain social/political critiques in these terms. There are visual references to the Vietnam War in the mass slaughter of groups of zombies in *Night of the Living Dead* and in the tangling jungle-like terrain through which victims attempt to escape in *Last House on the Left* and *Texas Chain Saw Massacre*. The ghastly, viscerally realistic violence may also entail references to the war, as Tom Savini notes in the documentary *The American Nightmare*. Again, as in the other two films, in *Night of the Living Dead*, Romero exposes several cultural oppressions or repressions by locating the U.S. public in both collectivities — that is, in the zombies and in the house-trapped nonzombies, in the monsters and in the victims. Each group — the apparently mindless drones and the supposedly intelligent, self-conscious survivors — can only become locked in a battle to annihilate the other. The film can spin several different ways. One interpretation is that the zombies represent the oppressed and/or repressed public who unconsciously operate only at the basest levels, blindly killing the other or, rather impassively, consuming the other at will, either way, annihilating, replacing, or assimilating the other through dispassionate, mechanistic, and regularized acts of violence. Another thematic thread, which is painfully evident in *Last House on the Left* as well (though with a slightly different inflection), involves the failure of government and municipal authorities to effectively deal with the serious problems posed by this devouring plague — as well as their failure to decipher the "good" people from the "bad" ones by judgments made on the physical appearance of the perceived "figure" of evil.[1] A third line of interpretation may set its sights on the film's representation of the news media and its apparent incapacity to do or say anything worthwhile amidst broad-scoped tragedy. The television and radio news reports in the film only serve to heighten the sense of panic in the viewers, as well as in the characters who watch and listen, effectively appealing to and heightening bourgeois anxieties to the point that they enlist in trigger-happy militias.

This new, independent wave of the modern horror genre, then, can be seen, at least in some fashion, to be expressing (whether consciously or not in its run) its ideas about the status of the American political and cultural situation, and it does so by inverting a classic horror technique. Instead of employing the grotesque to signify what is monstrous in the cultural other and what is alien to the ideology of what is deemed normative or status quo, these films reframe the normal and the familiar — including the traditional American family, a collectivity within the Jameson's privileged class — and codify them, instead, to appear as bizarre, repulsive, threatening, and strange — toward a kind of critique of the status quo in American society. The German playwright and critic Bertolt Brecht attempted something similar, though in the realm of theatre. Brecht's critiques, like some of those issued in *Night of the Living Dead, The Last House on the Left,* and *The Texas Chain Saw Massacre,* are leftist shots at the deterministic capitalist tendency to assign arbitrary values to people based on their "worth" for industry and to level those values when their worth becomes obsolete or is used up. Eugene Lunn, a Brechtian critic and historian, writes: "If, as Brecht believed, the capitalist 'normality' numbs the perception of history as endless change and human construction, and veils the contradictions between professed values and social realities, then the 'customary' must be seen as strange and unexpected, thus awakening the dreamer from a 'reified' sleep" (115).

This is not to say, however, that Brecht and these directors share the same performance aesthetic. Indeed, their aesthetics, as much as they can be compared, seem on different ends of the spectrum, since most horror depends, for its effects, on the spectators' emotional investments in it and reactions to it. What I am suggesting here is not that Craven and the others are Brechtians, but that Brecht's estrangement effects provide a helpful hermeneutical tool for thinking through how the grotesque images in these films function. Brecht describes the methodology for accomplishing this startling "shock" into wakefulness is his theory of *verfremdung* (alienation or estrangement) effects, or V-effects (Lunn 115). These are experimental theatrical means by which audiences are alienated from the characters and drama of a play — that is, they are the means by which Brecht attempts to "prevent simple audience 'identification' with individual characters" and with the emotional content in a given performance (117). These effects are produced through detached styles of acting; formal interruptions, such as songs; Brechtian "montage" narrative, which attempts to reveal reality as ever-shifting and contradictory; use of exaggerated costume and makeup; and many others (Brecht "A Short" 193). V-effects are employed in Brecht's epic theater in order to make the everyday world strange, to alienate "audiences from habituated mental assumptions," forcing them to rethink their relationships to the political and social structures of society with the hope that, eventually, they will become able to "truly master the social world" (Lunn 122). Terry Eagleton in his book *Literary Theory* summarizes the intention of V-effects well: Brecht uses "estrangement effects" to

> render the most taken-for-granted aspects of social reality shockingly unfamiliar ... [in order] to rouse the audience to a new critical awareness of them. Far from being concerned to reinforce the audience's sense of security, Brecht wants, as he says, to "create contradictions within them" — to unsettle their convictions, dismantle and refashion their received identities, and expose the unity of this selfhood as an ideological illusion [162].

Night of the Living Dead, The Last House on the Left, and *The Texas Chain Saw Massacre* all work to thwart easy identification with any character or group of characters in the narratives, particularly with the families. This is not a novel or original trajectory among the films I have been discussing. Burton, Gilliam, the Coens, and Lynch all experiment in different ways and to varying degrees with making the hum-drum dominant world seem odd, scary, or stupid; with bursting individual, class, and cultural fantasies; with shock effects, including "gross-outs," viscerally depicted violence, images of corpses, etc.; and with characters' capacities to elicit or alienate spectator identification. The difference with horror — why it would seem to benefit more from a Brechtian analysis than some of these other instances — is that it relies on shock, and the shock must be sustained, necessitating new levels of (usually negative, repulsive, threatening, etc.) grotesquery and spectacle. The difference for the horror films by Romero, Craven, and Hooper is that, while in some respects the agents of shock are certainly gratuitous, they are not without content, and their tendency to alienate, too, has purpose.

Craven's *Last House on the Left*, perhaps, enlists these sorts of narrative estrangement strategies most effectively through a system of character reversals. The film begins with juxtapositions of the average upper-middle class family in their secluded home in the woods and the parodical, dysfunctional gang "family" (perhaps centralized around the actual kinship of the father and son duo of Krug and Junior), making it easy for bourgeois viewers to choose to identify with the doctor, housewife, teenage daughter option rather than the delinquent alternative. But this possibility for identification only exists for half of the film. When Mari (the teenage daughter of the bourgeois family) is tortured, raped, and finally murdered by the gang of thugs, viewers who may have been willing to brave the ordeal of identifying with her through all of the demeaning violence and exploitation are prevented from doing so any longer because she is dead. The logical shift, then, is to identification with Mari's parents, who as yet do not know what has become of their daughter. Viewers can empathize with the bourgeois parents' coming anguish, and even become more morally outraged at the gang of monstrous villains when they pretend to be "plumbing insurance" agents who have had car trouble and take advantage of the Collingwoods' genial hospitality. But when Doctor and Mrs. Collingwood discover what has happened to their daughter at the hands of the very people whom they have invited into their home, the Collingwoods themselves become conniving, blood-thirsty monsters, sadistically enjoying themselves as they revel in the heat of their raving acts of vengeance.

This reversal shifts any possible comfortable audience identification away from the "upstanding" family. The only character left as this second wave of carnage begins is, perhaps, some tenuous identification with Junior, the (relatively) good-hearted junky slave and son of the gang's leader, Krug.

But, then Krug convinces him to "blow [his] brains out." Audiences are left to identify with either the sadistic Collingwoods, who, between them, have bitten off a man's penis (intentionally waiting until he reached the cusp of orgasm), slashed a woman's throat as she flailed helplessly on the side of a swimming pool, and cut a man in half (stem to stern, as it were) with a chain saw, or with the two bumbling idiots who compose the community's law enforcement, who arrive on foot after forgetting to put gas in their patrol car just in time to see Doctor Collingwood's chain saw surgery, and who are peripheral at best to the film's narrative.

With no comfortable point of identification left, then, audiences are forced to see this family, which at the outset of the film was irritatingly normal, as, instead, nearly as bloodthirsty and despicable as the gang of young people who murdered their daughter. Every character in the film comes under the critical inspection of the audience, and that audience can no longer identify with any of them. Instead, they are perhaps encouraged to move to consider the broader cultural and political structures — perhaps even the existential makeup of human beings — all in the context of which such grisly, grotesquely horrible acts of eroticized violence have occurred. Craven uses some of the darkest and most grotesquely realistic images of violence that had been captured in film up to the point when he directed *Last House on the Left*, but they can be interpreted as functioning with the plot analogously to how Brechtian estrangement effects are supposed to work in theater, the logic of which relies on the shock of the grotesque to call the audience's attention back to the social and political factors that background the action of the performance, or even to those cultural or political inconsistencies that may be extant in the audience's own social realities: for the late 1960s, the war in Vietnam and the grim press that accompanied it, Nixon-era political "ethics," as well as the various assassinations, riots, and instances of police brutality in the decade preceding the film, and the white, bourgeois American family's complicity in all of this shines out as an unnerving implication. Craven's film also seems to ask what kind of atavistic tribal unit the American family must be to have the capacity to love or mourn a dead daughter with a vengeance that is at once morally "righteous," brutally violent, and erotically decadent — and far beyond the realm of objective justice.

Night of the Living Dead, The Last House on the Left, and *The Texas Chain Saw Massacre* all attempt to "unsettle" audiences' convictions, and "dismantle and refashion their received identities" (Eagleton 162) by exhibiting disturbingly grotesque representations of the American family — and through the grotesque mode, used for the purposes of Brechtian-style estrangement — these films issue scathing cultural and political critiques on the most basic and utterly familiar of American social institutions: the family. So, as Brecht notes in his glosses on the estrangement effects of the grotesque paintings of Pieter Bruegel the Elder (Brecht, "Narrative" 157–59), as well as in other writings (notably, "*Praktisches zur Expressionismus*"), the grotesque mode in art functions almost naturally or implicitly as a contradictory means through which people (viewers, audiences, spectators, etc.) are estranged or alienated from easy, or lazy, art "appreciation" (qtd. in Lunn 87).

In *Texas Chain Saw Massacre*, the family receives a similar inflection. In the meal scene, after they capture Sally, the family of murderous cannibals can be seen as still grasping at the hollow shell of standard, middle class table manners: their "guest" (Sally) has a seat of honor at the head of the table (though she is tethered to an "arm" chair, which is apparently constructed of human arm bones); they dress for dinner (Leatherface even dons a suit and tie, along with his curled wig, and either a new skin-face-mask or at least some kind of fresh powder base); they also bring down the patriarch of the family (Grandpa) to join them (like an old suitcase out of the attack). When they decide it is time to do away with Sally, it is, of course, Grandpa who must (attempt to) "do the honors" — in good maintenance of the family tradition of having the "father" carve the festive bird, cut the roast, etc., acts which serve to display the symbolic phallic power of the father's position, as well as the deference that the others in the family display towards it. Here that power is impotent, as Grandpa is too enfeebled to perform the task of slaughtering Sally and is only capable of drawing a little blood from her scalp. This may hint at the wider social emasculation of the working class male through the politics of progress under modern capitalism, as Grandpa and his line have been rendered obsolete by the mechanization of the slaughterhouse industry (a running theme in the film).

It is this dinner scene that most powerfully illustrates the contradictory nature of bright and dark grotesque in *Texas Chain Saw Massacre*. Rick Worland remarks, "This scene of the family itself as the monster crystallizes around the dinner table, as if Norman Rockwell were gang-raped by Dali and Hogarth" (222). Wood also notes this scene in his analysis of the unnerving comic aspects of the film (93). This mealtime serves as a brief stay to the dizzying, cartoon-style chase scenes through which Hooper quickens the pace of the film. And though it begins as something of a formal occasion, this meal devolves into the family bickering at one another and finally to their maniacal laughter at Sally's frightened screams. The menu may well feature Kirk or Pam along with some mashed potatoes. The slaughter scene, the scene in which Sally is treated most like an animal, is probably the funniest and most disturbing few minutes of the film. As Leatherface and Hitchhiker hold Sally down like a skinny calf, Grandpa swings and drops the hammer over and over and over, grazing her scalp a few times. Hooper allows the action to go on for far too long, but that is part of what makes it effective grotesquery, and Hooper does something similar with all of the crazy laughing in the preceding moments. Further, at this table, the audience gets probably the best and most focused view of the family as a collective engaged in eating, drinking, yelling, laughing — things that "normal" families do — but that this family does exaggeratedly. By situating the unnerving and ludicrous behavior of this cannibal family within the normal, traditional structures of family mealtime, Hooper draws attention to the family itself *as a family* — as if to comment that this is when this family is happiest or at least when it is its truest self: gathered around a good meal with a young girl to kill. The whole scene seems so ordinary for these men that the audience, perhaps, recognizes something familiar, something of themselves — a faint hint of their own familial experiences — in a family that is so grotesquely alien, but one that is engaged in a traditionally, ideologically "good" family routine. As Wood remarks, "They are held together, and torn apart, by bonds and tensions with which we are familiar," resulting in the effect that "we cannot clearly dissociate ourselves from them" (92).

The "values" of the family, too, seem pretty closely associated with the run-of-the-mill, bourgeois American variety. Each brother has his role. "Old Man," the older brother (or father), holds the real power in the family and generally maintains what tenuous order is present there. Leatherface seems to fulfill a dual function as both brother and mother/sister/woman of the house. The wigs, make-up, the literal "applying of the face," the aprons, the cooking, his inhabitation of the kitchen, and his fits of (sow-squealing) hysterics — all of these seem in line with a paternalistic conception of femininity (to almost parodical proportions). Ironically, Leatherface wields the film's central phallic symbol, the chainsaw, which may refer, again, to his general emasculation within the operations of the family, but which, directed towards outsiders, reveals his obligation to protect and provide for his own (an ironic prototype of Sarah Palin's notion of the "mama grizzly" perhaps). Leatherface, in addition to exorcizing his frustrated and repressed energies and lusts via his "phallic chainsaw," as Wood remarks, in the role of "woman" (and/or mother), he must also wield brute phallic power but within the patriarchal vestiges of traditionally feminizing domestic roles (Wood 91). The "Hitchhiker" is clearly the rebellious teenager who antagonizes the rest of the family, but only to a degree which he knows is within the expectations of his role. Their family has an extreme respect for their forebears (who literally "live" above). And they seem to have invested much of themselves, their creativity, and their resources in their home, as the elaborate Dali-esque bone/feather "art" and the "found object" pieces in the yard, the peculiar kitchen specifications, etc. denote (Worland 218).

The grotesque in these depictions functions according to both Kayserian and Bakhtinian inflections, and therefore the film fits best with a conflation of the two polar theories. The human as meat analogy, which Hooper admirably and, at times, quite subtly sustains throughout the film, works well for both "bright" and "dark" grotesquery. The first appearance of the barbecue at Old Man's gas station should draw viewers' attention, especially after the establishing shots of the juicy corpses oozing in the sun at the film's outset. And after Leatherface, wearing his butcher's apron and skin mask, kills and dismembers Kirk and hangs Pam on a meat hook (and soon after puts her in a chest freezer), audiences may recall the Hitchhiker's conversation with Franklin in the van about the slaughterhouses and Hooper's eerie shots of those sprawling buildings out the van windows.

The American family receives a few possible critiques in Romero's *Night of the Living Dead*. First, the zombies are not only flesh-eating monsters, but they are also the brothers, sisters, fathers, mothers, etc. of the living nonzombies. Romero bookends the film with reminders of this theme: the pair of siblings encounter a zombie relative in the graveyard in the establishing scene of the film, and the young man, Johnny, (as "living dead") returns to the safe-house for his sister near the end of the film and violently drags her away from safety as other zombies nip and grab at her.

This version of the theme, too, reveals a family that turns in on itself, cannibalizes its children, parents, relatives out of blind — but very basic — hunger or desire.

Another layer is the construction of an American "family" within the Gothic space of the house under siege (a motif used in all three of the films). The characters throng to this farmhouse (again, an out-of-the-way safe-house in a proverbial "heartland" of America), and, as they do so, they become a kind of family: the last living nonzombies around — an American collective — under the (contested) leadership of Ben. Within this family are two actual family units, the Coopers (father, mother, and daughter) and the young lovers, who are exploded after only a few minutes. Because of the failure of this family-unit to get along together properly in the home, everyone ends up dead by the end of the film. One of the more dramatic and grotesque images in *Night of the Living Dead* is the scene in which Harry and Helen's "zombified daughter," Karen, assaults her parents, stabbing her mother over and over (Becker 51). Little Karen then begins devouring their bodies. The family is divided against itself and devours itself. It is a disgusting scene, but its grotesqueness functions according to the perceived contradiction between the innocence and youth of the little girl (who is 9 or 10 perhaps) and her wild but passionless deeds. Like Hooper, Romero allows many of the more disturbing images (such as the scene in which Karen stabs her mother) to occupy the screen for long periods of time without cutting away. These inconsistencies draw attention to themselves almost as grotesque V-effects, which can conceivably boomerang the audience's capacity for critique to what underlies analogous horrific situations in their own cultural or political lives, rather than allowing them to enjoy or appreciate the sheer spectacle of, or formal artistry behind, the carnage in the way one may approach the beauty of a scene of murder in a Caravaggio painting or something. The grotesque estranges such a perspective, renders it impossible.

Interpreting this radical wave of foundational modern horror films through the critical framework Robin Wood works out in "The American Nightmare" and through Jameson's comments on the political significance of modern Gothic films allows an opportunity to focus on some of the more notably grotesque elements in these films and their somewhat Brechtian function to alienate audiences from easy identification with characters and/or from film art "appreciation" — but all as the result of experimentation within the rudiments of the horror genre. Horror, in these films, then, becomes a vehicle that is made capable of a radical critique of the political and cultural situation of the America of the 1960s and 70s, and within this, of the ideological apparatus of the traditional (patriarchal) American family through its employment of the grotesque as part of the basic mechanics of the genre. While certain aspects of the films retain the residue of cultural oppressions of the age, the films' critical theses are transgressive in their subversion of cultural norms or ideology associated with the status quo. This approach complicates Jameson's notion of the function of a "U.S. Public" in classic horror by parsing it into a dynamic binary of sorts, but neither pole (the monster nor the victim) is elementally evil or good: they persist in intersecting, contradicting, and exchanging places with one another. Both are unmistakably American, though, and both are constructed within the sociopolitical contexts that emerge from the very heart of the primary ways in which bourgeois America has traditionally defined itself. Both are, by turns, pathetic, ridiculous, and terrifying.

VIII. Grim Reveries, or the Ambiguities

[N]o man can ever feel his own identity aright except his eyes be closed; as if darkness were indeed the proper element of our essences, though light be more congenial to our clayey part.

— Herman Melville, *Moby-Dick*

What unlike things must meet and mate.

— Herman Melville, "Art"

Tangling the Loose Ends

The grotesque as the conflict of opposites, or, more precisely, as the paradoxical complex of relationships among and between these various forms of duality, as they may be seen to function in the film-worlds of Tim Burton, Terry Gilliam, Joel and Ethan Coen, and David Lynch, has been the critical center of this study of the grotesque and its exegesis in contemporary American film. But I am also suggesting in the preceding discussion of slasher-horror and politics that the auteur approach should not be married to inquiry concerning the grotesque in film, for the strictures of genre filmmaking and genre criticism can invite novel explorations of what is possible within those bounds. Further, initiating such critical inquiry from a variety of perspectives (political, social, cultural theory, etc.), rather than from an auteur approach (even a "soft" auteur approach) singly, allows critical consideration of the conceptual slipperiness associated with the grotesque, and such a method can give rise to potentially fruitful ways to interpret its functions from the various theoretical positions from which one must begin if one is to have any hope of ascertaining its meaning. This study, though, investigates the directors it does because they slip into and out of genres, often merging them, minimalizing them, exploding them, and so on. Moreover, these filmmakers, often directly, explore the grotesque, and, though this study demonstrates these directors' engagement with the grotesque — Burton's through the duality of the "carnival" and the "official," Gilliam's through the related binaries of madness and sanity and mythic and rational thinking, the Coens' with attention to the paradoxically existential copresence of the catastrophic and the mundane, and Lynch's with an approach built around interpreting the uncanny effects of duality or multiplicity — a more thoroughgoing interpretation of the grotesque in contemporary American film can be apprehended by looking across the breadth of the films by these visionary directors.

The preceding chapters illustrate various positions that can be read as theses related to the particular director in question, but they also represent the incrementally invasive effects the grotesque can be seen to have on culture itself— moving centripetally from "culture" to "subject." While Burton's and Gilliam's films can be placed within related cultural and ideological binaries of the conflicting poles associated with carnival and its official other, imagination and rationality, madness and sanity, and the threats of each to its other, the Coens' films, in my reading, attempt to depict the effects of such conflicts in the ambiguous, exploded moments of the interval in which they reach their climaxes in particular characters' lives. This interpretation places the Coens' films *within* the "parallax gap" (to borrow Žižek's phrase once more), the "moments of extremis" (to use Harry Crews' language), between or within the conflict of opposites, which reveals this gap to be fraught with energy, anxiety, and movement or the notable absence thereof, none of which really reach a point of conveying meaning beyond the ambivalent excesses of these "charged" moments themselves (Žižek, *Parallax* 4; Crews in *Searching for the Wrong-Eyed Jesus*). Lynch's films, then, transport the effects of such conflicts to within the subject itself— in the forms of fantasies, nightmares, and variously manifested threats that emerge from within the subject or from some metaphysical "outside" that works its way within. His films feature such "internalized" variations on these related binaries or dualisms in which many of the formerly "external" conflicts recur within the mind or are reproduced from within the self, within which the subject recognizes itself in a new and troubling way.[1] Each approach centers in on a different emphasis of the manifestation of the conflicts of opposites, and each examines the grotesque in a way that can be interpreted as characteristic of his/their (in the case of the Coens) cinematic style to represent as film-worlds the contexts in which such dialectical paradoxes of the grotesque arise and affect the human condition. And one could look to other contemporary filmmakers, such as Quentin Tarantino, Jim Jarmusch, Paul Thomas Anderson, Spike Jones, Wes Anderson, and Darren Aronofsky, among others, whose work may, at times, suggest similar but stylistically unique variations of grotesque.

The Grotesque as Metaphysical Parallax: Melville and the Paradoxes of Forbidden Wisdom

Perhaps an even more appropriate analogy for dialectically paradoxical relations of opposites out of which grotesque art is born than the Moebius strip, then, is the human condition. Herman Melville's short poem, "Art," is instructive in articulating the dual nature of art itself and humanity with it: art here captures, represents, and paradoxically transcends the conflicts and oppositions inherent to human being as well as those inherent to its highest form of expressing itself, of its communication:

> In placid hours well pleased we dream
> Of many a brave unbodied scheme.
> But form to lend, pulsed life create,
> What unlike things must meet and mate:
> A flame to melt — a wind to freeze;
> Sad patience — joyous energies;
> Humility — yet pride and scorn;
> Instinct and study; love and hate;
> Audacity — reverence. These must mate
> And fuse with Jacob's mystic heart,
> To wrestle with the angel — Art [262].

The epigraph above from Melville's *Moby-Dick* relates something of this relationship, too, in its preoccupation with light and dark, body and essence, self and world, his protagonist thrown between and among them (55). In context, the quote arises out of one of Ishmael's many reflections in a seemingly insignificant moment early in *Moby-Dick*. Ishmael observes that in bed, in order to feel most at home with himself and in his surroundings, "I have a way of always keeping my eyes shut.... Because no man can ever feel his own identity aright except his eyes be closed; as if

190

darkness were indeed the proper element of our essences, though light be more congenial to our clayey part" (55). The scene becomes more interesting and troubling with the inclusion of another layer of meaning with the next sentence: "Upon opening my eyes then, and coming out of my pleasant and self-created darkness into the imposed and coarse outer gloom of the unilluminated twelve-o'clock-at-night, I experienced a disagreeable revulsion" (55). Not only does one find in this pericope Melville's inversion of the more common Christian identification of human essence (the soul or spirit) with light (God, the "divine spark," inner light, etc.), but Ishmael's commentary divides even darkness against itself, as that which is "self-created," internal, metaphysical, comforting, homely and that which is imposed, external, gloomy, coarse, and alien to the open eye, to the embodied essence, the "clayey part." Ishmael's "disagreeable revulsion" arises from the tables being turned on him: his expectation and control over his own navigation of himself in the world is made impotent by the world, whether by its malevolence or by its dumb indifference. The inner has been externalized against his will. This banal maxim of his identity has been universalized rather dramatically in the world outside, and his recognition of it brings revulsion because its familiarity is alienated. It is a brief instant of Ishmael's experience of the uncanny logic of the grotesque — a kind of metaphysical parallax — but in form it provides a structural analogy between the human condition and the philosophy of the grotesque.

And Melville does not stop here. He braids another strand into this line, for the simultaneity of conflicting opposites in Ishmael's blackness is parallel to Ishmael's turn on whiteness some hundred or so pages later. In the chapter "The Whiteness of the Whale," Melville develops the "vague, nameless horror" that whiteness is capable of in addition (and opposition) to its capacity for refining and enhancing beauty (157). Whiteness is associated with "whatever is sweet, and honorable, and sublime," but it is also the "the crowning attribute" of what is terrible in the polar bear, the white shark, the white squall, the dead, ghosts, and the list goes on (158–61). Bradley Johnson, in *The Characteristic Theology of Herman Melville: Aesthetics, Politics, Duplicity*, observes that in Ishmael's philosophical economy, the fundamental terror of such whiteness is "that it is simultaneously surface and depth, emptiness and fullness, life and death; both the 'very veil of the Christian's deity' and the defining mark of this deity's absence" (88).

Part 4. Into the World and Back Again

Hubert Dreyfus and Sean Dorrance Kelly, in *All Things Shining: Reading the Western Classics to Find Meaning in a Secular Age*, identify a corpus of instances of this peculiar logic throughout *Moby-Dick* (in defense of a different thesis). In addition to Melville's reflection on whiteness, they point also to his preoccupation with paradoxes and contradictions in the describing the white whale's almost Yahwehic stratagem of at once revealing and concealing himself from his devotees/murderers (172). They refer to the luscious remains of the whale from "A Bower in the Aracides," the skeleton of which has been woven over with vines: "Life folded Death," Ishmael utters, "Death trellised Life; the grim god wived with youthful life" (Melville 360). And Dreyfus and Kelly also identify the "unseen weaver" from this passage — the deity who, by the electric hum of his own creative act, deafens himself to his creation and those created mortals to each other — with the object of Pip's maddening vision in "The Castaway" (Melville 360, Dreyfus and Kelly 179). In the horrifying experience of being left behind, of being isolated in the middle of an endless sea, of having his "infinite soul ... carried down alive to wondrous depths, where strange shapes of the unwarped primal world glided to and fro," Pip sees "God's foot upon the treadle of the loom" (Melville 334). The consequence of the ship-keeper's grim reverie is a forbidden wisdom that obliterates his ego, leaving behind a vacant and mad, but paradoxically wise, fool (of Shakespearean proportions). He is thereby rendered radically open to the knowledge he has gained: he has seen the ultimate truth of the universe, and "what he has learned is that there is no deep, underlying truth there to see" (Dreyfus and Kelly 179–80).

What Melville develops in *Moby-Dick* through Ishmael's perspective, then, is a conception of the human condition, one that, in a way, prefigures the paradoxes of "Art," published forty years later. And the upshot of Pip's wisdom from the depths of the primordial chaos shares the same philosophical trajectory as Ishmael's earlier conclusions about whiteness and his reflections on his experience of darkness. As Johnson puts it, quoting Schelling, Ishmael "is consumed by the melancholic (and thus creative) implications of 'the incomprehensible *base of reality in things*, the indivisible remainder, that which with the greatest exertion cannot be resolved in understanding but remains eternally in the ground'" (88). Whiteness, darkness, truth — for Ishmael, they are "indivisible remainders" behind, within, between things, joining us with the world, our ideas with material objects

192

around us, cutting us off from the world, from things, from ourselves — they are backgrounds upon which the comic and tragic drama of life persists simultaneously as we fruitlessly exert ourselves in our attempts to bring resolutions, to make them. They are parallel but particular blanknesses that can devastate and horrify as much as they astound or delight because they invite contradiction, opposition, confliction, combination, fragmentation, synthesis, and scission — not only of those phenomena which would be "written" upon them — but also in the various ways in which they may touch each other, in which they "meet and mate" (to use Melville's words in "Art"). This is the philosophical territory of the grotesque: the grotesque names this level of our conflict-ridden interchange ("exertion" in the quote from Schelling, "to wrestle" in the Melville poem) with reality aesthetically expressed.

As with Ishmael's uncanny moment of recognition in the dark, his realization about the ineffability of whiteness, or Pip's mad sea-born sagacity, our categories, the contents of these categories, the meanings and associations with which they are invested, and the crippling effects their confusion entails for us — these are the junctures whereat the grotesque can emerge as the (metaphysical) aesthetic context within which such confusion arises, can be recognized, and/or expressed. It works according to a principle of macerated mimesis in its isolation, amplification, inversion, division, unification, etc. of any of the competing poles of the paradoxes between which human being finds itself drawn: light and dark, high and low, inside and outside, body and essence, contentment and anxiety, creation and destruction, life and death, good and evil, pleasure and pain, transcendence and obfuscation, the divine and the demonic, movement and stasis, self and other, official and carnival, imaginativeness and bleak materialism, reason and madness, mythic and modern, and the list goes on. Whether the grotesque finds expression as a literary mode, an artistic style, an aesthetic dimension, a pattern of thought (archetype, etc.), a metaphysical reality, a social ideology, or something else, it is utterly bound up with the human. Perhaps this is why its fruits seem forbidden but necessary. Perhaps this is why it can elicit desire and disgust, laughter and revulsion — or, simply put, love and hate and everything that comes with them — all at once. The grotesque is caught up with the breadth, depth, and confusion of what it means to be human.

So, I close this study by returning, in a way, to the darkness of Plato's cave. But Melville reminds us, having perhaps internalized Plato's message, that within and around and between the flickering images of light that we perceive in the world there (or indeed in its cinematic analog) is darkness, an uncontrollable, multivalent, and ungraspable absence that paradoxically bespeaks its presence as some mysterious "other" aspect that is within us, making us who we are, but that threateningly dwarfs or nullifies us as we recognize that it is not ours, that we have not created it, and that it is an identical opposite to the whiteness and light, which, at first glimpse, seemed the medium of our enlightenment: Life folding Death, Death trellising Life (to borrow a turn from Melville). As far as I can tell, the grotesque is something like the context through which we begin to approach the recognition of Melville's dynamic truths of darkness and light, which seem to metaphorize the "charged" paradoxes being human. It names the "charged" "spaces" wherein the slippage between our structures (be they artistic, linguistic, symbolic, etc.) and the reality they reach for is dramatized. And, perhaps, as Plato's Socrates realizes in "The Apology," the starting-place for learning wisdom from paradox is an honest curiosity and a philosophical sense of humility, one with which he enters the heart of the paradox itself: "For I'm only too aware that I've no claim to being wise in anything great or small" (652).

Chapter Notes

Preface

1. I should admit here that my interpretations of both Bacon's and Seuss's work is rendered in very broad strokes: apologies to Baconians and Seussians alike. I fully admit that that there are exceptions to the general picture painted here.

Introduction

1. In *Film Genre: Hollywood and Beyond*, Barry Langford argues that even as narrative cinema emerged as melodrama, a concept he uses to describe pregeneric cinema of the silent period, films are already being drawn toward generic poles, often associated with the class positions of viewers. He identifies melodramatic pathos as the center around which films as different as Griffith's *Birth of a Nation* and Chaplin's *The Kid* orient themselves, even as such films gravitate towards the confines of the genre film (42–43).

2. Bordwell and Staiger, in "Historical Implications of the Hollywood Cinema," challenge the degree to which "New Hollywood" breaks the conventions of "Old Hollywood." They point to the "process of stylistic assimilation" to the aesthetics of European art films among New Hollywood filmmakers as analogous to the workings of a similar process at work in Old Hollywood's integration of the aesthetics of German Expressionism and Soviet montage. Such a move, though it appears to be an aesthetic rift, fits into the narrative of how classical Hollywood cinema has functioned in the past (373). While such an argument provides a nuanced interpretation of this fraught historical "moment," it changes relatively little of the narrative Cook unfolds, though it does provide an argument for the continuity of Classical Hollywood across aesthetic categories rather than locating it necessarily with structures that had sustained it in Old Hollywood.

3. To some degree, locating the grotesque in contemporary, specifically, "American filmmakers," is a distinction both convenient and artificial. Just as my inclusion of Hitchcock in the brief historical sketch of American filmmaking may be challenged by the mere fact of his British nationality, similar challenges could be made to my treatment of Terry Gilliam as an "American" filmmaker, since his career in film has only intermittently returned him to the United States and since a minority of his films have been funded with American money (the latter of which could also be leveled at the ascription of "American" to some of Lynch's films). While I fully recognize these limitations to the selection of my material, I could defend my choices by pointing to the American citizenship of each filmmaker (none of whom, to my knowledge, has renounced his citizenship), the influence of their films on American cinema, etc. Either

way, the convenience of being able to gather the four directors together for the purposes of study outweighs what may amount to the (minor) imprecision of calling them "American."

4. See Chapter VII.

Part 1

1. See Harpham's discussion of Kant and Hegel on the grotesque in *On the Grotesque: Strategies of Contradiction in Art and Literature*, 180–85, Schopenhauer's "The Artist and the Sublime," and (along with it) M. A. R. Habib's discussion of Schopenhauer in *A History of Literary Criticism and Theory*, 503–7.

Chapter II

1. I should qualify that the designation of the artists mentioned in Doty's essay, whose art was collected and exhibited in the Whitney Museum of American Art for the project for which the essay was written, as "avant-garde" may be problematic, since the collection includes such diverse material as political cartoons, comic book illustrations, and photographs that may or may not qualify the artists behind them as "avant-garde." However, the impulse behind this collection certainly seems to derive from such a position, and, indeed, most of the work for the exhibition would probably fit quite well with what the term describes.

Chapter III

1. Although there has been some controversy over the degree to which *The Nightmare Before Christmas* is Burton's own film, as it was directed by Henry Selick, whom Burton asked to direct the film while Burton himself was shooting *Batman Returns* and *Ed Wood* (Selick qtd. in Felperin 104). Selick made the film, though Burton, who acted as producer for *Nightmare*, apparently maintained "creative control" over the way in which Selick developed the poem and sketches Burton had produced as a young animator at Disney (Smith and Matthews 147). The film was released under the title *Tim Burton's The Nightmare Before Christmas*, and many on the team (notably, Denise Di Novi, Caroline Thompson, Danny Elfman, Rick Heinrichs, Catherine O'Hara, Glen Shadix, and Paul Ruebens aka Pee-wee Herman, among others) Selick put together to make the film are Burton regulars (Smith and Matthews 144–45, 149–51). Selick put the matter this way in an interview with Leslie Felperin: "It's as though [Burton] laid the egg, but I sat on it, so it came out looking like both of us" (105). See the note on the auteurist approach (section III) in the Introduction.

2. Burton comments on the comic aspect of a headless character in an interview with David Mills: "Without a head" the character is "kind of almost funny.... [Y]ou start to laugh and you get kinda excited and it becomes a fantasy character" (149).

Chapter IV

1. I will be focusing in this chapter on Gilliam's films, but I will not be including his film work with the Monty Python comedy group. While his animations between

the Python sketches and *Monty Python and the Holy Grail,* which Gilliam co-directed with Terry Jones, are certainly grotesque in various ways and merit some scholarship, the Python material seems to reflect more equally shared labor between members of the group than those films in which Gilliam is at the creative helm. Further, Ellen Bishop has already written a rather exhaustive essay on the grotesque in *Holy Grail.* For more on this see Bishop's "Bakhtin, Carnival and Comedy: The New Grotesque in *Monty Python and the Holy Grail.*"

2. I am thinking here of Kayser's discussion of the experience of the grotesque in the act of reception of the culturally "unfamiliar" (181). He discusses the possible disjuncture between the producer's intention in making art and its possible reception as grotesque by those unaffiliated with the cultural vocabulary of images. Thomson's notion of the "unintentional grotesque" may also fit here (65).

3. The Moon King is so Cartesian that his head and his body retain separate names, Ray and Roger, respectively. Gilliam throws in as many jokes aimed at Descartes as possible. The floating, moon-head king despises his body: "I haven't got time for flatulence and orgasms." The cogito of the king is predictably arrogant about his intellectual pursuits, at one point explaining to the Baron: "I, that is, the head, where the brilliant and important parts are located, is now ruling the known universe. And that which I don't know, I create: Cogito ergo es: I think, therefore, you is!" This episode provides another layer of *Munchausen*'s critique of the "age of reason," here, via a novel inversion of Bakhtinian "degradation": instead of "the lowering of all that is high, spiritual, ideal, and abstract," which the moon sequence does, of course, on one level, Gilliam elevates the grizzled, aged, mad, Munchausen, and next to the too Cartesian Moon King, the baron seems quite sane and able-bodied (Bakhtin, *Rabelais* 19).

4. By "too alive," I am referring to the excessive powers of Munchausen's servants: the dwarf whose lung capacity is inestimable, the impossibly strong giant, and the marksman whose eyes can see for hundreds of miles unaided.

5. For Gilliam on archetypes and mythology, see the chapter on *Jabberwocky* in McCabe's *Dark Knights and Holy Fools*; chapters 4 and 8 in *Gilliam on Gilliam*; and his interview with Jerdi Costa and Sergi Sanchez, "Childhood, Vocation, and First Experiences of a Rebel Dreamer."

6. See Gramsci's *Selections from the Prison Notebooks,* "State and Civil Society" (206–76) and Althusser's *On Ideology* (especially pages 1–51).

Chapter V

1. For discussions of the Coens and postmodernism, pastiche, culture, reception, etc. see Chapter 2: "The Coen Brothers: Postmodern Filmakers," (especially pages 44–45 and 51–60) of R. Barton Palmer's *Joel and Ethan Coen.* See also Allan Smithee's "What Condition the Postmodern Condition Is In: Collecting Culture in *The Big Lebowski,*" *The Year's Work* in Lebowski *Studies,* 255–75.

2. Paul Martin and Valarie Renegar also draw out the connection between *The Big Lebowski* and Bakhtin's theory of the carnivalesque in "'The Man for His Time': *The Big Lebowski* as Carnivalesque Social Critique." In this essay, they catalog the film's adherence to the carnival aesthetic, highlighting *The Big Lebowski*'s tendency toward inverting social hierarchies in the film's utilization of grotesque realism and "structural and grammatical experimentation" (304).

Chapter VI

1. Lynch qtd. in Rodley x.

2. As I noted in Chapter II, Meindl's situation of the grotesque within Heideggerian metaphysics more thoroughly and beautifully frames his theory of the concept within broadly existential philosophy (see Meindl, 28–35), but for the present purposes, I think teasing out his reliance on and mutual integration of Bakhtin's and Kayser's theories is enough to move the argument along.

3. Ultimately, Hurley undermines this distinction between horror and Gothic by embracing a much broader definition of Gothic literature that would encompass horror as well. She claims that Gothic reemerges from time to time. Gothic plots tend toward the exorbitant; Gothic settings are "overcharged" with an oppressive atmosphere of foreboding and fear; and it is generally preoccupied with deranged human subjectivity and "extreme behaviors." Gothic concerns itself with communicating excess in its navigation and management of the cultural taboos (193–94). The distinction, I think, still points to the shifts in Lynch's use of images that I discuss in the rest of the paragraph.

Chapter VII

1. This is one place where a race reading fits as well: one of the interviewees in *The American Nightmare* also made mention of the image of a young black man being shot, especially after the assassinations of Malcolm X and M. L. King, was an especially bold and political decision for Romero to include.

Chapter VIII

1. These associations with directors need not be hard and fast "rules" by which the ascriptions I am noting here "need" to take place for the sake of my thesis. Indeed, in more isolated cases of this or that film, these interpretations are nearly interchangeable, as far as the directors who produce them: for example, Lynch's *Wild at Heart* bears stylistic resemblances to the characteristically physical features that I point out in my interpretation of the Coens' films; *The Hudsucker Proxy* owes much in its depiction of urban cityscape to Gilliam's *Brazil*; Gilliam's *Tideland* works in a similar thematic vein to Lynch's approach to the ambiguously fused mind-worlds created by characters in his films; and one could work this circle around among this group of filmmakers a number of times and arrive at similar approaches to their resemblances.

Works Cited

Adorno, Theodor W. *Aesthetic Theory*. Trans. and ed. Robert Hullot-Kentor. Min-
neapolis: Minnesota University Press, 1997. Print.
_____. *The Culture Industry*. 1991. Trans. Anson G. Rabinbach, et al. Ed. J. M. Bern-
stein. London: Routledge, 2003. Print.
Althusser, Louis. *On Ideology*. 1971. London: Verso, 2008. Print.
The American Nightmare: A Celebration of Horror from the Golden Age of Fright. 2003.
Dir. Adam Simon. New Video Group. 2004. DVD.
Ashbrook, John. *Terry Gilliam*. Harpenden: Pocket Essentials, 2000. Print.
Auerbach, Erich. *Mimesis: The Representation of Reality in Western Literature*. 1968.
Trans. Willard R. Trask. Princeton: Princeton University Press, 2003. Print.
Bakhtin, Mikhail. *Rabelais and His World*. 1968. Trans. Helene Iswolsky. Bloomington:
Indiana University Press, 1984. Print.
_____. *Speech Genres and Other Late Essays*. Ed. Caryl Emerson and Michael Holquist.
Trans. Vern W. McGee. Austin: Universtiy of Texas Press, 1986. Print.
Baudelaire, Charles. "Hymn to Beauty." Trans. Dorothy Martin. *Flowers of Evil: A
Selection*. Ed. Marthiel and Jackson Mathews. New York: New Directions, 1955.
29–31. Print.
_____. "Reversibility." Trans. F. P. Sturm. Marthiel and Jackson Mathews 41–43. Print.
Becker, Matt. "A Point of Little Hope: Hippie Horror Films and the Politics of Ambiva-
lence." *The Velvet Light Trap* 57 (2006): 42–59. Print.
Bennett, Andrew, and Nicholas Royle. *Introduction to Literature, Criticism, and Theory*,
2d ed. London: Prentice Hall, 1999. Print.
Bergan, Ronald. *The Coen Brothers*. New York: Thunder's Mouth, 2000. Print.
Bergson, Henri. *Laughter*. Trans. Cloudesley Brereton. New York: Macmillan, 1928.
Print.
Bishop, Ellen. "Bakhtin, Carnival and Comedy: The New Grotesque in *Monty Python
and the Holy Grail*." *Film Criticism* 15.1 (1990): 49–64. Print.
Blackburn, Simon. *Plato's Republic: A Biography*. New York: Atlantic, 2006. Print.
Blake, William. *The Marriage of Heaven and Hell*. Oxford: Oxford University Press,
1975. Print.
_____. "The Song of Los." *Blake: Complete Writings*. Ed. Geoffrey Keynes. London:
Oxford University Press, 1972. 245–48. Print.
Bordwell, David. "The Classical Hollywood Style, 1917–60." Bordwell, Staiger, and
Thompson 1–84. Print.
_____, and Janet Staiger. "Historical Implications of the Classical Hollywood Cinema."
Bordwell, Staiger, and Thompson 365–85. Print.
_____, and Kristin Thompson. *Film Art: An Introduction*, 6th ed. New York: McGraw-
Hill, 2001. Print.

_____, Janet Staiger, and Kristin Thompson. *The Classical Hollywood Cinema: Film Style and Mode of Production to 1960.* New York: Columbia University Press, 1985. Print.

Bosch, Hieronymus. *Altar of the Hermits.* Palazzo Ducale, Venice. Painting.

_____. *The Last Judgment.* Genaldegalerie der Akademie der bildenden Kunste, Vienna. Painting.

Boyd, Katrina G. "Pastiche and Postmodernism in *Brazil.*" *Cinefocus* I (1990): 33–42.

Breskin, David. "Tim Burton." Fraga 37–88. Print.

Brecht, Bertolt. "Alienation Effects in the Narrative Pictures of the Elder Brueghel." *Brecht on Theatre: The Development of an Aesthetic.* Trans. and Ed. John Willett. New York: Methuen, 1957, 157–59. Print.

_____. "A Short Organum of Theatre." *Brecht on Theatre: The Development of an Aesthetic.* Trans. and ed. John Willett. New York: Methuen, 1957. 179–205. Print.

Brottman, Mikita. "Kinda Funny Lookin': Steve Buscemi's Disorderly Body." *The Coen Brothers'* Fargo. Ed. William G. Luhr. Cambridge: Cambridge University Press, 2004. 77–91. Print.

Browning, Tod, dir. *Dracula.* 1931. Universal, 2006. DVD.

_____, dir. *Freaks.* 1932. Warner Bros., 2004. DVD.

Burton, Tim. *The Melancholy Death of Oyster Boy & Other Stories.* New York: HarperCollins, 1997. Print.

_____, dir. *Alice in Wonderland.* Disney, 2010. Film.

_____, dir. *Batman.* 1989. Warner Bros., 2009. DVD.

_____, dir. *Batman Returns.* 1992. Warner Bros., 2009. DVD.

_____, dir. *Beetlejuice.* 1988. Geffen, 2008. DVD.

_____, dir. *Big Fish.* 2003. Columbia, 2004. DVD.

_____, dir. *Charlie and the Chocolate Factory.* 2005. Warner Bros., 2005. DVD.

_____, dir. *Edward Scissorhands.* 1990. Fox, 2000. DVD.

_____, dir. *Ed Wood.* 1994. Touchstone, 2004. DVD.

_____, dir. *Frankenweenie.* 1982. Disney. *Tim Burton's the Nightmare Before Christmas.* Special ed. 1993. Touchstone, 2000. DVD.

_____, dir. *Mars Attacks!* 1996. Warner Bros., 2004. DVD.

_____, dir. *Planet of the Apes.* 2001. Fox, 2001. DVD.

_____, dir. *Sweeney Todd: The Demon Barber of Fleet Street.* 2007. Dreamworks, 2008. DVD.

_____, dir. *Tim Burton's Corpse Bride.* 2005. Warner Bros., 2006. DVD.

_____, dir. *Vincent.* 1982. Disney. *Tim Burton's the Nightmare Before Christmas.* Special ed. 1993. Touchstone, 2000. DVD.

_____, dir. *The World of Stainboy.* 2000. *The Tim Burton Collective.* Web. 15 Jan. 2010.

_____, prod. *Tim Burton's The Nightmare Before Christmas.* 1993. Touchstone, 2000. DVD.

Camus, Albert. *The Myth of Sisyphus and Other Essays.* Trans. Justin O'Brien. New York: Vintage, 1955. Print.

_____. *The Stranger.* Trans. Matthew Ward. New York: Vintage, 1988. Print.

Carroll, Lewis. *Alice's Adventures in Wonderland.* 1865. New York: Barnes and Noble, 2004. Print.

Carroll, Noel. *The Philosophy of Horror, Or Paradoxes of the Heart.* New York: Routledge, 1990. Print.

Cassuto, Leonard. *The Inhuman Race: The Racial Grotesque in American Literature and Culture.* New York: Columbia University Press, 1997. Print.

Chaplin, Charles, dir. *The Gold Rush*. 1925. Warner, 2003. DVD.

_____, dir. *The Kid*. 1921. Warner, 2004. DVD.

_____, dir. *Modern Times*. 1936. Warner, 2003. DVD.

_____, dir. *Monsieur Verdoux*. 1947. Warner, 2004. DVD.

Childers, Joseph, and Gary Hentzi. *Columbia Dictionary of Modern Literary and Cultural Criticism*. New York: Columbia University Press, 1995.

Childs, Elizabeth C. "Eden's Other: Gauguin and the Ethnographic Other." *Modern Art and the Grotesque*. Ed. Frances S. Connelly. Cambridge: Cambridge University Press, 2003. 175–92. Print.

Chion, Michel. *David Lynch*, 2d ed. Trans. Robert Julian and Trista Selous. London: British Film Institute, 2006. Print.

Christie, Ian, ed. *Gilliam on Gilliam*. London: Faber and Faber, 1999. Print.

Ciment, Michel, and Hubert Niogret. "The Logic of Soft Drugs." Trans. Paul Buck and Catherine Petit. Woods, *Joel and Ethan Coen* 167–173. Print.

Clark, John R. *The Modern Satiric Grotesque and Its Traditions*. Lexington: University Press of Kentucky, 1991. Print.

Clayborough, Arthur. *The Grotesque in English Literature*. London: Oxford University Press, 1965. Print.

Coen, Joel, dir. *Barton Fink*. 1991. Fox, 2003. DVD.

_____, dir. *The Big Lebowski*. 1998. Universal, 1998. DVD.

_____, dir. *Blood Simple*. 1985. Circle, 2001. DVD.

_____, dir. *O Brother, Where Art Thou?* 2000. Touchstone, 2001. DVD.

_____, and Ethan Coen, dirs. *Burn After Reading*. 2008. Universal, 2008. DVD.

_____, dir. *Fargo*. 1996. MGM, 2000. DVD.

_____, dir. *The Hudsucker Proxy*. 1994. Warner Bros., 1999. DVD.

_____, dir. *Intolerable Cruelty*. 2003. Universal, 2004. DVD.

_____, and Ethan Coen, dirs. *The Ladykillers*. 2004. Touchstone, 2004. DVD.

_____, dir. *The Man Who Wasn't There*. 2001. Universal, 2002. DVD.

_____, dir. *Miller's Crossing*. 1990. Fox, 2003. DVD.

_____, dir. *Raising Arizona*. 1987. Fox, 1999. DVD.

_____, and Ethan Coen, dirs. *No Country for Old Men*. 2007. Paramount, 2008. DVD.

_____, and Ethan Coen, dirs. *A Serious Man*. 2009. Focus, 2010. DVD.

_____, and Ethan Coen, dirs. *True Grit*. Paramount, 2010. Film.

Comentale, Edward P. "'I'll Keep Rolling Along': Some Notes on Singing Cowboys and Bowling Alleys in *The Big Lebowski*." Comentale and Jaffe 228–252. Print.

_____, and Arron Jaffe, eds. *The Year's Work in* Lebowski *Studies*. Bloomington: University of Indiana Press, 2009. Print.

Conley, Matthew. "Imagining the Past: The Films of Terry Gilliam." MA Thesis. Middle Tenn. State U, 1999. Print.

Cook, David A. *A History of Narrative Film*, 3d ed. New York: Norton, 1996. Print.

Coppola, Francis Ford, dir. *Apocalypse Now*. 1979. Paramount, 2004. DVD.

Corliss, Richard. "Battier and Battier." Woods, *Tim Burton* 77–79. Print.

Costa, Jerdi, and Sergi Sanchez. "Childhood, Vocation, and First Experiences of a Rebel Dreamer." Sterritt and Rhodes 170–83. Print.

Coughlin, Paul. "Acting for Real: Performing Characters in *Miller's Crossing* and *Fargo*." *The Journal of Popular Culture* 41.2 (2008): 224–44. Print.

Danow, David K. *The Spirit of Carnival: Magical Realism and the Grotesque*. Lexington: University Press of Kentucky, 1995. Print.

Works Cited

Dargis, Manohla. Rev. of *Big Fish*, dir. Tim Burton. Woods, *Tim Burton* 174–75. Print.

Denby, David. "Babes in Cinema Land." Woods, *Tim Burton* 37–39. Print.

Domino, Christophe. *Francis Bacon: Painter of a Dark Vision*. New York: Discoveries, 1997. Print.

Doty, Robert. *Human Concern/Personal Torment: The Grotesque in American Art*. New York: Whitney Museum of American Art, 1969. Print.

Douglass, Edward. "Director of the Living Dead." Woods, *Tim Burton* 183–86. Print.

Dreyfus, Hubert, and Sean Dorrance Kelly. *All Things Shining: Reading the Western Classics to Find Meaning in a Secular Age*. New York: Free Press, 2011. Print.

Eagleton, Terry. *Literary Theory*. Minneapolis: University of Minnesota Press, 2001. Print.

_____. *Walter Benjamin Or Towards a Revolutionary Criticism*. 1981. Brooklyn: Verso, 2009. Print.

Ebert, Roger. Rev. of *Alice in Wonderland*, dir. Tim Burton. *Rogerebert.com. Chicago Sun-Times*, 3 March 2010. Web. 8 March 2010.

_____. Rev. of *Blue Velvet*, dir. David Lynch. *Rogerebert.com. Chicago Sun-Times*, 19 Sept. 1986. Web. 26 Aug. 2010

_____. Rev. of *The Brothers Grimm*, dir. Terry Gilliam. *Rogerebert.com. Chicago Sun-Times*, 26 Aug. 2005. Web. 10 July 2010.

_____. Rev. of *The Imaginarium of Doctor Parnassus*, dir. Terry Gilliam. *Rogerebert.com. Chicago Sun-Times*, 6 Jan. 2010. Web. 14 July 2010.

Eco, Umberto, ed. *On Ugliness*. Trans. Alastair McEwen. New York: Rizzoli, 2007.

Edelstein, David. "Burton's *Alice*: a Curious Kind of Wonderful." *Fresh Air*. National Public Radio, 4 March 2010. Web. 8 March 2010.

_____. "Odd Man In." Fraga 31–36. Print.

Falsani, Cathleen. *The Dude Abides: The Gospel According to the Coen Brothers*. Grand Rapids: Zondervan, 2009. Print.

Fellini, Federico, dir. *Fellini-Satyricon*. 1970. MGM, 2001. DVD.

_____, dir. *Juliet of the Spirits*. 1965. Criterion, 2002. DVD.

Felperin, Leslie. "Animated Dreams." Woods, *Tim Burton* 102–107. Print.

Foucault, Michel. *Madness and Civilization: A History of Insanity in the Age of Reason*. 1965. Trans. Richard Howard. New York: Vintage, 1988. Print.

Fraga, Kristian, ed. *Tim Burton: Interviews*. Jackson: University Press of Mississippi, 2005. Print.

Freud, Sigmund. *Beyond the Pleasure Principle*. Trans. James Strachey. New York: Norton, 1961. Print.

_____. *Civilization and Its Discontents*. Trans. James Strachey. New York: Norton, 2010. Print.

_____. *New Introductory Lectures on Psycho-Analysis*. Trans. and ed. James Strachey. New York: Norton, 1964. Print.

_____. *The Uncanny*. Trans. David McLintock. New York: Penguin, 2003. Print.

Freund, Karl, dir. *The Mummy*. 1932. Universal, 2008. DVD.

Frye, Northrop. *Fearful Symmetry: A Study of William Blake*. 1947. Princeton: Princeton University Press, 1990. Print.

Gabriel, Markus, and Slavoj _i_ek. *Myth, Madness, and Laughter: Subjectivity in German Idealism*. London: Continuum, 2009. Print.

Gilliam, Terry, dir. *The Adventures of Baron Munchausen*. 1989. Sony, 1999. DVD.

_____, dir. *Brazil*. 1985. Universal, 1998. DVD.

_____, dir. *The Brothers Grimm*. 2005. Miramax, 2005. DVD.

Works Cited

_____, dir. *Fear and Loathing in Las Vegas*. 1998. Universal, 1998. DVD.

_____, dir. *The Fisher King*. 1991. Sony, 1999. DVD.

_____, dir. *The Imaginarium of Doctor Parnassus*. 2009. Sony, 2010. DVD.

_____. Interview with Phil Stubbs. *Dreams*. Smart. Aug. 2005. Web. 14 July 2010.

_____. Interview with Paul Fischer. *Dark Horizons*. Dec. 2009. Web. 14 July 2010.

_____, dir. *Jabberwocky*. 1977. Sony, 2001. DVD.

_____, and Terry Jones, dirs. *Monty Python and the Holy Grail*. 1975. Sony, 1999. DVD.

_____, dir. *Tideland*. 2005. Velocity/Thinkfilm, 2007. DVD.

_____, dir. *Time Bandits*. 1981. Criterion, 1999. DVD.

_____, dir. *Twelve Monkeys*. 1996. Universal, 2005. DVD.

Gilmore, Richard. "*No Country for Old Men*: The Coens' Tragic Western." *The Philosophy of the Coen Brothers*. Ed. Mark T. Conrad. Lexington: University Press of Kentucky, 2009. 55–78. Print.

Gramsci, Antonio. *Selections from the Prison Notebooks*. Ed. and trans. Quintin Hoare and Geoffrey Nowell Smith. New York: International, 1997. Print.

Grant, Barry Keith. *Film Genre: From Iconography to Ideology*. New York: Wallflower, 2007. Print.

Griffith, D.W. *Birth of a Nation*. 1915. Alpha, 2005. DVD.

Habib, Rafey. *A History of Literary Criticism and Theory: From Plato to the Present*. Oxford: Blackwell, 2008. Print.

Hamilton, Edith. *Mythology*. 1942. New York: Little, Brown, 1998. Print.

Harpham, Geoffrey Galt. *On the Grotesque: Strategies of Contradiction in Art and Literature*. Princeton: Princeton University Press, 1982. Print.

He, Jenny. "An Auteur for All Ages." *Tim Burton*. New York: MOMA, 2009. 17–23. Print.

Hitchcock, Alfred, dir. *The Birds*. 1963. Universal, 2000. DVD.

_____, dir. *Marnie*. 1964. Universal, 2006. DVD.

_____, dir. *Psycho*. 1960. Universal, 1998. DVD.

_____, dir. *Rope*. 1948. Warner Bros., 2006. DVD.

_____, dir. *Shadow of a Doubt*. 1943. Universal, 2001. DVD.

_____, dir. *Spellbound*. 1945. Starz/Anchor Bay, 1999. DVD.

_____, dir. *Strangers on a Train*. 1951. Warner, 1997. DVD.

_____, dir. *Vertigo*. 1958. Universal, 1998. DVD.

Hoberman, J. "Pax Americana." Woods, *Tim Burton* 138–43. Print.

Hopper, Dennis, dir. *Easy Rider*. 1969. DVD. Sony, 2002.

Hurley, Kelly. "British Gothic Fiction, 1885–1930." *The Cambridge Companion to Gothic Fiction*. Ed. Jerrold E. Hogle. Cambridge: Cambridge University Press, 2002. 189–208. Print.

Jameson, Frederick. *Postmodernism, or, The Cultural Logic of Late Capitalism*. Durham: Duke University Press, 1991. Print.

Jenkins, Mark. Rev. of *Imaginarium of Doctor Parnassus*, dir. Terry Gilliam. *Npr.org*. National Public Radio, 23 Dec. 2009. Web. 14 July 2010.

Jerslev, Anne. "Beyond Boundaries: David Lynch's *Lost Highway*." Sheen and Davidson 151–164. Print.

Johnson, Samuel. *Preface to Shakespeare*. *The Plays of William Shakespeare*. 1765. New York: AMS, 1968. Vol. 1 of 8. v–vlxxii. Print.

Johnson, Bradley A. *The Characteristic Theology of Herman Melville: Aesthetics, Politics, Duplicity*. Eugene: Pickwick, 2012. Print.

Works Cited

Jung, Carl Gustav. "The Psychological Function of Archetypes." *The Modern Tradition: Backgrounds of Modern Literature.* New York: Oxford University Press, 1965. 648–653. Print.

Kafka, Franz. *The Trial.* Trans. Willa and Edwin Muir. New York: Schocken, 1992. Print.

Kaleta, Kenneth C. *David Lynch.* New York: Twayne, 1993. Print.

Kayser, Wolfgang. *The Grotesque in Art and Literature.* 1963. Trans. Ulrich Weisstein. New York: McGraw-Hill, 1966. Print.

Keaton, Buster, perf. *The Navigator.* Dir. Donald Crisp. 1924. Image, 1999. DVD.

_____, perf. *Steamboat Bill, Jr.* Dir. Charles Reisner. 1928. Image, 1999. DVD.

Kember, Joe. "David Lynch and the Mug Shot: Facework in *The Elephant Man* and *The Straight Story.*" Sheen and Davidson 19–34. Print.

Kierkegaard, Soren. *Concluding Unscientific Postscript to Philosophical Fragments.* Ed. and trans. Howard V. Hong and Edna H. Hong. Princeton: Princeton University Press, 1992. Print.

Knight, G. Wilson. "*Lear* and the Comedy of the Grotesque." *The Wheel of Fire: Essays in Interpretation of Shakespeare's Sombre Tragedies.* London: Oxford University Press, 1930. 175–93. Print.

Kubric, Stanley, dir. *Dr. Strangelove, Or: How I Learned to Stop Worrying and Love the Bomb.* DVD. Sony, 2001. DVD.

Langford, Barry. *Film Genre: Hollywood and Beyond.* Edinburgh: Edinburgh University Press, 2005. Print.

The Last House on the Left. 1972. Dir. Wes Craven. MGM, 2002. DVD.

Lowe, Andy. "The Brothers Grim." Woods, *Joel and Ethan Coen* 162–66. Print.

Lunn, Eugene. *Marxism and Modernism: An Historical Study of Lukacs, Brecht, Benjamin, and Adorno.* Berkley: University of California Press, 1982. Print.

Lynch, David, dir. *The Alphabet.* 1968. *The Short Films of David Lynch.* Absurda/Ryko, 2006. DVD.

_____, dir. *The Amputee.* 1974. *The Short Films of David Lynch.* Absurda/Ryko, 2006. DVD.

_____, dir. *Blue Velvet.* 1986. MGM, 2002. DVD.

_____, dir. *Dune.* 1984. Universal, 1998. DVD.

_____, dir. *The Elephant Man.* 1980. Paramount, 2001. DVD.

_____, dir. *Eraserhead.* 1976. Absurda/Ryko, 2006. DVD.

_____, dir. *The Grandmother.* 1970. *The Short Films of David Lynch.* Absurda/Ryko, 2006. DVD.

_____, dir. *Inland Empire.* 2006. Absurda/Rhino, 2007. DVD.

_____, dir. *Lost Highway.* 1997. Universal, 2008. DVD.

_____, dir. *Mulholland Dr.* 2001. Universal, 2002. DVD.

_____, dir. *The Straight Story.* 1999. Disney, 2000. DVD.

_____, dir. *Twin Peaks: Fire Walk with Me.* 1992. New Line, 2002. DVD.

_____, dir. *Wild at Heart.* 1990. MGM, 2004. DVD.

_____, and Mark Frost, creators. *Twin Peaks.* Pilot and 29 episodes. 1989–90. Paramount, 2007. DVD set.

MacTaggart, Allister. *The Film Paintings of David Lynch: Challenging Film Theory.* Chicago: Intellect, 2010. Print.

Magliozzi, Ron. "Tim Burton: Exercising the Imagination." *Tim Burton.* New York: MOMA, 2009. 9–15. Print.

Martin, Paul, and Valerie Renegar. "'The Man for His Time': *The Big Lebowski* as Carnivalesque Social Critique." *Communications Studies* 58.3 (2007): 299–313. *Academic OneFile*. Web. 3 March 2010.

McCabe, Bob. "Chemical Warfare." Sterritt and Rhodes 135–40. Print.

———. *Dark Knights and Holy Fools: The Art and Films of Terry Gilliam.* New York: Universe, 1999. Print.

McCarthy, Cormac. *No Country for Old Men.* New York: Vintage, 2005. Print.

McFarland, Douglas. "Philosophies of Comedy in *O Brother, Where Art Thou?" The Philosophy of the Coen Brothers.* Ed. Mark T. Conrad. Lexington: University Press of Kentucky, 2009. 41–54. Print.

McGowan, Tod. *The Impossible David Lynch.* New York: Columbia University Press, 2007. Print.

Melies, Georges. *Voyage to the Moon.* 1902. *The Magic of Melies.* Facets, 2002. DVD.

Meindl, Dieter. *American Fiction and the Metaphysics of the Grotesque.* Columbia: University of Missouri Press, 1996. Print.

Melville, Herman. "Art." *Herman Melville: Selected Poems.* Ed. Robert Faggen. New York: Penguin, 2006. 262. Print.

———. *Moby-Dick, Or the White Whale.* 1851. New York: Dover, 2003. Print.

Merschmann, Helmut. *Tim Burton: The Life of a Visionary Director.* Trans. Michael Kane. London: Titan, 2000. Print.

Milbank, Alison. "Divine Beauty and the Grotesque in Dante's *Paradiso.*" *Yearbook of English Studies* 39 (2009): 155–68. *Academic OneFile.* Web. 13 Feb. 2010.

Miles, Margaret. "Carnal Abominations: The Female Body as Grotesque." *The Grotesque in Art and Literature: Theological Reflections.* Ed. James Luther Adams and Wilson Yates. Grand Rapids: Eerdmans, 1997. 83–112. Print.

Miles, Robert. *Gothic Writing, 1750–1820: A Genealogy.* Manchester: Manchester University Press, 2000. Print.

Mills, David. "One on One: Tim Burton." Woods, *Tim Burton* 147–50. Print.

Modleski, Tania. "The Terror of Pleasure: The Contemporary Horror Film and Postmodern Theory." *The Horror Reader.* Ed. Ken Gedler. London: Routledge, 2000. 285–93. Print.

Morson, Gary Saul. "Dialogue, Monologue and the Social: A Reply to Ken Hirschkop." *Bakhtin: Essays and Dialogue in His Work.* Ed. Gary Saul Morson. Chicago: University of Chicago Press, 1986. Print.

Mottram, James. *The Coen Brothers: The Life of the Mind.* Dulles: Brassey's, 2000. Print.

Mulvey, Laura. *Fetishism and Curiosity.* Bloomington: Indiana University Press, 1996. Print.

Newman, Kim. "The Cage of Reason." Woods, *Tim Burton* 156–60. Print.

———. Rev. of *Mars Attacks,* dir. Tim Burton. Woods, *Tim Burton* 143–45. Print.

Night of the Living Dead. 1968. Dir. George Romero. Synergy, 2008. DVD.

O'Connor, Flannery. "On Her Own Work." *Mystery and Manners: Occasional Prose.* Ed. Sally and Robert Fitzgerald. New York: Farrar, Straus and Giroux, 1969. 107–18. Print.

———. "Some Aspects of the Grotesque in Southern Fiction." *Mystery and Manners: Occasional Prose.* Ed. Sally and Robert Fitzgerald. New York: Farrar, Straus and Giroux, 1969. 36–50. Print.

Olson, Greg. *David Lynch: Beautiful Dark.* Lanham: Scarecrow, 2008. Print.

Works Cited

Page, Edwin. *Gothic Fantasy: The Films of Tim Burton*. London: Marion Boyars, 2007. Print.

Palmer, R. Barton. *Joel and Ethan Coen*. Urbana: University of Illinois Press, 2004. Print.

Parkinson, David. *History of Film*. 1995. London: Thames and Hudson, 1997. Print.

Pascal, Blaise. *Pensées (Thoughts)*. Trans. W. F. Trotter. Mineola: Dover, 2003. Print.

Pearson, Roberta E. *Eloquent Gestures: The Transformation of Performance Style in the Griffith Biograph Films*. Berkeley: University of California Press, 1992. Print.

Pelegrin, Allison. "Funeral Dawn." *The Zydeco Tablets*. Cincinnati: Word, 2002. 19. Print.

Penn, Arthur, dir. *Bonny and Clyde*. 1967. Warner Bros./Seven Arts, 1999. DVD.

Plato. "The Apology of Socrates." Trans. C. D. Reeve. *The Norton Anthology of World Literature*, shorter 2d ed. Ed. John Bierhorst, et al. New York: Norton, 2009. 648–69. Print.

———. *The Republic*. Trans. C. D. C. Reeve. Indianapolis: Hackett, 2004. Print.

Poe, Edgar Allan. "The Fall of the House of Usher." *Great Short Works of Edgar Allan Poe*. Ed. G. R. Thompson. New York: Harper & Row, 1970. 216–37. Print.

Punter, David, and Glennis Byron. *The Gothic*. Malden: Blackwell, 2004. Print.

Rea, Steven. "Birth of *Baron* Was Tough on Gilliam." Sterritt and Rhodes 47–51. Print.

Reed, Cory A. "*Batman Returns*: From the Comic(s) to the Grotesque." *Post Script* 14.3 (1995): 37–50. Print.

Rev. of *Raising Arizona*. *Variety* 4 Mar. 1987. Woods, *Joel and Ethan Coen* 45–46. Print.

Richardson, John H. "The Joel and Ethan Story." Woods, *Joel and Ethan Coen* 81–87. Print.

Robson, Eddie. *Coen Brothers*. London: Virgin, 2003. Print.

Rodley, Chris, ed. *Lynch on Lynch*, rev. ed. New York: Faber and Faber, 2005. Print.

Ross, Christine. "Redefinitions of Abjection in Contemporary Performance of the Female Body." *Modern Art and the Grotesque*. Ed. Frances S. Connelly. Cambridge: Cambridge University Press, 2003. 281–91. Print.

Rowell, Erica. *The Brothers Grim: The Films of Ethan and Joel Coen*. Lanham: Scarecrow, 2007. Print.

Russo, Mary. *The Female Grotesque: Risk, Excess and Modernity*. New York: Routledge, 1994. Print.

Salisbury, Mark. "Graveyard Shift." Woods, *Tim Burton* 150–55. Print.

———, ed. *Burton on Burton*. Rev. ed. London: Faber and Faber, 2006. Print.

Santayana, George. *The Sense of Beauty: Being the Outlines of Aesthetic Theory*. 1896. Ann Arbor: University of Michigan Press, 2006. Print.

Schaefer, Dirk. "The Film Music of Danny Elfman." *Tim Burton: The Life and Art of a Visionary Director*. Trans. Michael Kane. London: Titan, 2000. 143–62. Print.

Schneider, Steven Jay. "The Essential Evil in/of *Eraserhead* (or, Lynch to the Contrary)." Sheen and Davidson 5–18. Print.

Schoenberg, Arnold. "An Artistic Impression." Trans. Leo Black. *Style and Idea: Selected Writings of Arnold Schoenberg*. 1975. Ed. Leonard Stein. Berkeley: University of California Press, 1984. 189–91. Print.

Schopenhauer, Arthur. "The Artist and the Sublime." *The Essential Schopenhauer*. Ed. Wolfgang Schirmacher. New York: Harper, 2010. 133–49. Print.

Searching for the Wrong-Eyed Jesus. Dir. Andrew Douglas. 2003. Image, 2003. DVD.

Seesslen, Georg. "Crimewave." Seesslen and Korte 17–39. Print.

_____, and Peter Korte, eds. *Joel and Ethan Coen.* Trans. Rory Mulholland. New York: Limelight, 2001. Print.

Seuss, Dr. (Theodor Geisel). *Fox in Socks.* 1965. New York: Random House, 1993. Print.

Shapiro, Marc. "Explaining *Beetlejuice.*" Fraga 3–8. Print.

Sheen, Erica, and Annette Davidson, eds. *The Cinema of David Lynch: American Dreams, Nightmare Visions.* New York: Wallflower, 2004. Print.

Smith, Jim, and J. Clive Matthews. *Tim Burton.* London: Virgin, 2007. Print.

Smithee, Allan. "What Condition the Postmodern Condition Is In: Collecting Culture in *The Big Lebowski.*" Comentale and Jaffe 255–75. Print.

Stanfield, Peter. *Horse Opera: The Strange History of the 1930s Singing Cowboy.* Urbana: University of Illinois Press, 2002. Print.

Steig, Michael. "Defining the Grotesque: An Attempt at Synthesis." *Journal of Aesthetics and Art Criticism* 29 (1970): 253–60. Print.

Sterritt, David. "*Fargo* in Context: The Middle of Nowhere?" *The Coen Brothers' Fargo.* Ed. William G. Luhr. Cambridge: Cambridge University Press, 2004. 10–32. Print.

_____, and Lucille Rhodes, eds. *Terry Gilliam: Interviews.* Jackson: U of Miss. P, 2004. Print.

Stevenson, Robert Louis. *The Strange Case of Dr. Jekyll and Mr. Hyde. The Strange Case of Dr. Jekyll and Mr. Hyde and Other Stories.* Ed. George Stade. New York: Barnes and Noble, 2003. 3–78. Print.

Texas Chainsaw Massacre. 1974. Dir. Tobe Hooper. Dark Sky, 2006. DVD.

Thompson, Hunter S. *Fear and Loathing in Las Vegas: A Savage Journey to the Heart of the American Dream.* 1971. New York: Vintage, 1998. Print.

Thompson, John O., ed. *Monty Python: Complete and Utter Theory of the Grotesque.* 1982. London: British Film Institute, 1984. Print.

Thomson, Phillip. *The Grotesque.* London: Methuen, 1972. Print.

Van Boeschoten, Robert. "Revisited." *Culture and Organization* 11.4 (2005): 269–74. *Academic OneFile.* Web. 14 Aug. 2010.

Vidler, Anthony. *The Architectural Uncanny: Essays in the Modern Unhomely.* Cambridge: MIT Press, 1992. Print.

Watt, Ian. *The Rise of the Novel: Studies in Defoe, Richardson, and Fielding.* Harmondsworth: Penguin, 1963. Print.

Whale, James. *Bride of Frankenstein.* 1935. Universal, 1999. DVD.

_____, dir. *Frankenstein.* 1931. Universal, 1999. DVD.

_____, dir. *The Invisible Man.* 1933. Universal, 2000. DVD.

Wiene, Robert, dir. *The Cabinet of Dr. Caligari.* 1921. Kino, 2002. DVD.

Wilde, Oscar. *The Picture of Dorian Gray.* 1891. New York: Dover, 1993. Print.

Wood, Edward D., dir. *Plan 9 from Outer Space.* 1959. Image, 2000. DVD.

Wood, Robin. *Hollywood from Vietnam to Reagan.* New York: Columbia University Press, 1986. Print.

Woods, Paul A., ed. *Tim Burton: A Child's Garden of Nightmares,* rev. ed. London: Plexus, 2007. Print.

_____, ed. *Joel and Ethan Coen: Blood Siblings.* London: Plexus, 2003. Print.

Worland, Rick. *The Horror Film: An Introduction.* London: Blackwell, 2007.

Yates, Wilson. "Francis Bacon: The Iconography of Cricifixion." Adams and Yates, *The Grotesque in Art and Literature* 143–91. Print.

_____. "An Introduction to the Grotesque: Theoretical and Theological Considerations." *The Grotesque in Art and Literature: Theological Reflections.* Ed. James Luther Adams and Wilson Yates. Grand Rapids: Eerdmans, 1997. 1–68. Print.

Zacharek, Stephanie. Rev. of *Tim Burton's Corpse Bride*, dir. Tim Burton. Woods, *Tim Burton* 187–88. Print.

Žižek, Slavoj. *The Art of the Ridiculous Sublime: On David Lynch's Lost Highway.* Seatle: Walter Chapin Simpson Center for the Humanities, 2000. Print.

_____. *Enjoy Your Symptom: Jacques Lacan in Hollywood and Out.* New York: Routledge, 1992. Print.

_____. *The Parallax View.* Cambridge: MIT Press, 2006. Print.

_____, and John Milbank. *The Monstrosity of Christ: Paradox or Dialectic?* Ed. Creston Davis. Cambridge: MIT Press, 2009. Print.

Index

Index